1250

THE SILVER BULLET
AND OTHER
AMERICAN WITCH STORIES

The Silver Bullet
and other
American Witch Stories

Edited by
Hubert J. Davis

JONATHAN DAVID PUBLISHERS, INC.
MIDDLE VILLAGE, N. Y. 11379

THE SILVER BULLET AND
OTHER AMERICAN WITCH STORIES

Copyright © 1975
by
HUBERT J. DAVIS

No part of this book may be reproduced in any manner without
written permission from the publishers. Address all inquiries to:

Jonathan David Publishers
68-22 Eliot Avenue
Middle Village, New York 11379

Library of Congress Cataloging in Publication Data

Davis, Hubert J
    The silver bullet, and other American witch stories.

    1.   Folk-lore—United States.   2.   Witchcraft—
United States.   I.   Title.
GR105.D33   398.2′2′0973   75-11953
ISBN 0-8246-0199-8

Printed in the United States of America

TABLE OF CONTENTS

ACKNOWLEDGEMENTS

I am deeply indebted to Michael Plunkett and his staff in the Manuscript Department of the Alderman Library of the University of Virginia for making the manuscripts in their folklore collection of the W.P.A. Virginia Writers Project available to me, and to the Alderman Library, and the Virginia State Library for permission to use these materials.

My profound thanks is extended to the following organizations for permission to use materials from their publications: The American Folklore Society, The Hoosier Folklore Society, The North Carolina Folklore Society, The Southern Folklore Society, The Tennessee Folklore Society, The Texas Folklore Society, and the University of North Carolina Press.

Far too many people have been involved in this project as sources of information and contributors to be listed individually, but I am grateful to each of them. I owe special thanks to my wife who served as critic, editor and typist.

HUBERT J. DAVIS

Portsmouth, Virginia
1975

INTRODUCTION

Among the more interesting jobs created by the W.P.A. (Works Progress Administration) during the depression years of the 1930s was the Virginia W.P.A. Writers Project. The idea was to have a group of collectors fan out among the coves and hollows of the Appalachian Mountains and record the beliefs, superstitions, and traditions of the mountain folk. These stories were then transcribed and sent to Richmond with the intention of publishing a book on Virginia folklore. This ultimate goal was never accomplished, and the hundreds of stories collected were eventually placed in the archives of the University of Virginia, in Charlottesville.

This book draws heavily on the Virginia Project. But it proceeds from the assumption—borne out by investigation—that the folk tales of the mountain folk were heavily influenced by the experiences of their ancestors many of whom were of Scottish, Irish or German origin and who settled in Virginia, Texas, New York, Pennsylvania, Kentucky, Indiana, Tennessee, North Carolina and Arkansas. It also includes tales about Cajuns, Indians and people of Spanish backgrounds.

More than five hundred stories were studied and considered, and what emerges is a pattern in which belief in witches plays a significant role. The belief in witches, which these mountaineers had in common, stems from the views—often stretching back to the Bible—held by their ancestors in Europe.

It is not sheer accident that certain themes recur so often in the folklore of these mountain folks. Certain beliefs were basic to their way of life, the most important one being that when something went wrong, more likely than not, a witch was involved.

The physical setting of the mountains themselves provided ideal settings for witches to work, and for stories about them to develop. The hills and valleys were sparsely populated and were covered with forests, vines and bushes which made many spots dark and foreboding. One such area was in Carroll County, Virginia, described in "Aunt Nancy Bobbit and Witch Mountain." Witch Mountain was a high, rugged mountain with several cliffs that cast weird shadows. The sun was rarely visible and most of the time the peak was shrouded in mist.

The type of houses in which these mountaineers lived gave rise

1

to many witch stories. Their log cabins usually had rock chimneys at one end which emerged from large fireplaces used for cooking, heating and, to a certain extent, illumination.

Many occult ideas grew around these chimneys and fireplaces. It was thought that a witch's spell on a person could be broken by taking some urine from the bewitched person, putting it in a bottle, and hanging it inside the chimney. If the heat broke the bottle and evaporated the urine within seven days, the spell would be broken. We see this in "The Quaker Doctor and His Magic Bottle," where a father is directed to take some hair, some nail cuttings, and some urine from his wife, his child and himself, put them in a bottle, and place the mixture in hot ashes in order to break a witch's spell over the child.

The rough surface of the outside chimney provided an ideal place for hornets, wasps and mud daubers to build their nests. Since these insects were a deterrent to anyone who might want to approach the chimney, the idea developed that only witches could hide things between the loose rocks of a chimney. In "A Conjure Bottle in the Chimney," a witch uses a magic bottle to bewitch a young girl. A white witch—a good witch—called in to treat her, finds the bottle in a crack on the outside of the chimney. It contains a small cross, a small ball of hair, the vertebrae of a rat, and several herbs. The white witch burns the contents and throws the bottle in the river, thus breaking the spell on the girl.

A popular way of breaking witches' spells was to burn the forehead of the bewitched person with a branding iron heated in a fireplace. The idea was that by branding the bewitched person, the bewitcher would be incapacitated. Many instances are found among these stories in which a bewitched person has a treatment applied to a specific part of the body and the sorcerer is subsequently incapacitated in that very same spot.

The early settlers in America found wild game to be the best source for meat. Rich vegetation supported bears, wolves, panthers, deer, raccoons, buffalo, wild turkeys, pheasants and squirrels. The pioneers depended upon their trusty ball-and-cap rifles to capture this game. Sometimes, wet powder, faulty caps, dirty guns or other malfunctions caused the hunter to miss his target, leading him to believe that either the gun or the game was bewitched. In "Lige Hall's Bewitched Rifle-Gun," Lige twice misses a wildcat at close range and has to consult two white witches before the spell is removed from his gun. He is instructed to rob an Indian grave, get a jaw-bone, scrape some powder from it, and mix it with his gun powder in order to break the spell.

Mountain people were very dependent upon milk, so their cows were extremely important to them. The cows were "belled" and allowed to roam about in the woods and graze. Often, they were bitten by rattlesnakes or copperheads, causing many days of horrible suffering before dying. The cows were often chased or frightened by bears, panthers or wolves. Some of them ate poisonous weeds. If these experiences did not kill them outright, it did make them behave strangely, and refuse to give milk. In "The Devil Gets into a Heifer," a witch sprinkles some white stuff on a cow's withers when Bessie Sue won't sell her the cow. That night, when they try to milk the cow, she kicks, snorts, bawls, and cuts all sorts of monkey shines—very unusual behavior for her.

When a housewife tried to churn her milk and the butter wouldn't come, some nearby witch would be accused of casting a spell on the milk, the churn, or the cow. Placing a piece of red flannel cloth *under* the churn, or a silver coin *inside* the churn, might break the spell. If these remedies failed, the milk was taken out to the barn lot and placed in the hog trough, where it was slowly whipped out of the trough with a bundle of thorns.

Being isolated, these mountain folks lived social lives that centered around their own large families. During bad weather, and especially during the long winter evenings, families gathered around the fireplace to roast chestnuts, pop corn, drink, tell stories, solve riddles and sing ballads. These tales, songs and conundrums were repeated to neighbors whom they met at the grist mill while waiting for a turn of corn to be ground, or at the village store. Before long, one family's story became everyone's story.

Many old timers knew a great many witch stories and revelled in telling them. Of course, each time a story was told, it gained a little here and lost a little there. Story tellers usually vied with each other to see who could tell the biggest or wildest yarn, and this yielded a wide variety of fantastic and unbelievable tales.

Aside from casual social contacts, people got together at what were known as "workings." These were community efforts to help a particular family get a job done quickly. They included shuckings, hog killings, quiltings, bean stringings and log-rollings. Such activities usually ended in drinking, story-telling, dancing and ballad singing.

One of the most fascinating things about mountain folks to outsiders is their colorful way of speaking. Some of their expressions are adaptations of archaic English usage. "Poke," originally meaning "pocket," was adapted to mean "sack" or "bag." "Aunt" or "uncle" were used in referring to an older person to whom one wished to show some respect, although the person might not be related. Placing the word "old"—e.g. Old Pete—before a name usually implied some measure of scorn.

Other expressions evolved from the state of poverty that was widespread in the mountain region. Clothing was scarce, so, during warm weather, boys up to the age of ten were permitted to go around in a shirt, without bottoms. Boys not old enough to justify the expense of a pair of pants during warm weather, were called "shirt-tail boys."

In addition to these particular expressions, there were, of course, those easily understood by anyone, but peculiar to the folks of the mountain regions. Expressions like: "mean as a wildcat," "nervous as a rattlesnake," "low as a snake's belly," "feeling poorly," "about to be a ghost" (dying), and "hurt-done" (bewitched).

You may notice that, in the course of this book, the name of James T. Adams appears very often as a collector of these stories. Adams had the advantage of knowing a large number of people in the area of southwestern Virginia where he worked. He was a native of the area and came from a large family of pioneer settlers. His older relatives, in particular, knew many of the witch stories which they grew up on, and they were anxious to relate them. To some of these older relatives, witchcraft was an active belief instead of just a curiosity, and a few were said to be practitioners of witchcraft.

It should be pointed out that many of the stories located in manuscript form were in need of fleshing out. Accordingly, in such cases, the author consulted the back issues of American and British folklore journals where some of these stories exist in slightly different forms, and obtained the needed material to round out the stories.

The stories that follow have been arranged in four categories: how to become a witch, how witches work, how to counteract witchcraft, and witchcraft for money and mischief. There is no special significance to these groupings, and any number of other arrangements might have done just as well. But, the arrangement we have decided upon is logical and presents the material in a viable form.

PART ONE

HOW TO BECOME A WITCH

INTRODUCTION

Three groups of people among the early settlers in America were considered to be witches. Possibly the largest group consisted of people physically deformed, and those who lived in strange settings. Imperfections in one's physical appearance were thought to be the work of the Devil, and all who suffered from them were thought to be associated with him. If a person had a dried-up, wrinkled face, snaggle-teeth, stringy white hair, or beady eyes, and lived alone, he or she was often accused of being a witch. Aunt Nancy Bobbit, in the second story of this section, acquired the reputation of being a witch because she was old, feeble, dirty, and queer, and lived alone in a narrow, dark, isolated hollow.

Another group accused of witchcraft consisted of those who a) did not openly reveal their religious beliefs, or b) whose beliefs differed markedly from those of the average member of the community. The early settlers brought with them from Europe the idea that heresy was synonymous with witchcraft. This was one of the reasons why the Melungions were thought to be witches. If a group of people seemed to hold no religious beliefs, they were said to be witches, and were blamed for any unusual natural phenomenon for which local people could find no logical explanation.

A third group of people accused of witchcraft consisted of people of unusual intelligence and personal magnetism, or those having the ability to faith-heal or hypnotize.

Why did people want to become witches? Some wanted to do harm to their neighbors; others wanted to enliven their otherwise drab existence. This craving for excitement is the reason why the young adolescent, Jonas Dotson, wants to become a witch in "Delivered up to the Devil." He is bored with his dull, routine farm chores and with his father's self-righteous moralizing against the devil. When the Reverend Dotson finds out what is happening to his son, he immediately accuses the mother of Jonas' girl friend of witchcraft, and says she is trying to deliver his soul to the devil just like Saul was delivered to the Philistines.

To become a witch, one had to be sponsored by a witch, and had to go through a ritualistic ceremony. The would-be witch had to swear allegiance to the devil, worship him, and promise to obey him faithfully. "The Devil, a Beetle, and the Bleeding Toe" describes the ritual by which Rindy Sue Gross becomes a witch. She has to dance in the woods for twelve nights and, on the thirteenth, she has to kill a black hen and let its blood spurt against a tree. The devil then appears from behind the tree and dances with her. He makes her sign an oath of loyalty to him, in her own blood, and then bites her on the shoulder to make a witchmark.

In the case of Jonas Dotson, his initiation begins on Friday, the thirteenth. But, since it has to be repeated three times, it takes three years for him to become a witch.

Both of these stories point up the idea that the numbers three and thirteen were considered by witches to have magical power —contrary to both the Greeks and Romans who thought thirteen was an unlucky number. A coven consisted of twelve witches and the devil made thirteen. Friday the thirteenth was the day on which witches held their sabbats or gathered to make their witchballs.

The pledge that Jonas Dotson makes when he becomes a witch is similar to that sworn by all witches at their initiation:

> As I dip the water with the ram's horn,
> Cast me, a cruel heart of thorn,
> As I now to the Devil do my soul lease.
>
> I also renounce Christ as my savior
> And promise the Devil my behavior
> 'Til my life on earth shall cease.
>
> May my black and evil soul be
> Of Christian love and grace free
> As this place is of grease.
>
> And when I become an evil crone
> From my outer skin to my inner bone,
> I'll never give Christians any peace.

CONJURE BONES AND BLOODY SUNRISE

The evening sun of our first hot June day dropped behind Piney Ridge just as Pa and I arrived on horseback at Granny Jordan's little two-story log cabin nestled in the woods. I was to stay with Granny for two weeks. After a big dinner of cornbread, cold buttermilk and fresh blackberry pie, Pa mounted his tired horse and headed back toward Norton. I was tired and sore from the long ride, but I insisted on helping Granny with the dishes before she tucked me into bed on the second floor. I remember that it didn't take long for me to fall asleep.

I awoke in the middle of the night screaming. Out of nowhere, something heavy, furry, with big black feet, sharp claws and shiny eyes thumped down on my chest, then sprang to the floor and away. Granny Jordan hot-footed it to my bed holding her little oil lamp.

"Thet cat skeered ye, didn't hit, honey child?" she asked.

Before I could answer her, she put her arm around my neck and explained what had happened: "You see, leetle one, them rafters air jest agin the logs. So when they built this cabin, they left a cathole in the roof."

Prowling witches! Ghosts! Falling cats! Sweet, understanding grannies; was any of this actually real, or was I dreaming? How these confused thoughts tripped over each other in my sleep-fogged brain! Needless to say, I didn't go back to sleep, but just lay there trembling, afraid to relax until daylight.

My first day's visit at Granny's was spoiled before it began, because at breakfast everybody laughed at my childish fears. They didn't understand how I could possibly mistake a cat for witches, but they blamed it on the fact that all my ten years had been spent in the city. Granny laughed at their chiding, but said she was sorry my visit had got off to a bad start, and promised to make it up to me: "Now, Sheila Jane, effen you'll help me churn this mornin', I'll tell you more witch stories than you've ever heard in all your life."

Collected by James Taylor Adams, Big Laurel, Wise County, Virginia, March 27, 1939. As told by his grandfather, Spencer Adams, who was then 87 years old.

They brought the big wooden churn filled with sour cream into the cabin and placed it in front of the fireplace. Granny dragged up her favorite rocker, sat down, and began the slow rhythmic motion of lifting the dasher and pushing it down through the cream. Her small, piercing black eyes sparkled like the coals in the fireplace, and a very serious expression came over her wrinkled, tanned face.

I reminded her: "Please, Granny Jordan, tell me all you know about witches."

"Well, chile," she drawled, "there's more to know 'bout witches than I could ever tell you in my lifetime, effen I live to be a hundred. But I'll tell you fust a few ways thet I've heard 'bout how witches are made. You take over the churn while I light my pipe."

She plucked her clay pipe from the mantle, poured some homemade tobacco into it from a glass jar, tamped it firmly with her forefinger, then stooped down and carefully removed a burning ember from the fireplace and put it in her pipe. She took several vigorous puffs to insure that the tobacco was alight, took her seat in her rocker and began:

"Many years ago, your grandpappy onct tole me the quickest way to git to be a witch wuz fust, to go out and ketch a big black cat. Then go and find a spring with a branch runnin' due east. Next, put a kittle on a hot fire, bile the water, then throw thet live black cat into the biling water. Let hit bile till all the meat comes offen the bones. Drain off the water, let the bones cool, then put 'em in a basket and tote 'em to the spring. Set down aside the spring and start a washin' them bones in the branch one at a time. Keep your eyes on the spring branch all the time, kase atter a while the Devil'll come down the stream and come torge you. The bone you're a washin' when you fust see the Devil is a lucky bone. The Devil'll make you take an oath to serve him, then he'll leave. As soon as he leaves you, throw all 'tother bones in the branch and put the lucky bone in your pocket. This lucky bone 'll make you a witch. But you'll have to pack the lucky bone with you all the time, kase effen you lose or forget hit, you'll lose your magic power."

By now, it was time for the butter to begin to form on the dasher and around the hole in the churn lid. Granny paused, tilted the top of the churn and peeked, but she didn't see any butter. "Laws a massy*, chile," she nervously announced. "Tain't nuthin in there 'cept foamin' cream."

Then, Granny Jordan glanced towards the window and, as she

* A mountain expression used as an exclamation. A corruption of the phrase "Lord have mercy."

stared out at the dripping trees, she continued, "Shore as hit's a rainin, honey, hit's the work of them evil witches. I'm afeared thet they've put a spell on this churn kase we've been talkin' 'bout them." Then, in an awed and cautious tone she said, "Sheila Jane, you hustle to the kitchen, wet the dishrag and bring hit to me."

I hurried to the kitchen, doused the dishrag in water, wrung it out a little and rushed back. Granny reached her bony hand under her long skirt to a secret pocket and pulled out a silver coin. She wrapped it in the wet dishrag, tilted the churn aside a little, and slipped the rag under the churn. She mumbled some unintelligible words under her breath, turned towards me and said, "I'll lay you a bet thet'll git shet of them pesterin' witches."

Then I begged, "Granny, could you tell me some more about witches?"

Granny glanced dubiously at the foaming milk as if wondering whether she ought to wait before talking any more about witches. She began: "I've been told thet annuder way to git to be a witch is to fust go to the top of a high mountain, throw rocks at the moon and cuss God Almighty. Then, go find a spring where the water runs due east. Take a brand new knife and wash hit in the spring jest as the sun rises. Say, 'I want my soul to be as free from the savin' blud of Jesus Christ as this knife is of sin.' Do this fer twelve days in a row. Effen on the thirteenth day the sun rises a drippin' blud, hit's a shore sign thet you're becomin' a witch."

Granny paused, raised the churn lid and peeped at the milk. She scowled discouragingly and said, "Let me churn a while."

Then, as if to get her mind off the drudgery of churning, she began: "I onct knowed a gal who got her mind set on bein' a witch. She tole me thet she went one dark midnight to the oldest witch woman there wuz to axt her how to git to be a witch. Natcherly, the old witch wuz all soured and mad as a hornet at somebody a knockin' on her cabin door at midnight, but she got up and let the gal in. But, when the old crone found out thet the gal had come to learn how to be a witch, she wuz tickled pink, and she danced a jig then and there.

"She tole the gal to go to the fireplace, ketch hold of her right foot with her left hand, and put her right hand on the top of her head and say, 'All betwixt my hands, I give to the Devil.' "

Granny paused, peeped at the foaming cream again, and dejectedly announced, "Them infernal witches air still a hellin' round thet milk. But, by tarnation, you jest wait, I'll drive 'em to hell in a turkey trot."

She removed the cover from the churn, folded her hands together to make a cup, dipped them into the churn and came out with a double handful of foaming milk. She walked slowly and carefully to the fireplace and dumped the milk onto the hot coals. "Thet'll scorch their fanny and make 'em scoot," she boasted triumphantly.

Then, she replaced the cover on the churn, turned the churning over to me, and continued: "Annuder way to git to be a witch is to ketch a black cat, and scratch hit on hit's belly till it starts to bleed. Then, take this bloody black cat to a deep holler where there's a crick, build a fire on the bank, and bile thet cat till all the meat comes offen the bones. Sort out the cat's left shoulder blade and pour the rest of the awful stuff in the crik and watch hit float away. As hit gits outten sight say, 'In the name of Beelzebub, Succubus, and the Archangel of Hell, I pledge to be loyal to the Devil the rest of my born days. I promise never to pray to God agin, and never to darken the door of a church, and come Hell or high water, to allus be loyal to the Devil.' Then, bore a hole through the cat's shoulder bone, git a red woolen string and tie hit to the bone and wear the bone round yore neck."

Granny paused again, took another look inside the churn, grinned, and exclaimed, "Hit's come! Hit's come! The fire shore done the trick thet the dishrag couldn't do, and the butter's come!"

Then Granny explained to me, "Hit musta been kase we wuz a talkin' 'bout witches thet made 'em mad and so thet they spelled the churn. Now, I 'low the reason the dishrag and silver coin didn't drive 'em away, wuz thet hit wuz men witches what spelled the milk. You have to burn them men witches to break their spell."

AUNT NANCY BOBBIT OF WITCH MOUNTAIN

Witch Mountain, in Carroll County, is about seven miles northeast of Hillsville, Virginia. It got its name more than a hundred and fifty years ago when a clan of people who believed in and practiced witchcraft settled there. It consists of high, rugged terrain with several cliffs that cast weird shadows. Where there is enough soil, tall pines grow and spread their arms into the misty haze which always seemed to enshroud them. The sun never seems to shine there, and the jarring cries of bats are the only night-time sounds.

Hosiah Ward, of Bridle Creek, lived in that area and tells this story:

"As a shirt-tail boy of ten, I felt mighty grown up when my mother let me go alone on shank's mare* to visit my granny. Her cabin rested along the base of Witch Mountain about a mile from our house. I always ran the whole distance, and my little heart thumped like a trip hammer every jump of the way.

"An old Irish woman, affectionately known as Aunt Nancy Bobbit, lived alone up a narrow dark hollow not too far from my granny's cabin. A lot of people in the community, including my mother, thought that Aunt Nancy was a witch. My mother warned me to stay away from the cabin. But my granny, who had known Aunt Nancy from childhood, assured me that, though she was queer, feeble and a little dirty, she was not and never had been a witch. She was a lonely, harmless old woman who needed companionship, so Granny would let me visit Aunt Nancy and neither of us would tell my mother."

"It was clear to me that Aunt Nancy enjoyed my visits because she encouraged them. She always had walnuts and hickory nuts for me to crack and stacks of maple sugar cakes to eat. Of course, I loved

Collected by I. M. Warren, Roanoke County, Virginia, June 9, 1939. This story was told to P. E. Crowder when he was a child by Hosiah Ward of Bridle Creek, Carrol County, Virginia. Witch Mountain lies about seven miles north of Hillsville, in Carrol County, near Big Island Creek.

* A widely used mountain expression meaning "to travel by foot" or "to walk."

13

the good things to eat, but, most of all, I enjoyed Aunt Nancy's exciting stories. She would thrill me with her blood-curdling tales of the narrow escapes of the pioneers from wild animals and Indians and the exciting exploits of her late husband who had been a long-hunter* and Indian fighter years ago. She seemed to have an endless supply of witch stories, too. I don't recall her ever having told me the same tale twice.

"Aunt Nancy was a firm believer in witches and their magic, and she told me that the mountains hereabouts were full of witches still. She said that she knew of a whole coven—twelve witches and the Devil—and that she knew them all personally, including the Devil. Since she knew so much about them, it is no wonder that people thought she was a witch herself.

"When I was ready to leave after one of my visits, she would always warn me to be very careful while walking through the woods alone, since witches were anxious to catch little boys and she knew of several who had been carried away by them. Sometimes, they'd take them and make them work for them, and some they'd bewitch so that they'd be queer for the rest of their lives.

"Aunt Nancy had stirred my imagination and curiosity with her stories, and I decided that I wanted to be a witch when I grew up. So I asked her how people got to be witches.

"She began to talk: 'Becoming a witch is not simple, son. Fust, you should give very serious thought to hit.' Then, she paused, filled and lighted her clay pipe and, between puffs, she continued, 'Effen a body wuz shore he wanted to be a witch, what he has to do is to swap his soul to the Devil for the soul of some wicked dead person. He'd have to promise to do what the Devil told him the rest of his life. Hit would be easier to become a witch effen you wuz the seventh son of a seventh son, but ennybody who wants to be a witch bad enough can get to be one.'

" 'Fust, he'd have to climb to the top of the highest knob on Witch Mountain and tote either a black cat or a black hen. Then, he'd have to find the Indian graveyard at the place nigh where the two Indian trails cross. There he'd have to draw a big ring in the dust 'bout fifteen feet acrost, and dance in this circle each morning at the break of day for eight mornings in a row. Then, on the ninth morning, he'd have to put one hand on the top of his head and 'tother on the sole of his foot and say, "I give all betwixt my two

---

* During the period of exploration and settlement of the frontier, hunters would often go into the wilderness to hunt bear, buffalo, and other fur-bearing animals. They would take supplies with them and often stay for months. These hunters were known as "long hunters."

hands to the Devil. I swear I'll do everything he axts of me.' "

"'Then, the Devil comes right up over the edge of the cliff and nips him on the shoulder so hit bleeds. Then, the Devil tells him to wet his finger in the blood and sign an X to this pact. Then, the soul of the wicked person swaps places with his soul, and he'd be a witch. Then, the Devil will say some magic words over the cat or the hen and change hit into an imp. Or, if you'd rather, the Devil will change the imp into a toad, a crow or a beetle.' "

THE DEVIL, A BEETLE AND A
BLEEDING TOE

Rindy Sue Gose was a dried-up, snaggle-toothed, peculiar old woman with stringy white hair and eyes like a snake. She lived over near Indian Rock Creek with her husband, Gary Ben Gose, in a dirty, dark log cabin.

One night, during the dark of the moon, in dog-days*, Clint Hill and Jeff Thorn were out in the woods hunting and they treed a coon. The weather turned bad, and it took them quite a spell to get the coon out of the tree. It was late, near midnight, and they were on their way home when they met Rindy Sue Gose. Clint picks it up:

"We mighty nigh run smack dab into her, she wuz joggin' along so fast with her head in the clouds. She didn't see us, so me and Jeff sneaked right quiet like behindst her through the woods. She went way back on Wolf's Head Ridge. When she come to a stoopin' birch tree, she stopped, picked up a stick and drawed on the ground a big ring round thet tree. Then, she made a cross in the ring and sed some mumble jumble sich as we'd never heard afore. Then, she heisted her dress to her knees and started to dance. She danced fer 'bout five minutes and then made a beeline torge her cabin.

"Now, me and Jeff 'ud both heard that effen a woman wants to be a witch, she goes to a birch tree and dances and the Devil 'ud come and dance, and he'd make the person a witch. So, we lowed something wuz in the wind, so we figgered we'd watch her. Well, fer the next twelve nights, effen she didn't come to thet *same* white birch tree, make a cross in the ring, dance fer a spell, then go back to her place.

"Then, on the thirteenth night, she put a cross in the ring and danced jest atter midnight like she'd done on 'tother twelve nights,

Collected by Cornelia Berry of Rockbridge County, Virginia, May 7, 1939. It was told to her by Woodrow Ciarose who had recently moved to Rockbridge from Cambridge, Maryland.

* A six week period between July 3rd and August 11th which usually coincided with the rainy season. It was a widely accepted superstition in the mountains that during the dark of the moon of this season both wild animals and witches were most active. Hence, this was a period of night-time hunting.

16

'ceptin' this time she didn't go home. She had brung a black hen with her, and atter the dance, she slit the hen's neck and let the blood spurt outten agin the tree trunk. Then, she throwed the dead hen as fur back in the woods as she could. When hit landed, the Devil stepped outten behind the tree. Neither me nor Jeff had ever seed the Devil, and we couldn't believe our eyes, but it must've been him. He had horns jest above his ears, his feet had hoofs like a deer, he had a long tail like a cow, and fiery eyes thet looked like two boiled eggs. Jeff and me wuz skeered stiff, and we wuz a shakin' in our boots, but we stayed there to see whut wuz a goin' on.

"Fust, Rindy Sue cut her finger with a knife, and when hit started to bleed, she opened a little Bible and 'peared to write sumpthin' in hit with the blood from her finger. The Devil then nipped her on the left shoulder to give her a witchmark so's she could suckle her familiar. Rindy Sue swore to give her soul to the Devil and to work for him the rest of her born days. Then, the Devil danced with her, and then went into the woods behindst thet tree. Rindy Sue tuk off torge her cabin.

"Well, three days atter this happened, Old Jonas Sperky, the most onry, wicked old codger thet had ever been round here, died. Bless my soul, effen Rindy Sue Gose wuzzn't the fust to show up for his wake. She wuz a carryin' a little medicine bottle in her hand, and she wouldn't let nobody see whut wuz in hit. Now, we'd been told thet effen somebody got to be a witch, the most wicked one round 'ud die in three days' time. Then, his soul 'ud go into a frog, a rat, a cat or a beetle, and this varmint with the wicked soul 'ud be the witch's familiar. Now, me and Jeff figgered mebbe Rindy Sue had a beetle in thet bottle and thet Old Jonas' soul wuz a goin' into her beetle.

"Atter Jonas' funeral, Rindy Sue got to goin' from one place to annuder to borrer sumpthin. She borrered some spice frum Grannie Bond, and right away Grannie's hens all stopped a layin. Then, she borrered some soap frum Lil Coleman, and atter thet Lil couldn't get her butter to come when she churned. Si Weems lent her his corn knife, and then his gun wouldn't shoot straight.

"Old Rindy Sue come to my place and axt my old woman to borrer some meal, but I'd told her not to lend Rindy Sue nuthin'. When she told Rindy Sue she couldn't have no meal, Rindy Sue axt effen she could look at my hawgs. Since my old woman wuz afeard of her, she tuk her to the barn lot to see the hawgs and then she went home. The very next morning, all of them hawgs wuz stone dead.

"Now, this made me mad as a hornet, and I went over to Jeff

Thorn's place to talk to him 'bout hit. He told me thet Rindy Sue 'ud been there and borrered some wool cards* and atter thet, all his cows went dry. We grumbled and cussed up a blue streak, and 'lowed thet we'd just have to have hit out with her, come hell or high water. So, we went over to Gary Ben Gose's place and told him what his old woman had been a doin'. We swore to him effen he didn't do sumpthin' 'bout her, we'd do hit ourselves.

"Old Gary Ben wuz a triflin' sort of feller who allus acted like he wuzzn't 'zactly right in the haid, but he never had no bone to pick with nobody. So, he swore to us, effen we'd leave hit to him, he'd find out for certin effen Rindy Sue wuz a witch, and effen she wuz, he'd take care of her. We didn't put much stock in his promise, but we 'lowed hit wuz 'bout all we could do, so we waited.

"Gary Ben told us later what happened. That very night, he started to watch Rindy Sue, and when hit come time to bed down, he locked the cabin door and hid the key. Then, he got in bed with his face torge the room, closed his eyes and started a snorin' real loud. Afore long, Rindy Sue sneaked real quiet outten the bed and made a beeline torge her trunk in a corner of the room. Gary Ben opened his eyes jest wide enuf to get a good look-see, and he watched her take out a little crock from the trunk, take the kiver offen hit and fetch out a little medicine bottle. She pulled out the stopper and a beetle came out in her hand. Then she held thet varmint nigh the witch mark on her shoulder, and hit grabbed on to hit and started a suckin' blood.

"Whilst thet beetle wuz a suckin her witch mark, Rindy Sue tuk offen all her clothes and rubbed some black stuff on her from the crock. She peeled offen her skin, folded hit and put hit in the trunk. Then, she poured some awful stinkin' stuff outten annuder bottle and rubbed hit on her hands and waved 'em in the air. Lo and behold she started drawin' up and in no time 'tall, she was 'bout the size of thet beetle. Then, her and thet beetle jest sailed acrost the room and outten the keyhole!

"Now, old Gary Ben had never seen no monkey shines like this afore, and he wuz so flabbergasted he couldn't move for a long spell. Then, when he did git his sense back, he started a thinkin' on whut he'd seed, and whut he could do 'bout hit. He made up his mind to a scheme to head her off.

"He got up, tuk her skin outten the trunk, unfolded hit and

---

* A flat board or paddle with a handle which has small metal teeth or spikes on one side which are not very long, but are very close together. A wool card is used to comb wool or other fibers free of tangles.

rubbed salt on the inside of hit. Then, he folded hit back and put hit in the trunk jest like he'd found hit, and went back to bed. 'Twarn't long afore Rindy Sue and her beetle come a creepin' through the keyhole, and Gary Ben started a snorin' again, but kept watchin' her.

"Rindy Sue made a beeline for thet trunk, put the beetle back in hit's bottle and put it in the trunk. Then, she got a bottle uf some green stuff and poured some in her hands. When she waved them in the air, right away she started to grow, and she growed and growed till she wuz the same size she wuz afore she tuk her skin off. Then, she got thet skin outten the trunk and tried to put hit on again. But, bless my soul, thet salt had made Rindy Sue's skin draw up and hit wuz too little fer her!

"Besides drawin' up her skin, the salt burned and stung her and made her mad as a swarm of bees. She throwed a fit then and there, a dancin' and screamin' and cussin'. She swore she'd witch Gary Ben so he'd turn into a horse thet she'd ride every night the rest of his borned days. She grabbed at him, but he jumped outten the bed. Then, she kicked at him, but he jumped aside. Her naked foot hit the bedpost and hurt her big toe somethin' awful. She yelled at Gary Ben to light the lamp so's she could see effen her toe wuz broke. Hit wuzzen't broke, but the blood wuz a oozin' out, and when Rindy Sue saw her own blood, hit broke her witch spell.

"So Gary Ben made her put on her skin and her clothes, and told her effen she ever done any more witchin', he'd kill her. But, Rindy Sue's skin was too little fer her, and she couldn't stand up straight. Atter thet, she walked all stooped over like an old woman.

"Gary Ben paid me fer my hawgs. The spells Rindy Sue had put on 'tother folks wuz broken, and she didn't do no more witchin.''

DELIVERED UP TO THE DEVIL

The fragrant odor of wood smoke diffused through the cold air as Reverend Hiriam Dodson's big boots crunched the frozen snow along the path beside the noisy creek. The shadows were straddling the ridges and dusk was deepening over the log cabin nestled in the hillside at the head of Mill Creek.

As Reverend Dodson approached, his hound dog, too lazy and cosy to abandon his warm rag bed under the porch, quavered a welcome. Hiriam lumbered up the steep porch steps, hung his overcoat over a peg on the wall, kicked the snow from his boots, and entered the cabin. He called out to his wife, "Nan, I'm shore froze stiff, and I'm hongry and tired as a dog. Hope you've got a lot of hot vittels a waitin'."

"Twill be ready afore long. Now, you jest stretch yore legs afore the fire and warm and dry yourself whilst I set the supper on the table," Nancy Sue answered. Then, she asked, "Hiriam, wuz there enough foregathered at the meetin' house to preach to? I 'lowed that mebbe not many 'ud come out this Sunday, sence hit's so close to Christmas and so cold."

"Wall, yep, I had a scatterin'. But I 'low they're a gettin' a bellyful of my preachin' 'bout how the Devil's a takin' over here through them Melungion* witches. Looks like we've got to take the bull by the horns and do sumpthin' besides preachin' 'bout hit," Hiriam drawled, rubbing his cold hands together and holding first one foot, then the other out to the blazing fire. "Where's Jonas?"

Instead of replying directly to his question, Nan said, "Come

Collected by James Taylor Adams, Big Laurel, Wise County, Virginia, May 17, 1939. Told to him by his grandfather, Spencer Adams. It was Spencer Adam's son, James Taylor's uncle, who became the witch. Spencer Adams, his father, and his grandfather were all hardshell Baptist Preachers.

*The Melungions are said to be people descended either from a group of Portuguese mutineers who appeared on the North Carolina coast many years ago and who intermarried with Indians and Negroes, *or* members of the Lost Colony on Roanoke Island who intermarried with Indians and Negroes. They are often referred to by such names as Ridgemanites, Black Waters, Ramps, and Melangos. The origin of the name is obscure. See Bell, Bonnie, *The Melungions*, Historical Society of Southwest Virginia, 1969.

on to supper. They'se sumpthin' I want to talk to you 'bout whilst we eat.''

Hiriam drew his chair up to the dimly lit table, filled his plate with steaming hot vittles, took a sip of buttermilk, and then looked straight at Nan and asked: "Is hit 'bout Jonas you want to talk? Why didn't you set a plate for him? Has he traipsed through this snow and ice to Mud Flats again to spark thet good-fer-nothin' little Melungion heifer?''

"Hiriam, hits worser then thet. Thet young'uns run off, and sez he ain't a comin' back to live with us no more. He sez he's tired of workin' hard all week for you, then a tryin' to learn how to preach on Sundays. He sez you won't give him any money and won't let him go out and do things like t'other boys. He sez you're barkin' up the wrong tree effen you think fer a minute thet he's a goin' to preach hellfire and damnation to these here mountain primitive Baptists like you and your pappy and your grandpappy's been a doin' ever sence the white people took this land frum the Indians. Sted of thet, he sez he's a goin' to larn to be a conjure man, and live offen the people. He sez he's a goin' to enjoy all the worldly pleasures you've denied him.''

Nan paused as her little round mouth puckered and her eyes filled with tears. She peered at Hiriam and, with an anguished sigh, continued: "Hiriam, you know we've tried to raise thet young' un in the fear of the Lord. We hain't never done nuthin' to spite him. What's got into him lately, I don't know. Thet little huzzy, Effie Goins' old mammy, is a witch, and she mought have put some quare idees in his haid.''

She paused again, stared ahead in agony, then continued, "Hiriam, in all my born days I hain't never heard sich a rigamarole. Thet boy wuz shore hog-tied and runnin' in circles. I couldn't b'lieve my ears when he sez mebbe he'd have a broomstick marriage* with Effie Goins and live out thar in thet old prospector's shack on Willer Crick. He sed he knowed you won't sign for them to marry, so when he gits of age he's a goin' to hang his hat with her family.''**

This aged couple, hearts overflowing with disappointment

---

*In the mountains, a common law marriage was often referred to as a "broomstick marriage." In the actual ceremony, a broomstick would be placed on the floor and, when the couple had stepped over the stick together, they were considered married.

**In the mountains, when a man went to live with his wife's family, he was said to "hang his hat" with her family.

and sorrow, sat together in the dim light and wept in silence. For either it would have been more merciful to have buried their youngest son.

Then, after what seemed to be an eternity, Hiriam said, "Nan, this is worser than all git out. You know thet young'un hain't paid me no mind for nigh onto a year now. He's been a goin' to them infares,* and workin's and a drinkin' and a hellin' round, and he's jest been a hankerin' for trouble. He ain't no good now."

Then righteous indignation crowded out Hiriam's sorrow, and he said, "Mind me, Nan, even effen he is our own flesh and blud, hit'll be over my daid body afore he ever darkens this door while he's a traipsin' round with thet pack of Melungion witches. Thet harebrained young'un is jest like Saul in the Bible. He's lost touch with the Lord. He's lookin' for a woman with a familiar speret, and I reckon he's found her kase old Liz Goins is knowed to be the chief witch amongst them Melungions. She'll deliver him up to the Devil, jest like Saul wuz delivered into the hands of the Philistines."

Then, in his best pulpit voice he quoted to Nan: "Hit sez in Exodus, 'Thou shalt not suffer a witch to live!' Again in Leviticus, 'A man also or a woman thet hath a familiar speret, er thet is a wizard, shall surely be put to death; they shall stone 'em with stones; their blud shall be upon 'em.' "

While Hiriam preached and ranted, Jonas Dodson, as he'd bragged to his mother he'd do, moved into the prospector's abandoned shack on Willer Crick. Then, he trudged over the ridge in the half light to Liz Goins' place on Mud Flats to work out some plans with Effie and to find out how to become a conjure man.

Jonas' approach to Liz' shack was heralded by the rasping grind of the frosty crispness under foot. A puny shaft of light shone feebly through the one dirty pane of glass left in the window, the rest being stuffed with paper and rags. When Liz swung the creaky door open, he smelled some fetid odors. She said in her husky voice, "We heard the crunchin' of the snow way down yonder, and 'lowed hit wuz you. Come into the house, and thaw out yore nose."

For more than fifty years this hovel had sheltered old Liz Goins and her numerous bastard young 'uns, most of whom disappeared

---

* In the mountains, after a couple was married, the wedding party and guests drank and socialized until early bedtime. At that point, the bride and bridegroom were put in a specially prepared bed upstairs, whereupon the revelers resumed their drinking and dancing. In the early hours of the morning they would wake the bride and groom, make them join the guests for more fun, and bid them farewell when the party was over.

as mysteriously as they had been conceived. She was sitting before the struggling little fire, and glanced up at Jonas from the corner of her eyes, then went back to gazing at the fire.

"Liz," Jonas asked, "what does hit take for you to make a conjure man outten me? I want the whole works: to be able to cast spells, to change into varmints, to fly through the air, to find lost things, and to do all tother things any warlock can do."

Without taking her eyes off the fire, Liz brushed back a strand of her Indian-straight black hair, and said, "The fust thing you got to git through your haid is whut witches air 'sposed to do. Witchcraft is the 'ligion of the Devil. Witches do everything whut God's 'ligion don't do. Witches promise to worship the Devil and to do zactly like he sez; to preach and spread the Devil's idees; never to tell nobody nothin' 'bout the Devil's plans, nor never tell who air witches. Onct the Devil lets you be a witch, 'tain't no changin' back, and in the end the Devil gets yore soul. So you shore better be sartin thet you want to be a witch afore you get into hit."

"I know all the things you're sposed to do atter you git to be a witch," Jonas interrupted her. "What I want to know now is how to git to be one."

"Wall, Jonas, I cain't make you a witch myself; hit's the Devil's work," Liz explained. "But mebbe sence I've served him nigh on to forty years, I could argue him to make you into a conjure man. Now, you jest stay here tonight. I've got some bizziness with the Devil tonight, and I'll axt him effen he'll have you and effen he will, whut you'll have to do to get to be one."

With that, she opened the door and disappeared, but reappeared with the first light of dawn as suddenly as she had gone. "Jonas," she said, "I've got a proposition frum the Devil for you. Nacherelly, he's suspicious of you, since yore granddaddy, yore daddy and you've all been a preachin' agin him and a fightin' him and his witches all these years. So you'll have to prove to him that you're shore this is whut you want to do. You'll have to swear to do zactly as he sez."

Jonas had some qualms on hearing this, but he'd gone too far to haul in his horns, so he told Liz he'd do anything the Devil asked him.

Liz then said, "This is whut the Devil wants the most: promise you won't never preach no more, nor go to a 'ligious meetin. Then, effen you git to be a witch, promise to do ennything you can to keep yore pappy frum preachin' agin witches. Now, hit ain't a goin' to be easy, and I 'low you mought have to try more'n onct afore you git in. Whatever happens, you have to foller 'structions zactly."

Jonas promised, "Yep, Liz, I'll do zactly whut I'm told to do."

So, following instructions, at midnight he sneaked into his father's field and stole one of the black rams. He killed it and cut off its left horn, hiding the rest of the carcass in the woods.

The next day being Sunday, he got a boy to steal a silver coin out of the collection plate of his father's church. He melted down the coin and made it into a silver bullet, which he put to soak in toad's blood. He also went to Gladeville where he bought a pewter plate. Next, he scoured the hills until he found a spring whose stream flowed directly east.

He then waited until Friday the thirteenth and returned to the spring as the morning turned gray over the ridge. He dipped some water from the spring with his ram's horn and poured it over the pewter plate. He did this seven times and repeated the verses Liz had taught him:

"As I dip the water with a ram's horn,
Cast me cruel with a heart of thorn,
As I now to the Devil do my soul lease.

I also renounce Christ as my Savior,
And promise the Devil my behavior
'Til my life on earth will cease.

May my black and evil soul be
Of Christian love and grace free
As this plate is of grease.

And effen I become an evil crone
From my outer skin to inner bone,
I'll never given any Christian peace.

Rain and shine, for eight mornings, Jonas came to the spring and repeated this ritual. On the ninth morning, he was supposed to become a witch and he took his gun and the silver bullet with him. He shot the bullet toward the sun as it came up over the ridge. They had told him that if the sun looked as if it were dripping blood as it came up, then he would be a witch. Jonas thought it did, and started home.

He had also been told that if he had become a witch, he would find a toad waiting for him when he got home which would be his familiar spirit or "imp." But, there was no toad near the door, look as he might. This meant that he hadn't passed, and he'd have to do this all over again the next Friday the thirteenth.

The second time, there was no familiar waiting, either. But Jonas was stubborn, and he tried the third time before he became a conjure man. This took him two full years, but he said it was worth the time and trouble. Liz told him that it took so long because the Devil distrusted him because of the preachers in his family.

Jonas Dotson lived to be an old man, and became notorious for his evil deeds as his father had been respected for his good work as a preacher. He harassed the people and became such a terror in the county that he was finally arrested by Old Doc Taylor and hanged at Wise Courthouse for a brutal murder.

PART TWO

HOW WITCHES WORK

INTRODUCTION

As in any other trade or profession, witches had a stock set of procedures which they used in plying their craft. Often, witches were accused of casting spells on animals, especially cows, horses and hogs. In "The Horse That Wouldn't Cross the Stream," George sets out to get a city doctor to attend to his wife who has been treated without success by a witch. Of course, the witch objects to bringing in a doctor, but George does so just the same. When he comes to a small river and begins to wade through it, his horse balks and refuses to go further. He drubs, beats and curses at the horse, but it won't move an inch. He gives up, turns around, and goes back home. He is convinced that his horse has been bewitched so that he could not fetch the doctor.

The witchball was a favorite tool of witches. In "How Witchballs Are Made," there is a detailed account of their manufacture. Witches shot them at animals and humans to cast a spell, or buried them on a path where the person they desired to bewitch would be sure to cross.

Witches used many herbs and plants to brew potions which were administered to people, among them deadly poisons like digitalis from the foxglove plant, and belladonna from henbane. These poisons could be administered slowly so that a witch could make a person ill without killing him.

A recurring theme in witch stories is the use of a magic bridle. This device turned people into horses on which the witch would ride at night. Della Barksdale tells, in "The Big Brass Pin," how a witch came through the keyhole into her bedroom, changed her into a horse, and rode her into town.

Witches, at times, changed themselves into animals in order to carry on their work more efficiently. In Europe, they were reported to have changed themselves into monstrous dogs and werewolves. In "The Indian Warlocks from Acoma," two Indians, riding to a tribal religious meeting, claim that two warlocks—male witches —turned themselves into coyotes. These men may have been under the influence of peyote or some other hallucinogen in preparation for the forthcoming ceremony. At other times, witches assumed the form of a cat to do their evil work.

Many stories tell of witches appearing in balls of fire and in strange lights. No doubt, the mountain people associated such manifestations with the fires of hell, but they can probably be explained physically as being caused by fox-fire, seepage of methane gas, or some form of lightning. In "A Ball of Fire," a blazing reddish-yellow ball of fire appears, skids aimlessly from side to side, then lodges against a tree trunk. This corresponds to a description of ball lightning.

It was generally believed in Europe—and the belief brought to America—that witches had two souls, one of which could leave the body and do evil deeds, while the other remained in the witch who was peacefully asleep in her bed. Perhaps this was the case in "The Invisible Witch," where a girl complains that an old woman is chasing and slapping her, although nobody else can see her.

Witches used many strange props or tools. Live bugs were placed in a bottle to indicate the direction in which it is best to look for lost objects. "The Strange Chestnut Tree" is used by Billy Jo Boggs to change into an animal and back again. The witch ladder was made of a long cord and interwoven and combined with the feathers of a black hen. Eutiquio finds one of these in the bruja's home in "The Witch of Cenescu." "The Indian Warlocks from Acoma" use a magic hoop through which they jump to change into coyotes, and then jump back again in order to change back into men.

One of the strangest of witch tools was the "hand of glory." This consisted of the right hand of a hanged felon, dried in a pot filled with salt, dragonwort, black pepper, niter and spices. It was used with a special ointment made from the fat of a hanged man's body, mixed with virgin wax. This mixture was spread on the fingers of the hand all of which were lit like candles. They issued an eerie blue flame, and gave off a gas which rendered people unconscious.

HOW WITCHBALLS ARE MADE

Miz Ison, a Melungion*, lived with his wife Kate and their ten children near the head of Mud Creek up Big Laurel Holler, not too far from Zollie and Izzy Snipes' cabin.

Kate had a very fine flock of black leghorn chickens of which she was very proud. Izzy Snipes took a fancy to one of Kate's big black roosters, and wanted to buy it. But, Kate thought Izzy was a witch, and she had been told never to let a witch have anything, because they would be able to cast spells on their former owner. So, Kate refused to sell Izzy the rooster.

One day, Kate was out in the barnyard gathering eggs and feeding her chickens, when she suddenly fell down as if she'd been shot. She was conscious, but unable to move or speak. Finally, one of the children came to look for her, and Miz moved her into the cabin. When they dumped the broken eggs out of her apron, they found a round hairy ball about the size of a chestnut burr, and it had a foul odor. Miz examined her and found a big blue spot on her left side just under her heart. Then, they knew that Izzy had shot her with a witchball because she had refused to sell the rooster.

Kate was all right the next day, but Miz was as mad as a wounded bear. He took that witchball and hot-footed it over to Zollie Snipes' place. He told Zollie what had happened and showed him the witchball. He said that if Zollie didn't do something about Izzy's shenanigans, the Melungions would handle it in their own way. Zollie was afraid of the Melungions, so he begged Miz to give him the witchball, and give him a chance to do something.

Now, Zollie wasn't sure Izzy was a witch, so while she was out milking, he searched the cabin for some evidence. He found nothing. Then, he sat down in front of the fire to think. After a while, he got up to throw the last log on the fire, and, as he moved the log, he thought he saw one of the hearthstones move. He examined it and found it was loose ˙so he pulled it up and found a dirty rag

Collected by Gertrude Blair, Roanoke, Virginia, June 10, 1939. Told to her by Aunt Lucy Skinner, who lived in Montgomery County, not far from Christiansburg, Virginia. This story has been handed down through at least four generations.

*See note on page 20.

under it. Under the rag was a small Bible. He took it out carefully, and under it he found six witchballs just like the one Miz had given him.

Zollie was afraid to touch the witchballs, so he replaced the rag and the stone, laid the witchball Miz had given him on the hearth, and began to examine the Bible. In the back of the Book of Revelations, he found what could barely be read as the name "Izzy Snipes X," which seemed to be written in blood. This was the oath of allegiance to the Devil she had signed. This was all positive evidence that she was indeed a witch, and Zollie was boiling mad as he waited for Izzy's return.

When she joined him in front of the fire, he told her of Miz' visit and of his discovery of the Bible and witchballs under the hearthstone. He was as mad as a wet hen and bellowed: "Izzy, effen you don't tell me all about this witchin' I'll throw you outten the snow and let them Melungions sick their dogs on you."

Izzy had to make a hangman's choice: If she blabbed about witchcraft, the Devil would beat her to death. On the other hand, she knew that Zollie meant what he said, and that it would be certain death if the Melungions caught her, because Miz wasn't the only one she'd given a hard time over the years. Then, she thought that if she told Zollie everything, and they both tried to get right with the Lord, she might get back her bonded soul from the Devil. So, she made up her mind to come clean with Zollie.

"I know you recollect, Zollie, thet when I wuz a young gal no more'n sixteen, I wuz awful purty, and jest 'bout as silly as enny gal could be. I wuz a greedy gut, too. I wanted a man; I wanted purty clothes; I wanted control over folks; I wanted nigh everthing I seed or thought of; I wanted things so bad thet I didn't care how I got 'em. As I look back now, I can see I didn't have nary a bit of gumption.

"You remember years ago, Zollie, when I usta go out at nights and tell you I wuz a goin' to see my sick sister. Well, I wuz a goin' to witch meetin's. No doubt 'bout hit, I wuz one of the fust in these hills to jine up with 'em. Yep, I traded with the Devil and promised I'd let him use my purty body durin' my lifetime, and get my soul when I die. He promised to keep me purty, make me rich, and give me power to cast spells over people and things. The Devil bit my big finger till hit bled, and, sence I cain't write, he took my hand in his'n and holp me write my name in thet Bible. Thet wuz my contract with him."

"Yep, I made thet out soon as I saw the Bible," said Zollie.

"Now, how did you make them witchballs?"

"Well, you have to make witchballs on Friday the thirteenth, so we had a special meetin' thet night. The Devil 'ud told us the meeting afore what every witch wuz supposed to bring. Effen she didn't bring hit, she had to kiss the Devil's bottom, and then bare her own bottom whilst the Devil gave her thirteen licks with a bundle of rose thorns. Ever' time a witch 'ud scream, she'ed get another lick."

Izzy frowned, thinking about how that rose thorn thrashing hurt, and what she was risking by talking about it. She almost stopped, but the sight of Zollie's lowering face made her go on: "When we met at the crossroads down nigh the graveyard, the Devil fust drawed a big ring 'bout nine feet acrost. The witches rounded up some firewood and built a big fire in the middle of hit. When hit started burnin' good, the Devil poured a mess of things on hit to make the blue, green, red and yeller flames. Then, he put a pot on to bile, and threw into hit a bottle of weazel's blood and a handful of dried baby's flesh. Then, each witch throwed in the stuff she'd brung into the pot, and the Devil throwed in any stuff they failed to bring. Atter this, we all joined hands and danced 'round the fire while the Devil chanted:

> A pair of dead spiders' legs,
> Guts and bladder of a black cat,
> Dead baby's toenails, buzzard's eggs,
> Blud of a weazel and tail of a rat.
>
> The eye of a big, fat sow,
> The whisker of a wildcat,
> A tit of a milk cow,
> And the brain of a bat.
>
> The foot of a toadfrog,
> The hair from a murdered man's wig,
> The dried turd of a feiss dog,
> The hair of a Poland-China pig.
>
> To this mystic myrrh,
> To make a witchball,
> I, the Devil, doth stir,
> To place curses on one and all.

"We let this brew bile for seven minutes then, whilst hit cooled, the Devil handed us candles made outten human grease. We lit the candles from the fire and marched 'round the ring till they were 'most burnt up, then threw them into the fire. Then the Devil took up blobs of the stuff from the pot and wrapped each one with hair each witch had cut from her haid, and this made the witchballs.

"Witches who'd brung what they'se supposed to got thirteen balls, and those who jest brung part got seven balls. This wuz all I got. Them that didn't bring nuthin' got only three balls. The Devil told us these balls 'ud have to last us till annuder Friday the thirteenth when we could make some more. Effen a witch lost one or let somebody steal one, the Devil would whup her with rose thorns. Thet's why people don't find witchballs: the witch slips back to git 'em so's she can use 'em agin."

So Zollie found out how witchballs were made, but not much else. He exacted a promise from Izzy that she would quit witching, but the promise was worthless, since the Devil never lets a witch back out on her contract, and the Devil gave her a thorough beating with rose thorns. Soon, she was back at her old tricks, but she was far more careful to conceal it from Zollie.

NO MILK ON SATURDAY

Around 1800, there lived a family of McCorkles on Bridle Creek in Grayson County. Frieda Lotz, whose children were all grown and away, was a widow and lived with them. She was known throughout the county as Granny Lotz, the witch.

Stephen Ward and his family lived on the adjoining farm and Granny Lotz often visited them. She was so old and forgetful that she often forgot to shut the gates after her, and Steve's livestock would get out. He got after Granny about this, and she became very angry. But, Steve didn't give a whoop.

Not long after their tiff, Steve's cow started giving bloody milk, and he blamed Granny for it. He said she'd witched the cow, and word of this got back to Granny Lotz. She was so angry that she swore she wouldn't let him rest from then on.

Now, Steve had never tangled with a witch before, and he didn't know just what to do, so he thought he'd better go over to see Dicey Osteen, who was known to be a witch doctor. Dicey agreed to tell him what to do to lift the spell, but he asked a high price for it.

The next morning, following Dicey's instructions, Steve milked his cow, brought the milk into the cabin and put it in a big flat pan. Then, he went out on a ridge and cut three birch withes and tied them together. He built a big fire under the pan of milk and, as it boiled, he flailed as much milk as he could out of the pan into the fire with the birch withes. As the milk burned with a blue-green flame, Steve saw Granny Lotz's face in the flames and he knew that it was indeed she who had witched the cow.

Just as the last drops of milk hit the fire, one of the McCorkle children ran in hollering: "Come quick! Granny Lotz is awful poorly and she thinks she's about to draw her last breath. She don't want to peg out with you mad at her. She wants you to come so's she can make things right with you."

But, Steve was so outdone with her that he yelled back, "Damn her old witchin' soul! You go back and tell her to die and go straight to hell where she orter been a long time ago! I don't want nuthin' to

Collected by P. E. Crowder of Potts Creek, Grayson County, Virginia, September 24, 1939. Told to him by Boyd A. Rhudy of Elks Creek, who had heard it from Hosiah Ward. This story is said to have happened around the year 1800 to a family on Bridle Creek in an isolated section of the county.

However, many others in the community went to see Granny Lotz while she was ill, and they said her eyes were almost smoked out. She had whelps on her face as if she'd been whipped with a switch. But, Steve's cow didn't give any more bloody milk.

Granny Lotz got better, and soon was hobbling about again. Then, Steve's cow wouldn't give any milk on Saturday mornings. It acted as if it'ed already been milked, so Steve put it in the barn every night, but he still didn't get any milk on Saturdays.

So, he went back to Dicey Osteen to ask his advice, and Dicey said that a witch was milking the cow before Steve got up. Steve said that this couldn't be, as he stayed in the barn Friday night, and the cow hadn't been milked. Dicey laughed fit to kill at this and explained that a witch could milk a cow in her own cabin by using a clean towel with a fringe on it. The towel was hung outside their cabin door by a new pin, and after some magic words were said, they could milk the fringe of the towel. Dicey thought perhaps Granny Lotz was doing this.

Steve flared up and said he wanted to get rid of Granny's spells once and for all, and he'd pay any reasonable price if Dicey could do it. But Dicey held out for every seventh animal that would be born on Steve's place for the next three years, and Steve had to agree.

Again, he followed Dicey's instructions. First, he paid one of the McCorkle children a quarter to steal one of Granny Lotz' dirty stockings. He put them in some creek water and boiled them, later pouring the water into a bottle. Then, he got a metal plow point and heated it red hot in the fireplace.

As the plow point was heating, one of the McCorkle boys came running to borrow some linament. He said that Granny had dropped a kettle of hot water and burned her legs real bad. But, Dicey had told Steve not to lend Granny anything, or it would destroy his magic, so Steve told the boy to get off his place before he sicked his dog on him.

After the plow point was red hot, Steve took it out of the fire and poured the dirty water out of the bottle on it.

Just as Dicey had told him, Granny Lotz' legs were badly burned, and she took a long time to recover. She did get better and was able to walk again, but this time it worked and Steve had no more trouble with her. The spell Granny Lotz had put on the cow was broken and she began to give her regular yield of milk.

FINDING THINGS THROUGH CLAIRVOYANCE

Theopolis Votsis, Dominick Amato and Bruce McRae worked together in the deep shaft mine at Caretta, West Virginia. They always changed into work clothes and left their street clothes in lockers topside before they descended hundreds of feet below in the elevator cage.

One afternoon, Bruce and Dominick, who were working as a team that day, had to clean up a slate fall after they had finished their cut of coal. This delayed them until most of the men had left the mine, and they were the last to come up the elevator. As they changed their clothes in the locker room, Bruce missed his favorite tartan shirt which he had worn that morning. They looked all over for it, but had to give up and Bruce wore an old shirt which Dominick had in his locker.

Bruce had heard that Nath Wrightson was a conjuror who could help people find lost items, and he decided to consult him on the way home, and persuaded Dominick to come along. As they walked along, Dominick became too hot, so he shed his overcoat and decided to leave it at the home of his friend Eric Ison, who lived on the edge of the camp. Then, an idea occurred to him and he asked Bruce if he didn't think it would be a good idea to test the conjuror's ability to find things by asking him where he had left the overcoat. Bruce thought this a fine idea.

When they reached Nath Wrightson's cabin, he greeted them both by name, though neither one knew him. He added, "Dominick, you are a Catholic and your name means 'belonging to the Lord.' And, before either of them could speak, he announced, "Bruce, you want me to find your tartan shirt. I know you prize it very highly because your grandfather sent it to you from Scotland years ago."

He then turned to Dominick and asked, "You want me first to tell you where you left your overcoat, don't you?" To their utter amazement, he proceeded to answer his own question by saying,

Collected by F. Dingus Huffman of Bartley, West Virginia, September 12, 1934, from W. D. Bishop who was told this story by his father. Story adapted by the author.

"You left it with Eric Ison because it was too hot and too heavy to carry. Now do you believe I can tell you where to find Bruce's shirt?"

They were both struck dumb by this, but when Nath stretched out his big, skinny hand, palm upward and asked, "Now, Bruce, are you ready to cross my palm with three pieces of silver in exchange for the whereabouts of your shirt?" Bruce gladly complied.

Nath bowed his head and seemed to go into a trance. After what seemed like an eternity, he broke the silence by saying, "Your shirt is a MacLeod tartan. It blends the colors of blue for the pure waters of Scotland, purple for the heather which covers the Highlands, and white for the snowy peaks. The shirt was sewn by a left-handed woman, possibly your grandmother. You have removed the second button from the top and are carrying it in your right front pocket as a good luck charm. Now, Bruce, you wouldn't have lost your shirt if your old woman hadn't given away some salt today. This is a very dangerous thing to do, because if it passes into the hands of a witch, it gives her the power to cause harm to any member of your family by simply uttering a wish."

After this long monologue, Nath opened his eyes and peered at his attentive listeners for a moment. Then, he bowed his head again, closed his eyes, and began to rock his torso right and left. He continued, "Just as there is a Holy Trinity of Father, Son and Holy Ghost, so we have a magic trinity to thrust out evil spirits. Upon returning home, you will find your tartan shirt has been returned by Theopolis Votsis, who carried it away from the pit. I have directed him through my magic trinity to return it at once."

Nath continued, "When you go home, get your old woman to wash and boil your shirt. When it is dry, sew on the button you've been using as a charm. This is the first step of the magic trinity. The second step is to rub some salt on your cat's head while saying ABRACADABRA, SATOR ROTAS.* For the third step, sleep tonight with your Bible under your pillow."

Bruce carried out Nath's instructions, and darn if he didn't find his shirt. He carried out Nath's instructions and never lost another thing from his locker.

---

* ABRACADABRA is an alphabetical acrostic. At one time, it was inscribed on a piece of parchment or on a metal plaque. It reads as follows:

```
A B R A C A D A B R A
A B R A C A D A B R
A B R A C A D A B
A B R A C A D A
A B R A C A D
A B R A C A
A B R A C
A B R A
A B R
A B
A
```

SATOR ROTAS is likewise an acrostic. It was inscribed on parchment or paper and reads as follows:

```
S A T O R
A R E P O
T E N E T
O P E R A
R O T A S
```

WITCHES! THAT'S TOMFOOLERY

Before the Civil War, an old woman named Della Purkey, lived way back on Piney Notch. She took to her bed, and people in the community refused to believe she was really ill. She was reputed to be a witch, and they said she could get up any time she wanted to work one of her evil spells.

Little Gus Purkey, old Della's ten-year old grandson, stayed with her and had to wait on her hand and foot. Her incessant demands didn't even stop at night, and it was rare that little Gus got a full night's sleep. His granny wouldn't let him go anywhere, not even home to see his parents. He was very lonesome, and when he was lucky enough to see one of his friends, he begged them to come to the cabin to spend the night with him. One or two did come, but they never stayed more than one night, and they never came again.

But, little Frank Ball was braver than the rest. He bragged that he wasn't afraid of witches; that it was a lot of tomfoolery. So, when Gus begged him to come and spend the night with him, he accepted and made up his mind that he would stay awake and find out what was really pestering Gus.

They went to bed soon after dark, and Gus was soon asleep. But, Frank stayed awake and felt increasingly uneasy. He tried to comfort himself with the sight of the big pied cat in front of the fireplace.

Before long, old Della yelled for Gus to get up and fetch her a drink of water, but Gus didn't wake. She screamed three times for him, but he was dead to the world. Then, Frank noticed that the pieds on that cat started to get bigger and bigger and brighter and brighter until he thought they must give off light. Then, the cat gave a leap and landed on Gus's chest. It just sat there, its eyes shining like silver dollars, looking first at Gus and then at Frank. Now Frank had heard tales of cats sucking the breath of babies and killing them, and he thought that was what the cat was up to, so he started hitting at the cat and yelling at him so that Gus finally woke up.

Collected by Emory L. Hamilton, Wise, Virginia, September 5, 1940. Told to him by Mrs. Belle Kilgore from Norton, Virginia, who heard it from her mother. Belle Kilgore was 82 years old at the time.

"What air you doin'?" Gus asked Frank, before he was awake enough to see the cat.

"Look, thet pied cat's on your chest!" answered Frank excitedly.

"Aw shucks, Frank, thet hain't no cat; thet's my granny's imp. She's sore at me fer sumpthin'. Did she holler fer me?"

"Yep, she yelled for a glass of water," Frank informed him.

The pied cat moved down to the foot of the bed, and Gus rolled out and got his granny a drink of water. As soon as he got up, the cat jumped down, went over to the fireplace, hunkered down before the fire and went to sleep again. It wasn't long before both Frank and Gus were fast asleep, and they weren't disturbed any more that night.

After breakfast, early the next morning, Gus told Frank that his oldest brother Glen was cutting timber on a ridge not far away, and since he hadn't seen any of his family for some time, he thought they ought to go over there and inquire about the family.

His granny forbade them to get out of sight of the cabin, so they climbed the ridge where they could watch Glen working with his team of bay horses but still keep the cabin in sight.

They had been watching for some time when Gus glanced down at the cabin and whispered to Frank, "Look!"

When Frank turned around, he saw Old Della coming out of the cabin carrying a broom. She went into the barn, came out with a bridle and went behind the barn. In a few minutes, she reappeared from behind the barn mounted on the biggest and prettiest black horse they had ever seen. She rode off toward Piney Notch, then came back and rode beside Glen's horses as fast as she could ride, turned and galloped on the other side of them. It scared Glen's horses so bad, they reared and broke their harness.

When this happened, Granny Purkey rode off cackling at the top of her voice. She disappeared from sight, circled around and headed for the barn again. She and the horse vanished behind it, and in a minute she came out the front without the horse, but carrying a bridle and her broom, and laughing fit to kill. She hung the bridle in the barn and hurried into the cabin.

When Frank and Gus got down to the cabin and peered in, Granny was in her bed moaning and groaning as if she were about to die. Frank took to his heels and lit out for home, and nobody ever heard him say again that witches were tomfoolery.

THE STRANGE CHESTNUT TREE

W. Patton Beverely of Norton, Virginia, told this story about his grandfather, Tine Beverely:

"One day, Tine followed Wagon Track Road back on the ridge between the forks of Clear Crick near Ramsey looking for some stray hogs. He came upon this strange chestnut tree standing all by itself. All of the trees and bushes around it were dead, but the tree was alive and loaded with chestnuts. Grandpappy went back to his cabin and told Granny, Sallie Ellen, that he was going up there and chop down the tree and get the chestnuts.

"But, Granny knew that the chestnut was a witches' tree, and she tried hard to persuade Grandpappy not to go. She told him that each year the tree would bear many chestnuts, but nobody ever got any because the nuts would stick in the burrs until freezing weather ruined them.

"Both Granny and Grandpappy knew that Old Billy Jo Boggs hung around the tree. He was reputed to be a witch who could turn himself into all kinds of animals and scare the living daylights out of folks when he was a snake or a panther or a bear. Old Billy Joe always had to come to that tree before he could change back to a man.

"But Grandpappy was as stubborn as a mule and as strong as he'd ever been in spite of his eighty-odd years, so he left at dawn the next day with his ax on his shoulder. When he didn't return by the time he should have, Granny got uneasy and went to a neighbor's place to get him to go with her to check on Tine.

"They went up Wagon Track Road to the chestnut tree and, so help me, if they didn't find Grandpappy lying there stone dead. He'd cut the tree about in half, and the ax was still in the tree. It looked as if he had just fallen away from the ax handle.

"When they turned him over and examined him, they didn't find a mark on him except a big blue spot on the calf of his leg. It surely looked like he'd been shot by a witchball, although of course

Collected by James Taylor Adams, Big Laurel, Wise County, Virginia, November 4, 1941. Told to him by Patton Beverly of Norton, Virginia, who heard the story as a child from his grandfather. His grandfather claimed he helped carry the victim to the cemetery.

they didn't find one since witches always take back their balls so they can use them again.

"That old chestnut tree stood there for many years just as Grandpappy had left it, since people wouldn't go anywhere near it after he was found dead there. Finally, lightning struck the tree, tore it to splinters and set it on fire. Every bit of it burned except the stump below where Grandpappy had been chopping."

THE BIG BRASS PIN

Not everybody in the little rural community of Riceville, Virginia, near Danville, believed in witches. Some of the people who found their hired help listless on the job were convinced that the stories the help told about witches pestering them at night so they couldn't sleep were fabricated to cover their night-time carousing. But, sometimes a hired hand *was* able to convince his master or mistress that he had really been bothered by a witch. Della Barksdale tells this story:

"I know they's such a thing as witches. Onct on a clear, moonlight night, a witch come through the keyhole in my cabin when I wuz jest a young'un. She come to my bed, changed me into a horse, and rode me to Riceville. She tied me to a tree clost to the store and disappeared.

"Whilest I wuz hitched to the tree, I seed sumpthin a shining in the moonlight on the ground, but hit was too far away for me to reach hit. Hit looked like one of them big brass pins folks wear in their shawls.

"Purty soon thet witch come back with her arms full of things she'd stole outta the store. She musta got in through the keyhole, stole them things, then unlatched the door and brought them out, 'cause I know the store wuzzen't open this late. Then, she rode me back home at a gallop.

"When daylight come, I wuz so tired, stiff and sore I couldn't hardly move. My missus axt what wuz wrong with me, and I tried to tell her 'bout the witch ridin' me. But, she jest flared up and sed, 'Hush up, chile, you're jest a tryin' to git outta work.' Then, she bust out laughin till her side shook, and she said, 'You ain't a goin' to git by with a wild tale like that. Grab that broom and start a sweepin! Witches don't ride you when you're pushin' a broom.'

"Then, I sed, 'Look, I can show you where that witch made welts on me when she wuz beatin' on me to make me gallop.' When I showed her these places, she laughed again and sed mebbe I'd been fightin' somebody, and they'd made them bruises.

Collected by Pearl Morrisett, Danville, Virginia, April 14, 1941. Told to her by Mrs. Della Barksdale, a seventy-two year old Negro woman who lived in Danville.

"But, I told her I could prove that I wuz tellin' the truth. She flared up and sed: 'There's no such thing as witches, and I'm goin to take you up on your offer. That'll show you.'

"So I tole her 'bout the big brass pin lyin' on the ground under the tree, and 'bout the things the witch had stole from the store. And, I axt her if she found the pin and axt Mr. Barker if he was missin' stuff from his store, would she believe me then. And she sed she would, but if she found I wuz lyin' to her, she'd whup the livin' daylights outta me.

"We hooked up the horses to the buggy, and made for Riceville. First off, we looked under that tree, and shore 'nuff, there wuz that big brass pin. The missus turned white as an egg, but sed she'd have to talk to Tom Barker 'bout the things missin' from the store. So, we went there, and she axt him if there wuz ennythin' different in the store when he opened up. He sed all the boxes of shoes and a big stack of clothes wuz heaped in a pile like somebody wuz lookin for somethin', and when he checked real careful, he wuz missing two pairs of woman's shoes and a whole lot of woman's things, besides a bottle of assafetida and a box of powdered sulfur.

"On the way back home, the missus sed, 'Bessie Bee, mebbe you're right, there must have been a witch around. Now we've got to do something to get rid of her.'

"So, ole missus went over to Fritz Hunsacker's to ask him what to do. He wuz a witch doctor, so he sed he would tell her how to get shut of the witches if she'd bring him two dominecker hens, a black shoat and a handful of acorns. When she took him all those things, he told her what to do and warned her to do zactly as he sed.

"Fust, we went out and kotch a big toad frog, and wropped hit in a black rag with hit's right hind foot stickin' out. Then, we got some hairs from the horse's tail, twisted them into a string, and tied the bag tight and hung hit to a tree nigh my cabin. Then, we nailed a horseshoe over the door so no more witches would come in.

"When that frog died and the bag rotted and dropped to the ground, I knew that the witch who had ridden me wuz dead. And that wuz the end of the witches botherin' round our place."

CAPTAIN SYLVATUS AND THE
WITCH OF TRURO

One of the strangest enchantments which ever befell the master of a sailing vessel overcame Captain Sylvatus. His ship was off Cape Cod Bay waiting for a favorable wind to push him around Race Point and into Boston harbor. He was carrying corn from North Carolina, consigned to a Boston merchant.

The captain, an elderly man, had a son who was already master of a vessel. While the ship was becalmed, Captain Sylvatus grew tired of the ship's fare, and went ashore near Truro to buy a bucket of milk. He bought it from an old woman whose red-heeled shoes could be seen beneath her linsey-woolsey skirt.

As soon as he returned to his ship, a favorable wind arose and he put out to sea. No sooner had they reached open water than the wind rose to a gale. Sails were ripped and then torn away, spars were broken, and finally the main mast went, leaving the little ship wallowing in the waves.

But, the behavior of the captain was the worst calamity of all. He made little effort to direct the handling of the vessel, became thin with a yellow complexion, and locked himself in his cabin early each evening. When his first mate tried to arouse him from his apathy, the Captain told him a strange tale. He declared that the milk he had bought from the old woman in Truro had been bewitched. He said that the old woman came to his cabin every night at moonrise and changed him into a horse. She would put a bit in his mouth, saddle and bridle him, and, all night long, she would ride him over the hills around Truro. They galloped along the combs, through the woods, up the dunes, across the inlets, and even down to Brook Island. When she released him just before dawn, he was too worn out to captain the ship.

The crew was getting desperate, since none of them knew navigation, so they pleaded with him to cast aside his delusions and put them on course again. But, the captain seemed to be under a compulsion to lock himself in his cabin each night and wait for the witch to come.

Based on a story in the *Journal of American Folklore*, Volume 14, Number 3, 1938. This story had been abstracted from *Narrow Land*, by Elizabeth Raynard, Houghton Mifflin, Boston, 1934.

Meanwhile, the ship drifted toward the Grand Banks. One morning, a sail was sighted and the crew raised distress signals. It was the ship of young Captain Sylvatus, and he brought his ship alongside and came on board his father's ship. His coming seemed to destroy the enchantment and to restore the old man's sanity. He roused himself to direct the needed repairs and set the ship on a correct course.

THE JACK-MA-LANTERNS

In 1942, Catherine Jones, a Negro practical nurse in Rockbridge County, Virginia, told this story she'd heard from her grandmother:

"Granny used 'ma' as the middle syllable instead of 'o' in jack o' lantern. She sed they 'ud lead you astray at night. You see, back in them days there wuzzen't lights a shinin' everwhere to guide a body like there is today. When the sun fell down, and there wuzzen't any moon, hit got skeery dark in the woods. Folks didn't have no flashlights ner lanterns neither, so effen ennybody wuz out at night, they'd try to find the light from a cabin outten the ridge and foller hit.

"Them hills wuz full of witches in them days. They done all kinds of things like spellin' people, witchin' varmints, and makin' folks sick. Sometimes, they done jest little mean tricks like leading folks astray with their jack-ma-lanterns like they done to my Grandpappy.

"Onct on a gloomy winter night, Grandpappy started out to see Hal Compton, whose cabin wuz way up on top of Horsepen Ridge. Hit wuz a right fur piece, but with the leaves all offen the trees, hit wuz easy to see the light in Hal's cabin from Grandpappy's place. Hit wuz as cold as the north wind, and the only sound he could hear wuz his own feet a crunchin' the leaves and twigs on the path, and an owl hootin' now and then.

"Grandpappy lost the path when he crossed the crick, but he saw a light and started to foller hit. The light led him 'round the hill, up the ridge and then into the thick woods. Then, he knowed he wuz lost, so he stopped and studied 'bout hit. He wuz mad as a hornet, kase he 'lowed he'd been a follerin' one of them jack-ma-lanterns.

"But Grandpappy knowed jest whut to do. He turned all his pockets wrong side out. Then, he drawed a ring in his path, made a cross on the ground, bowed his head and sed, 'In the name of the Father and the Son and the Holy Speret, drive these witches away with their evil jack-ma-lanterns.' When he looked up, he saw Hal Compton's cabin right nigh, but in 'tother direction then he'd been a headin.'"

Collected by Virginia Hale, Rockbridge County, Virginia, October 13, 1939.

THE BEWITCHED MUSKET

Barney Grisby and his father were getting ready to go hunting one day, when Barney asked his father a question that had been bothering him for some time.

"Why don't you ever use thet big rifle-gun a hangin' up there?" he asked.

"Kase hit hain't no good," he answered hurriedly. "And don't you ever tech hit," he warned, shaking his head to emphasize the point.

But, as Barney told his friend, Grant Boles, "Of course, thet jest made me as curious as a bluejay in a chicken yard. Ever since I could remember, thet musket 'ud hung on them deer horns over the fireplace. One day when everbody wuz outten the cabin, I tuk hit down and looked hit over real good. I couldn't see nuthin' wrong with hit, ner different from enny other gun, 'ceptin' hit wuz a little heavy. So, I put hit back on them deer horns, but I wuz dead set on findin' out all about thet gun.

"Twarn't long atter this till I cotched Paw when he wuz a feelin' pretty good atter some hooterns* of red-eye moonshine and his tongue wuz loose at both ends. So I axt him to tell me the story 'bout thet rifle-gun.

"Paw sed thet he'd brung thet gun with him when he come to the mountains many years ago. He got hit from his oldest brother, who tuk hit from a Yankee prisoner during the Civil War. Thet Yankee musta put a spell on hit, cause atter the War his brother tried to use it huntin'. The fust time he tuk hit outten the woods and shot hit, hit blowed off one of his fingers. So then he give hit to Paw.

"Paw tuk thet gun out and shot at a varmint from real close up, but the bullet missed hit by a mile. Then, he 'lowed the rifle-gun 'ud been witched and hit wuz bad luck to use hit, so he jest hung hit up on them deer horns and left hit there.

"But I wanted thet gun, and I told Paw sence I had never

Collected by Susan R. Morton, Haymarket, Virginia, January 21, 1942. Told her by Grant Boles of Antioch, Virginia, who was a friend of the chief character, Barney Grisby. The gun belonged to Barney's father, and was brought by him to the area after the Civil War.

*Mountain slang for a drink of whiskey. The term is also applied to the tin cup from which the drink is taken.

knowed my uncle, mebbe the curse wouldn't be on hit effen he 'ud give hit to me. So, he finally did, but he warned me to be very careful with hit, kase hit could hurt me. Natcherlly, I wuz as happy as a hive of bees in June clover, and I tuk hit down, tuk hit apart, and cleaned, oiled and shined hit up real good.

"I tuk hit out thet very day to hunt a rabbit er a squirrel. The fust rabbit I seed wuz so close I knowed I could kill hit, so I cut loose ker-bang! But, thet gun jest turned in my hands. The bullet hit a tree a long ways to the side of where I'd been a aimin'.

"I hunted through them woods the rest of the day, but I didn't see any more varmints, though I knowed them woods wuz full of 'em. I thought my Paw wuz right when he sed the gun wuz bad luck, and I wuz downfaced and low as dirt when I got back to the cabin.

"Atter a few days, I 'lowed I'd give thet gun one more chance, so I went out and soon saw a squirrel up a tree. I wuz shore I could hit him, so I cut loose and the tree limb fell offen the tree, but the squirrel jest flicked his tail and run off.

"Now, I wuz dead set on gettin' somethin', so I went on huntin' and afore long I come to a little branch and there wuz an old coon on the bank waitin' to cotch him a fish. So, I got real close and let loose. But, jest as afore, thet gun turned in my hands and the coon traipsed off into the woods, without a hair bein' teched.

"But, Holy Smoke! When I looked 'round, I saw I had hit a calf a way off to the left of thet coon, and kilt hit daid! Now, this scared the livin' daylights outten me, cause hit's a bad thing to kill somebody's brutes, and you could go to jail for hit. So I hired myself out to the man who owned the calf for three months to pay him fer hit.

"Atter thet, I went over to Little Bull Run River and throwed thet witched gun into the deepest hole I could find. Years later, some boys found it, but by thet time hit wuz so rusty that hit wuz no good."

WITCHCRAFT AND CHARMS

Ambrose Hyter, who lived in the mountain village of Cubage, Kentucky, had worn a charm around his neck since he was a child. The reason he did so is given in the following story:

When Ambrose was a little tyke, his mother sent him out on Elkhorn Ridge to fetch her quilting frames which she had lent to Nettie Baldt almost a year before. This put up old Net's dander because she had intended to keep the frames if she could. But, she got madder than a wet hen when little Ambrose, while turning the long frames to get them out the door, swept a jar of milk off the table which broke and spattered milk all over the floor. Old Net flew off the handle, boxed his ears, kicked his shins, and gave him a good drubbing.

After this, little Ambrose suddenly stopped eating even his favorite foods. He never complained or seemed to suffer any pain, but he stopped growing for two years. It was whispered around that Old Net, who was thought to be a witch, had put a spell on Ambrose.

At night, Ambrose developed a habit of leaving his bed, going outside and lying down in the back yard. This was dangerous, because there were many copperheads, rattlesnakes and wild varmints around. His parents were afraid for him, and would fetch him in and put him to bed.

Then, one day a neighbor, Milt Lotz, stopped to talk to Matthias Hyter about some timber. He asked about little Ambrose, and when the father sadly described his worsening condition, he said, "Matt, if I were you, I'd take the child over to Pineville to see Lige Slagle, who's supposed to be a white witch."

"Do you think Amby is bewitched, Milt?"

"Sure as shooting, he is, Matt. Nobody would stop eating and waste away like that if he wasn't under a spell."

"Do you really think Lige could do him any good?" asked Matt.

"Well, you know these pill doctors can't cure them that's hurtdone [bewitched]. You ought leastwise to give Lige a try," insisted Milt.

This story was told to Carrie M. Compton, Hazard, Kentucky, October 3, 1928, by his father, who was sixty-eight years old at the time.

Matt said nothing more, but stood staring off into the distance for a long while. Come Sunday morning, Matt was up with the chickens, and he told his old woman, "I'm a going to take Amby over to Pineville to see Lige Slagle today."

Kate said, "I think that's a plum good idea, Matt. Nothing else we've tried so far has helped a smidgeon. I surely hope Lige can do something."

So Matt and Ambrose got a soon start and traipsed over ridges, through hollers and across streams until the shank of the day before they reached Lige's cabin.

"Hi, Matt!" Lige called out, and before Matt could say a word he continued, I see you've brought that runt of your'n to see me. I knowed you'd come, but why in tarnation didn't you come a long time ago? It's most too late now, but I'll do the best I can. Come on up and set on the porch."

After they had exchanged a few pleasantries, Lige disappeared into the house and came back carrying a Bible, a large house key and a piece of string. He placed the key in the Bible on the Twenty-third Psalm, closed it and tied the string around it. Then, he suspended the Bible from a nail, got down on his knees, and recited the Lord's Prayer aloud. He got up, waved a hackberry branch over the Bible and mumbled some strange words which sounded like "po-se-non sul-nec-re se-bella-vers."

Then, he said, "Look, Matt, didn't you see that key turn?"

Matt hadn't been watching the key all that closely, but he agreed with Lige that it had turned.

Lige continued, "Yep, Matt, it was old Net Boldt who's hurt-done your young'un. Now he won't ever grow no more if we can't break her spell or leastwise bridle the spirits she's got working on him. You've waited a long time to come to me, and them spirits have set root and growed in him jest like an acorn grows into a big oak tree. Now, if you can't pull a sapling up, the next best thing is to trim the branches. That's what we're going to have to do with this evil spirit that's holding Ambrose back. But the boy will have to do exactly as I tell you."

Matt was pleased to hear some encouraging news, so he readily promised that he'd see that Ambrose did whatever was necessary.

Lige then got a small square of paper and wrote a charm on it. He showed it to Matt, although he knew Matt couldn't read it. It looked like this:*

*See note on page 38.

```
A B R A C A D A B R A
A B R A C A D A B R
A B R A C A D A B
A B R A C A D A
A B R A C A D
A B R A C A
A B R A C
A B R A
A B R
A B
A
```

Then, he folded the piece of paper into a small square, covered it with a piece of green silk cloth, and tied it securely with a string. He tied it to a leather thong and put it around Ambrose's neck. He instructed Ambrose never to take it off, even when he washed or changed his clothes.

Matt paid Lige for his services and he and Ambrose trudged home. After this, Ambrose started eating and growing again. Of course, he never made up for the two years' lost growth, but he did grow to be a fairly large and healthy young man.

One day, Ambrose put on some old clothes to help his father get in some hay. He was leading the horse and Matt was pitching hay into the wagon. When they came to the end of the field, instead of turning the horse and wagon, Ambrose just kept on going. Matt shouted at him, but he paid him no mind at all. He seemed to be in a trance. Matt ran to the horse and stopped him just in time. A few steps more and Ambrose would have led the horse right over the cliff and they would have fallen about a hundred feet onto some rocks.

Matt led the boy home and began to undress him to put him to bed. He found that the charm was missing from around his neck, so he left Ambrose in bed and went back to the field to look for the charm. He found it and put it back around Ambrose's neck. He came to with a start, and was all right after that. But, he wore this charm as long as he lived.

THE DEVIL GETS INTO A HEIFER

Milk was one of the most important foods of the mountaineers and the sale of butter was an important source of income. Everyone kept a cow or two. They were cheap to maintain. They were simply "belled" and turned out in the woods and hollows to graze. As long as the family cow stayed healthy, things were fine. If something happened to them, though, it was a serious matter.

Belle Kilgore of Norton, Virginia tells this story:

"My Paw, Jed Kilgore, told me that my Maw, Sallie Lou Kilgore, onct had a young heifer as purty as any critter you ever seed. Now, Bessie Sue Slagel, who lived over nigh Seltzer's Rock, took a shine to thet heifer. Ever' time she'd come by, she 'ud banter Maw to sell her thet heifer. Onct she cotched Maw in a bad temper, and she wuz tired of bein' pestered 'bout thet heifer ennyway, so she told Old Bess there wuzzen't enough money in the mountains to buy her. Besides, she'd promised the preacher the fust calf thet she had, and she didn't want to hear enny more 'bout buyin' her.

"Atter Maw and Bessie Sue 'ud jowered awhile, Old Bess jest sulled up, kase she wuzen't uster bein' outdone. So she sez, 'Sallie Lou, effen you don't sell thet heifer to me, you'll be sorry.' Then, she patted and rubbed thet heifer, and afore she started home, she took a poke outten her dress pocket and shook some white stuff all over the cow's withers.

"Thet night when the heifer come in from the woods and Maw hunkered down to milk her, hit wuz a fright the way thet critter carried on. She hooked, she kicked, she snorted, she bawled, she fidgeted, and she cut all kinds of monkey shines. Allus afore this, she'd been as mute as a mouse, and never paid no mind to Maw milkin' her.

"Maw finally got her settled down a little, but, when she started round t'other side, thet heifer took off goin' round and round like a chicken with hit's head cut off. Paw seed whut was goin' on, so he started torge her. Maw cringed aginst the fence, and hollered to Paw to stay back. He ran back when thet heifer lunged at him, a buttin' and a slingin' her haid.

Collected by Emory L. Hamilton, Wise, Virginia. Told to him by Mrs. Belle Kilgore.

"All of a sudden, thet cow knuckled under and plopped down on the ground. Froth ran outen her mouth, and she rolled her glassy eyes back in her haid, and Maw figgered she'd be daid in no time t'all. Now Maw had a real hang-dog look, cause she'd raised that heifer from a little calf, and had humored and petted her jest like she wuz one of her young'uns.

"Now, the fust thing thet popped into Maw's haid wuz whut Old Bessie Sue Slagel 'ud sed to her 'bout thet heifer. She told this to Paw and 'splained how Old Bessie 'ud rubbed the heifer and put thet white powder on her.

"Everybody for miles around knew that Old Bessie wuz a witch, and Paw got so mad he could a whupped a wildcat. He fired loose and sed, 'Damn her low-down, Devil-owned soul, effen thet heifer dies, I'll take my rifle-gun and blow her brains outen her logy head!'

"Now, I allus heard thet effen you could cotch a witch and whup her, or effen you threatened her and really meant hit, you'd break the witch spell. But, no indeedy, Paw wuzzen't 'bout to quit with a threat. He built him a fire right there beside thet heifer. While the fire got started, he went into the cabin and got some dried henbane and nightshade leaves, powdered them up, added a gob of sulfur and a pinch of copperas, and brought hit back to the fire. Then, when the fire wuz burnin' real hot, he throwed this mess into hit, and got down on his knees and said the Lord's Prayer.

"Shore enough, all this 'peared to take off thet witch spell. In no time t'all, thet heifer started to switch her tail, twitch her nose, quivver, and kicked and staggered up. Maw held outen her hand and thet critter come and licked hit jest like she'd allus done.

"My Paw and Maw kept thet heifer for a long time, and nuthin' ever went wrong with her enymore. Old Bessie Sue Slagel never come round pesterin' Maw bout buying thet heifer again."

THE QUAKER DOCTOR AND HIS
MAGIC BOTTLE

A beautiful and healthy little daughter was born to Tim and Ada Calder, who lived in the Pennsylvania mountains. She filled their lives with happiness and contentment. They were so pleased with the baby that they named her Dorothy because Tim had heard that the name meant "a gift from God." From infancy, she was active and happy, and at three years of age she was a strong and beautiful child.

Then, suddenly little Dorothy's health vanished. Within a few weeks' time, she had degenerated into a squalling, miserable child with fear and agony in her eyes. Her firm, round pink body became as flabby as a sponge, and her skin became a clay-like yellow. At night, she would utter inarticulate cries.

Fear and apprehension gripped Tim and Ada. They were so heartbroken that no words could convey their suffering. Ada and a neighboring yarb doctor administered all the potions and poultices which they knew how to concoct, but to no avail. Finally, Ada concluded that Dorothy had been ill-wished and suggested to Tim that they consult a Quaker doctor who was noted for his skill in over-looking [breaking spells]. At first, Tim laughed and ridiculed her superstitious ideas, but as time passed and little Dorothy got no better, he finally yielded to Ada's pleas and they set out to Bedford to consult the Quaker doctor.

Upon arrival, Ada took Dorothy into the doctor's house while Tim put the horses in the stable and fed them. Ada explained Dorothy's symptoms to the doctor's assistant, but she made no mention of her suspicion that the child had been bewitched. The assistant examined Dorothy and asked some questions, then went into another room to confer with his master. He returned, asked more questions, and went back for a second conference.

Then, a tall, distinguished looking man with thick white hair and a well-trimmed moustache slipped quietly into the room. His kind blue eyes briefly rested on the mother, but he didn't speak.

Told by Peter Quillin of Bedford, Pennsylvania, in November, 1941. At that time, he was sixty-eight years old. He had heard the story from his grandfather while he was a boy.

With a serious mien, he began at once to examine little Dorothy. His graceful hands explored her entire body, and he was just finishing when Tim entered the room. The doctor glanced at him, but still said nothing.

"Is the child hurt-done [bewitched]?" Tim asked with fear.

"Yes!" replied the doctor in his kind, melodious voice. "As sure as the morning sunrise, she has been bewitched."

"Kind sir, can you do anything for her?" inquired Ada, her voice trembling with sorrow and fear.

With a stern, pointed look, he replied, "If thou wilt do as I tell thee, I can."

Ada's face flushed with a flicker of hope. She hastened to assure him, "Indeed, we will do anything you tell us."

"Well, then," he said, "take some of the hair of wife, husband and child; some of the cuttings of thy finger nails and toe nails; some of the water of all three of ye, and three black straight pins and put all this in a bottle and cork it. Then, on next Friday night, when you rake the fire, put the bottle under the stuff you rake up. But, before you do this, place three very small candles on the hearth. As you light each candle, say, 'In the name of the Father and the Son and the Holy Ghost.' When the candles are all lighted, both of ye kneel down and say the Lord's Prayer aloud. Then, after the candles have burned out, rake the coals and put the bottle under them. And remember, whatever happens, don't let any woman enter your house for three days."

Tim and Ada hurried home to carry out these instructions. Since little Dorothy had been restless at night and had cried out as if she were having bad dreams, they moved her bed near the fireplace. Then, they prepared the bottle, lighted the three candles and said the prayer. They waited until the candles burned down, then put the bottle under the raked coals. To their pleasant surprise, Dorothy was soon fast asleep and she didn't move nor make a sound the rest of the night.

Ada and Tim also slept soundly that night. Tim rose at the crack of dawn, broke the fire, and carried out the ashes to riddle them.

While he was in the back yard, Ada heard a thrashing in the bushes, followed by steps approaching the front door. She opened the door and was startled by the bleating laugh of Old Betty Orts, the witch. She remembered the doctor telling her not to let any woman enter the house, so she stood in the doorway. The gnarled old crone glared at Ada with her beady eyes and demanded in a threatening voice, "Does your old man have to riddle them ashes that way?"

But, Ada had reached the breaking point, and she unleashed months of pent-up anger and frustration on the old woman. "God have mercy on your wicked soul! I'll beat you to a bloody pulp," Ada shouted as she grabbed her by the sleeve and hit her over the head with the long iron poker. Blood gushed from the old woman's forehead and began to trickle down her wrinkled face. Old Betty was completely flabbergasted by this sudden attack, but as soon as she recovered, she took to her heels and vanished into the woods.

When Ada regained her self-control, she found herself clutching the bloody poker in one hand and a fragment of Old Betty's dirty sleeve in the other. She hastened inside, heated a pot of water, and boiled the piece of sleeve for seven minutes. She then removed it from the water, dried it, and threw it on the fire. It burned with an eerie greenish-blue flame and left no trace of ashes.

Now, Ada recognized that they had thrice overlooked the bewitchment: once with the good Quaker's magic bottle, again by drawing blood from the witch's brow, and finally by boiling and burning the fragment of her clothing. One or all of these exorcisms must have worked, since little Dorothy began to improve from that time. In a few weeks, she was well again, and in too few years to please her fond parents, had grown up to be a beautiful young woman.

THE PELLAR AND THE GOLD WATCH

In the autumn of 1851, the road to Owing's Mill parsonage was a jolting, dusty ten miles by buggy through the foothills of the Maryland mountains and just a little smoother ride the last three miles through a wide valley. But, on this day, the three people in the buggy, Reverend Hines, and his wife and his foster daughter, Judith, were to be the guests of honor at a dinner party which the Reverend Barry Duncan was giving for his fellow clergyman, and they thought the trip well worthwhile.

During the evening's merrymaking, Judith slipped upstairs to her hostess' bedroom to re-arrange her hair. She saw a beautiful gold watch hanging on the wall which so intrigued her that she took it down to examine it more closely. Then, she returned it to its place on the wall. When she started out of the bedroom door, she stopped as if an invisible hand had been placed on her shoulder. She turned and stared for a long while at the beautiful watch. She soon rejoined the party and entered into the amusements for the remainder of the evening.

After the guests had gone, Mrs. Duncan went to her room and immediately missed her watch. She searched the room, and then the entire house, but failed to find it. The next day, she made tactful inquiries among her guests of the evening before, but found no clues.

Finally, in desperation, she called in the police. They suspected her servants, a poor widow and her daughter, who had been in the house the night of the party. These women had always borne excellent characters, and were very hurt when the police insisted on searching their homes. Nothing was found.

When the police failed to turn up a single clue, Mrs. Duncan sent for Old Etta Baines, a pellar*, or white witch, who was noted for finding lost articles. Old Etta and her husband came at once.

Old Etta was told how the watch had disappeared during the party and who the guests were. She went into a trance and became

This story was told by James E. McCall of Owings Mill, Maryland, March 17, 1937.

*A Scottish-Irish term for a white witch.

limp as a rag. Her husband bent over her and muttered a few words, and then all was silence. Her head bowed and her eyes closed, Etta suddenly began to speak: "I am going over a hill and down into a valley onto a beautiful plain. I arrive at the gate to a large house which I open and enter. I go into the house and ascend the stairs. Here, I see a young woman clothed in a beautiful pink dress take the watch off the wall, examine it, then replace it. Then she disappears."

There was a slight pause, then Etta began speaking again: "Now I approach a country home. I hear the shouts of children at play in the back yard. I go out in the yard and see three children being cared for by a beautiful young girl. This is the same young woman who wore the pink dress at the party. I see a beautiful gold watch hanging from her neck inside her dress. She is very apprehensive. She has been trying to get rid of the watch, but is too fascinated by it to destroy it. She is afraid to try to sell it or to give it to anyone."

Mrs. Duncan was visibly shaken by these words. Could this old pellar be wrong? She was reluctant to believe that Judith Hines, the adopted daughter of her friends, could have taken the watch. As much as she wanted to recover the watch, she did not want to embarrass her friends.

When she told this story to her husband, he was not at all disposed to believe it. But, thinking of the agony of his poor servants who had been under suspicion, and knowing that finding the watch would clear them, he decided to carry on an investigation.

Judith's boxes and trunk were searched, but in vain. But, when she was searched, the watch was found where the old pellar had said it was. This wise old woman said this was not the first thing Judith had taken, nor would it be the last: "She can't control her urge to steal. You see, she is a kleptomaniac."

THE BRASS SCREW

Everybody for miles around the mountain community of Sandy Ridge knew that a large clan of Melungions lived there. Their odd habits, clannishness and wicked ways had earned them a reputation as witches.

Boyd T. Bolling, of Flat Gap, Virginia, narrates a story his father had told him about this clan:

"Way back yonder, when the Bollings fust settled in these hills, there wuz an old man, a Melungion who lived outten Sandy Ridge. His name was Aaron Wooten, and he wuz knowed fur and wide as a gun witch.

"Uncle Jerry Bolling onct met Aaron outten the hump of the Ridge. He stopped Uncle Jerry and sed with an evil whisper, 'Jerry, let me see thet gun.'

"Now, Uncle Jerry wuz a good man who wuzzen't afeard of hell ner high water, but sence he knowed witches wuz evil and wicked and in cahoots with the Devil, he wuz afeard of Aaron Wooten. And folks sed Aaron 'ud take your rifle-gun and look hit over to see effen there wuz any brass in hit. For some reason, witches can't spell brass, so effen he didn't find any in the gun, he'd spell hit and hand hit back. Then, he'd dare you to step back a few paces and shoot at him with the gun. So Old Aaron 'zamined Uncle Jerry's rifle-gun and handed hit back to him and sez, 'Jerry, I want you to shoot at me with thet gun.'

"But Uncle Jerry, nervous as a rattlesnake, sez, 'Aaron, mebbe I hadn't orter.'

"Old Aaron laughed fit to kill and sez: 'Now, Jerry, you wouldn't be weak-kneed, would you?'

"Then, he walked away about ten paces and sez: 'Jerry, have you got a white liver?'

"Now, this kinda riled Uncle Jerry, but he didn't want to kill Old Aaron. So, he tuk good aim and cut loose with thet rifle-gun and shot the tip of Aaron's left ear clean off.

"Well, Sir, this skeered Old Aaron so much he shook in his

Collected by James Taylor Adams, Big Laurel, Virginia, February 26, 1942. Told to him by Boyd J. Bolling, of Flat Gap, Virginia, who heard this story from his father when he was a child.

legs, his teeth chattered, and he hollered, 'Jerry Bolling, you tried to kill me!'

"Then, atter he found he wuzzen't hurt too bad, he sidled up to Jerry and sed, 'You've tricked me!'

"When Uncle Jerry seed that Aaron wuz all flustered, he 'splained to him that he'd jest fixed his gun and had lost a screw outten hit. So he put in a brass screw in hit's place.

"This larned Old Aaron a lesson, and he never axt anybody to shoot at him atter thet."

A BALL OF FIRE

Soon after the turn of the century, near a small village in Indiana, a family of Tinsleys moved into a dilapidated old house which had wide cracks between the vertical boards which were used as the walls of the house. The wind whistled through and raindrops oozed in between the boards. The Tinsleys covered these cracks at once with narrow strips on the outside.

Whenever someone became ill in the house, there was a rattle and clatter which sounded as if someone were running around the house with a stick held against the strips of the siding. The Tinsleys searched the place thoroughly, but found no evidence whatever of anyone being on the property. The Tinsleys were so plagued by these noises that they moved out of the house.

Another family by the name of Powell moved in, consisting of a father, two sons and a daughter. The Powells were also bothered by the same rattle and clatter which had driven the Tinsleys away, but the noise now was accompanied by a faint blue light which danced about the room and moved restlessly from one room to another. When the family would be awakened by the noises, the light would appear very faintly at first, then brighten and hover over a bedpost or other piece of furniture.

One night, the two Powell boys and their father decided to go hunting. They were scarcely out of the house when Old Kate Hiller appeared and asked to borrow some salt. Now, Naomi Powell had heard that Old Kate was a witch, and she was mortally afraid of her. So, she gave her the salt without delay in order to get rid of her as quickly as possible.

After a long, hard night of chasing raccoons and trudging over hills and valleys, the hunters came upon a fence and sat down to rest before climbing it. Suddenly, a blazing reddish-yellow ball of fire appeared in front of them. It skidded to and fro aimlessly, then lodged on a near-by tree trunk. Its color faded to a pale blue and it gradually assumed a human form. The phantom thrashed and squirmed about like an entrapped animal trying to free itself. This terrifying apparition froze the hunters motionless. Finally, the

This story was told to Margaret Pruett by a retired school teacher who had been told the story by her parents.

youngest boy managed to get to his feet and shoot at the phantom. It vanished like a streak of lightning.

When the tired, trembling hunters finally stumbled into the house, it was to find that Naomi was in bed, stricken suddenly by some strange malady. Most disconcerting of all, Old Kate Hiller was seated by the fire stirring a potion of yarbs with which to treat her. Naomi said she had come to the house shortly after she had been stricken by her illness and offered to treat her.

The three men were completely flabbergasted to find Old Kate there. They had heard about her being a witch, and had already begun to suspect that she was behind the curse of weird noises and eerie lights in the house. Now, here she was in the house, posing as a yarb doctor and treating Naomi. They just didn't know what to make of it, or what to do about it.

The father and the oldest boy silently leaned their guns in the chimney corner where they kept them. However, when the youngest boy started toward the corner, he was so nervous and distraught that he got his foot hung over the chair rocker and lost his balance. In an effort to avoid falling, he grasped his gun in such an awkward way that he pulled the trigger. The charge grazed Old Kate's forehead and lodged in the ceiling over her head. Blood trickled down her dirty, wrinkled face, and she screamed, "You've killed me." She bolted for the door and ran away in the night.

Naomi began to feel better at once, and the next morning she was well enough to be out of bed. After this, they never saw the light nor heard the noises again. They all agreed that the hunting incident was connected in some way to the happenings in the house. And they were sure that the drawing of blood from above the nose of Old Kate had broken her spell over Naomi.

GRANDPAPPY WUZ A WITCH

John Boyd Bolling, of Flat Gap, Virginia, tells this tale about his grandfather, Jim Tom Baker, of Baker's Flats:

"Grandpappy Jim Tom Baker moved around a lot before finally settlin' down at the head of the Cumberland River in a place called Baker's Flats. He wuz a conjure man, and people were afeard of him and made his life not worth living, which wuz one reason he moved so much. He got married and sired a whole passel of young'uns, among them, my uncles Jerry and Jim, and, of course, my mammey.

"By the time I remember them, Jerry and Jim were grown men with cabins of their own and families. Uncle Jerry wuz a kind of yarb doctor for both varmints and men. Even then, Grandpappy kept on conjurin'.

"One morning, Uncle Jerry heard a rifle-gun go off way back on Carmel Mountain nigh Baker's Flats. Right off, he thought hit sounded like a witch's gun. Now, everybody believed that a witch could shoot his gun and as fur as hit wuz heard in the woods, they'd be 'rung.' That is, a whole patch, fur as the gun sounded, 'ud be hagged and nobody's gun could kill a deer nor other varmint inside thet ring.

"Twarn't long atter this till Uncle Jerry went a huntin'. He sneaked up on a whole caboodle of deer and shot pimeblank at 'em, but he didn't hit nary a one. Hit wuz jest like thet for a long while, so he quit huntin' fer a spell. Then, he tuk his rifle-gun apart, cleaned the lock and the pan, oiled hit, got him some fresh powder and new flints, and went a huntin' agin. But he didn't do nary a bit better.

"So, Uncle Jim figgered mebbe his rifle-gun wudden't be spelled, so he went a huntin'. He run into a mess of deer so close he mought a kilt some of 'em with the butt of his gun effen he'd tried. He fired pimeblank at them deer, but he never hit nuthin'. He tried agin with the same luck. Then, a wild turkey lit on a limb right in front of him and he tuk dead aim and fired away 'C-bang.' The sound of his gun skeered the turkey, but he missed hit a mile. He

Collected by James Taylor Adams, Big Laurel, Virginia, February 4, 1942. Told to him by Boyd J. Bolling, of Flat Gap, Virginia, whose father told him this story about his grandfather, Jim Baker.

knowed then thet his gun wuz spelled jest like Jerry's.

"But Uncle Jerry knowed jest whut to do. He went out and cut him a bunch of hair from his boar hawg. Then, he got him a dust of sulfur, a bit of asofetida and chinked in a little cayenne pepper, dabbed this with molasses, and rolled the hawg hair into this mess. Then, he moulded him a bullet of lead and wropt this round hit. He tuk out lickety split torge Caney Ridge where he found a scrawny whiteoak sapling. He tuk out his knife, skinned back the bark, and drawed a picture of Old Jim Tom Baker. He stepped back thirteen steps and let loose with thet special bullet. As he shot at the picture, he sed, 'In the name of the Father, the Son and the Holy Speret, break the spell of this witch.' His bullet hit clost to where he'd drawed Jim Tom's hand over his heart.

"He hadn't been back in his cabin more'n a minute till Jim Tom's old woman come over like a house afire and axt to borrow his wife's quiltin' rods, but wuz told hit wuz in use. In two shakes of a sheep's tail, Granny wuz back again, this time to borry windin' blades*, but wuz told they wuz in use, too. Now this didn't set so well with Granny, but she edged into the woods agin.

"But, the next mornin', afore they got up from the breakfast table, she wuz back agin a scratchin' at the door. This time, she wuz fit to be tied, and sed, 'Jerry, effen you don't come over and do sumpthin' fer yore pappy right off, he won't live till sundown.'

"Now, Uncle Jerry thought his Pappy had suffered enough and would be cured of his conjurin', so he sharpened his special lance he used to bleed a risen er to lance a boil, and set off with his mammey. When he 'zamined old Jim Tom, he found a big blue spot on the side of his body nigh his heart, and his left hand wuz all swoll up and black as midnight, like hit had blood pizzen. Uncle Jerry lanced his side and his thumb and cotched the blood in a little dish.

"Purty soon, Jim Tom got to where he could move and wuz right peart. When he raised up and saw his own blood in thet dish, he sed, 'Jerry, the jig's up. You've foxed me!'

"You know, effen a witch sees his own blood, this ruins his power to be a witch. So atter this, they never had no more trubbel with their guns being witched by Jim Tom's huntin' ring."

---

* A device for winding yarn in preparation for spinning.

THE HORSE THAT WOULDN'T
CROSS THE STREAM

Dog-tired from roaming the ridges and woods, Old Lizzie Steele dumped the contents of her hickory-bark basket on the porch of her little cabin. She had been out gathering ginseng and sassafras roots, and henbane, burdock and nightshade leaves which she used in preparing her simples*. She was a granny doctor, and so much in demand that she found little time to replenish her supplies. She set to work immediately sorting them out and tied them into little bunches which she hung on pegs along the wall.

George Trevitt's old woman, Denise, got real poorly and had been laid up for so long that she had wasted away to a bag of bones. George worried a lot about her, and finally went out on Kent's Ridge to fetch Old Lizzie to doctor her.

Matilda Sexton, Denise's neighbor, picks up the story:

"Dees had right much fever, chills and the shakes, but hit 'peared like Old Liz knew jest whut to do fer her. Fust, she made poultices of pimpernel weed, then some sarsaparilla and catnip tea, and doctored her with all the simples she knowed how to make. But, Dees jest kept a goin' down hill, till she thought she wuz about to meet her Maker. She wuz so skeered, she begged George to fetch a city doctor from the county seat.

"Now, 'course this didn't set well with Old Liz, and she pleaded with George to wait a few more days and she wuz sure Dees 'ud be on her feet by then. She told George that part of the trubbel wuz that Dees wuz bein' witched, but she sed she knew how to take off the spells and then Dees 'ud get better. But, atter three days, Dees wuz no better, and George sed he wuz a goin' to get the city doctor. Liz left in a huff at this, but she sed she'd be back after the doctor had done his job.

"So George went over to Tim Saxby's place to axt him to go to the county seat and git the doctor. Tim set out lickety split right

Collected by James Taylor Adams, Big Laurel, Virginia, May 26, 1941. Told to him by his sister-in-law, Polly Hughes, aged seventy-four, who heard it as a child from Uncle Dave Sexton's wife.

* Tonics, brews, ointments or poultices that were prepared and used by granny doctors. They contained such local herbs as foxglove, mugwort, ginseng, henbane, and sassafras.

away, 'cause hit wuz a fur piece. He rode down the holler, over the ridge, and outten Clinch Valley. Then, he come to a river and rode his horse into the middle of the river, when, all of a sudden, the horse stopped dead in his tracks. Tim thought the horse wanted a drink of water, so he let up on the reins, but the horse didn't drink. Then, Tim had a strange feelin' that sumpthin' er somebody 'ud climbed up on the horse behind him. A shiver run up his spine when he looked back and didn't see nuthin'. So, he pulled in the bridle reins and sed 'Giddup!' But, the old horse didn't move. Then, he beat, and he drubbed, and he cussed, and he tried everythin' he knowed to get that horse to move, but it wouldn't budge an inch.

"Finally, he give up and turned the horse around and got outten the water. As soon as he did, he felt whatever wuz behind him get offen the horse. So he turned the horse torge the water agin, but she went to the middle of the river and stopped agin. However much Tim beat and kicked her, she jest wouldn't move, so Tim came outten the river and went down the bank a piece and tried to cross at annuder place. The same thing happened when he got to the middle of the river: whatever hit wuz climbed back on the horse and hit would't move. Tim wuz so skeered, he turned thet horse torge home and galloped all the way like the devil wuz atter him.

"He went to George's house and told him whut had happened, and they both 'lowed thet Old Liz musta hagged his horse. George axt Tim to go over to Coon Crick and talk with Wes Wardell, who wuz a witch doctor, to find out whut to do. Tim paid Wes two dollars, and Wes told him whut to do to break the spell.

"So George and Tim set out to do whut Wes told 'em. George went outten his pasture and cotch a black yearlin' calf, and Tim holped him to butcher hit. They saved the blood, built a big fire, and burnt hit. Then, they cut a big square chunk of lean meat outten the right frunt quarter, tied a string to hit, and, 'zactly at midnight, they hung hit in the chimney.

"Now, Old Liz hadn't come back to see 'bout Dees, but on the third day atter they'd hung thet piece of meat in the chimney, she showed up afore sunrise. George noticed thet she had her right shoulder tied up with a rag, so he axt her whut wuz wrong. She sed a horse had kicked her, and she axt George to give her a few mustard and beet leaves to make a poultice out of. Now, George had been warned by Wes thet she mought come to borrer sompthin' when they started breakin' the spell, and effen he let her have ennythin', hit 'ud keep the spell from bein' broke. So George 'lowed he didn't have none.

"Then, she axt for some sarsaparilla to make some tea, but George wouldn't let her have none. Then, Liz flared up and left the place in a huff, but she showed up agin three days later and wanted to borrer some sugar. George told her he didn't have none. Then, she axt him to lend her his huntin' knife so's she could cut some roots and yarbs, but George wouldn't let her have hit. So, she give George a whoppin' tongue-lashin' and left.

"Seven days atter George hung thet wad of raw meat in the chimney, things happened jest as Wes 'ud sed hit would. Old Liz wuz found dead in her bed. Her right shoulder had a big rotten hole in the same place as thet chunk of meat they'd cut outten the calf's shoulder. When George heard Liz wuz dead, he reached up in the chimney, pulled down thet chunk of rotten meat, tuk hit outten the ridge and buried hit. 'Twarn't no time atter this till Dees started a mendin' and wuz feeling peart agin."

BALL OF FIRE AND EMPTY ROCKER

Mountain people often had to travel great distances to a grist mill to have their grain crushed. One Saturday, Grandpappy Eli Proffit took a wagon load of grain to Jonathan Hooker's mill over near Hillsville, the county seat of Carroll County, to have it crushed for feed.

Julia Mae Proffit picks up the story:

"One Saturday, Grandpappy took a wagon load of grain to Jonathan Hooker's mill to have hit crushed for feed and to have some corn ground into meal. Hit wuzzn't fur from the mill to the county seat, so he went over there to pay his taxes while the miller wuz a grindin' his corn. He saw Vic Stout and his old woman, Ginny, in town. They'd bought some things a little heavy to carry, so Grandpappy told 'em to up 'em in his wagon and they'd all walk home alongside the wagon.

"On the way, they come to a place in the road where a big tree had growed so clost to the road thet there wuzzen't room for 'em all to walk betwixt the tree and the wagon, so Vic and Ginny walked 'round the tree on t'other side. All of a sudden, a ball of fire big as a cabin hovered right over 'em. Hit filled the air with a kind of hummin' and a burnt smell. Then, as they come to an open place, hit come down to the ground and started a rollin' torge 'em. The air wuz still, and not a leaf rustled. They all shook in their boots, and couldn't move. Them horses snorted, then reared up and jumped to the side and 'most turned the wagon over. Effen they hadn't, hit 'ud a hit and killed 'em. Then, the ball jest rolled right smack dab into the side of the hill and disappeared. Hit left the air a stinkin' like burnt meat and burnt sulfur.

Grandpappy, Vic and Ginny jest stood there a shakin' like dogs in a wet sack. Atter Grandpappy kinda got holt of hisself, he 'lowed to Vic they musta made the witches mad by walkin' on one side of thet tree with him on t'other back there at thet narrow place in the road and they'd sent thet ball of fire atter them. But, Grandpappy knowed jest whut to do. In a flash he outten with his pocket knife,

Collected by Bessie C. Scales, Danville, Virginia, January 10, 1941. Told to her by Julia Mae Profitt, who heard it from her father, who had heard the story when he was a boy.

cut a hole in a sack of cracked corn, and strewed hit acrost the road behindst the wagon 'bout three er four inches wide. He sed when the witches come to the corn, they'd have to stop and count the pieces and, afore they could finish, the spell 'ud wear off.

"Then, he cut seven hairs from the tail of each horse and buried 'em in separate little graves in the dirt of the road in front of the wagon. He 'splained thet, when the wagon rolled over 'em, this 'ud break the spell so the witches couldn't hurt 'em the rest of the way.

"Vic and Ginny thanked Grandpappy fer haulin' their goods, and left him at the barn where he turned offen the road. He went on to the barn, unloaded his grain, unharnessed his horses, fed 'em, gathered up his things, and headed fer the cabin. Bless my soul, effen he didn't hear two pairs of footsteps behind him. He thought it mought be Vic and Ginny, but when he looked, there wuzzen't nobody there 'tall. Then, there wuz a rustlin' like the footsteps had run by him. He had a sinkin' feeling in his stomach, and he walked in fear and dread till he got inside the cabin.

"When he walked into the room, there wuzzen't anybody there, but both rockin' cheers wuz a rockin' up a storm with nobody in 'em. He lit a shuck* outten there and hollered fer Polly. When he told her 'bout thet big ball of fire, the footsteps a follerin' him, and then the rockin' cheers, her eyes nigh popped outten her haid. At fust she didn't believe him, but when he told her thet Vic and Ginny 'ud seen the ball of fire, she wuz flabbergasted.

"The next day, Grandpappy told Tom Altizer and his old woman 'bout the witches, and they 'lowed mebbe he'd been a hittin' thet bottle of red-eye a little too hard, but they both knowed he'd never drunk enough to see things. Then, they studied on hit fer a whet, and decided thet mebbe somethin' bad wuz about to happen. Silas Prophett come along and told 'em thet he'd seed the ball of fire, too. He sed Jess Gross, a conjure man from out on Hickory Spur, 'ud told him thet witches could throw balls of fire only jest afore somethin' bad wuz about to happen, and thet Jess 'lowed mebbe there wuz a goin' to be a war or sumpthin else awful. Shore 'nuff, hit warn't no time 'tall afore the Civil War broke out."

* A mountain expression indicating a very quick departure from some dangerous or explosive situation.

THE BEWITCHED BOAT

Rod Collins, who lived near Lynchburg, Virginia, was a notorious gambler. Once, in a poker game with Dick Greer and some other fellows, he lost more money than he had, but he promised to pay them later. Old Dick was hard-hearted and onery, and Rod was afraid of him, so he knew he had to find the money to pay him soon.

Now, this was back before the Civil War, and Rod had a big farm which he worked with slaves. One of them was a wizzened old crone who was reputed to be a witch, but she had the prettiest young daughter you ever saw. Her name was Betsy, and soon after Rod lost his money in the poker game, a slave buyer from Norfolk named Abe Goldstein, came by and saw Betsy. He knew he could get a high price for her, so he sounded Rod out about selling her. Rod had never thought about selling any of his slaves, but this seemed like too good a chance to get some ready cash to miss, especially as Dick Greer had told him he wanted his money soon, or it would be too bad for Rod. So he sold Betsy to Abe for a good sum.

Abe took Betsy and the other slaves he'd bought down to the river and loaded them on his boat, put his supplies on board, cast off, and prepared to set off down the James to Norfolk. Well, sir, that boat wouldn't move an inch. They pushed it, they pulled it, they pried it and they swore at it, but it just stuck there like it was frozen in an ice cake. They unloaded the supplies and tried again, but the boat wouldn't move. Then, they unloaded some of the slaves, but again it didn't budge. Then, they took off more slaves, Betsy among them, and the boat floated right away.

Of course, there was no doubt about it, that boat had been hagged. But Abe was hardheaded and stubborn, and didn't give up easy. So, he reloaded the boat with everything and everybody except Betsy and sent it down the river. Then, he bought him a buggy and two good horses, and prepared to take her to Norfolk by land. He loaded his buggy, told Betsy to get in, climbed in himself, and told the horses to 'giddup'. The horses started to pull, but their feet began to slip, and that buggy didn't move an inch. Abe got out

Collected by Susan B. Morton, Haymarket, Virginia, March 7, 1939. Told to her by Elizabeth Carter, who heard it from her grandfather, Josiah Conklin, of Potts Creek, Virginia.

and told Betsy to get out, too, and the buggy moved with no trouble 'tall. So Abe knew the buggy had been hagged also.

But, Abe wasn't about to give up. He unhitched the horses, told Betsy to get up on one and mounted the other. But, when he said 'giddup', his horse moved off, leaving Betsy's standing like a statue. So Abe switched horses with Betsy, but her horse still wouldn't move an inch.

This time, Abe gave up in disgust, hitched the horses to the buggy and drove off, leaving Betsy to find her way back to Rod Collins' farm. He knew he'd been swindled and decided it must have been Betsy's mother who had bewitched the boat, the buggy and the horses so he couldn't take her away.

THE INDIAN WARLOCKS FROM ACOMA

Many years before white men came to the Southwest, two Indian braves mounted their burros and headed north from the sun-baked city of Acoma, New Mexico. It was a beautiful Indian-summer day, decked out with gay fall colors and capped by a clear blue sky.

Before they had ridden very far, they saw two other Indians walking in the distance. When they overtook them, they immediately recognized the travelers as two Indian warlocks*—members of the Witch Society of Acoma.

"Where are you going?" the warlocks inquired.

"We are going to Laguna, the enchanted mesa," the mounted Indians answered.

"Why are you going to Laguna at this time?" they asked.

"It is now the season for our yearly pow-wow. There, we will dance, feast, and our medicine men will drive out evil spirits."

"And, when do you expect to get to Laguna?" the conjurers demanded.

"We will be there before the frosty wolf-moon** rises tonight," replied one of the men.

"Ah! We shall see you there. We, too, are going to the council festival. Though we are walking, we will get there long before you do! We will be there before noon today," boasted one of the conjurers.

The mounted travelers said no more. They prodded their slow-moving burros and soon left the warlocks behind.

"Those two warlocks bother me," said one of the riders. "I have a bad feeling that they are coming to our pow-wow with evil plans. Did you hear them say they would be at Laguna by noon?

This story is found among the Pueblo Indian tales published in the *American Journal of Folklore*, Volume 49, Number 4, 1936.

* A male witch.

** An October full moon. It is also known as the "wolf-moon" or the "country moon." For five or six nights in a row, it rises early giving the long October nights a silver brilliance. Coon hunting is excellent during this time of the month. When wolves in the forest were plentiful, they would howl at this full moon.

That's not possible. They must be witches, and we had best stay away from them."

After they had ridden a few miles farther, they heard a coyote wailing mournfully behind them. They looked back and saw two coyotes running toward them. The coyotes caught up with the riders, passed them, and were soon out of sight. But, as they passed, one of the coyotes said to the other in a low voice, "Though we are on foot, and they on burros, we can travel much faster than they do."

"Surely those coyotes must have been the Acoma warlocks," one Indian rider said to the other. "Warlocks sometimes do change into coyotes in order to hide their wicked deeds. I am afraid they will do us harm."

Before they had gone very far, they met the coyotes coming back. They circled the burros warily, and, as they passed, one coyote said in a low voice, "I see they are still here. They don't seem to be moving very fast on their burros. We will be at Laguna and have our work done before they arrive."

Then, both the coyotes barked viciously at the burros, scampered off, and disappeared into the woods. Before long, the Indians saw the coyotes approaching them again. This time they made a smaller circle around the burros, eyed them menacingly, howled, and again fled for the woods.

"If we aren't careful, these warlock-coyotes will surely kill us," one of the Indians said to the other. But, after this, they saw no more of them.

The coyotes arrived at Laguna at noon. They passed through their magic hoops and changed back to men before they entered the festival grounds.

The sun had set before the other two Indians arrived on their burros. They were trembling and almost overcome with fear and apprehension. They dismounted and immediately accused the two warlocks of changing into coyotes, but the warlocks denied knowing anything about the coyotes. No one would listen to their accusations. The frightened Indians were *positive* that they were talking to the same two warlocks who had changed themselves into coyotes.

These tall warlocks from Acoma were handsome fellows who were very attractive to women. That evening, they met the beautiful Indian maiden, Isleta, sister of the medicine man, Taos, and daughter of the tribal chieftan, White Eagle. They decided at once that they would abduct her and take her back to their witch cave in the enchanted mesa. So, they set to work to win her over with charm and flattery as well as their handsome persons. This worked so well that they were able to arrange a meeting with her for the next day.

When Isleta went to the river for water the next evening, the two warlocks were there to meet her. First, they tried to persuade her to run away with them to Acoma. She was flattered to be asked by two such handsome men, but she thought she ought to get her father's permission.

"But, what if your father will not give his permission to go?" inquired one of the warlocks.

"Then, I cannot go," was Isleta's reply.

So, one of the warlocks invoked his magic on her. He waved his hand swiftly over her face without touching it. This caused her to make strange grimaces, to roll her eyes about, and finally to fall into a trance, staring blankly into space.

Then, the other warlock took over. He sprinkled some white powder on her ebony locks and said, "Panak, Kanap, Tuefor," three times. Then, he said, "In the name of all the evil spirits, I command you to fall asleep. Isleta immediately fell into a deep slumber.

They put her through a magic hoop and changed her into a coyote, after which they jumped through the hoop themselves and changed into coyotes. They awakened the sleeping coyote and the three started to Acoma, traveling over the hills and cliffs as coyotes do.

When they reached the witch cave on the enchanted mesa, the warlocks prepared a soft warm bed of pelts for Isleta. They put her through the magic hoop again and changed her back into a lovely copper-skinned, raven-haired beauty. The warlocks asked her if she knew where she was and how she got there, but she had suffered a total loss of memory and did not know.

Now that she was inside the magic cave, she could never escape without the help of a good witch. The conjurers congratulated themselves on their good fortune in abducting this beautiful girl. They built a fire and roasted some meat, vegetables and Indian corn-pone, and had a feast. Then, they burned some dried henbane* in the fire. Its magic aroma filled the cave and brought a deep and restful sleep to the three travel-worn Indians.

At Laguna, Isleta's parents were worried when she failed to return from the river with water and began to inquire about her. A

*A poisonous plant with an unpleasant odor, clammy leaves, and a narcotic juice which grows in dry waste ground.

little boy reported having seen the two warlocks talking to her. They searched the village and the festival grounds but found no trace of her. When they went to the riverbank, they found her leather water pitcher and saw the coyotes' tracks in the mud.

When word of the coyote tracks and the missing Isleta spread, the two Indians from Acoma again told their story about the warlocks changing into coyotes, and this time some of the people believed them. Taos was certain that the conjurers had taken Isleta away with them.

Isleta's father, the tribal chieftan White Eagle, then called a council meeting. His braves agreed that if Taos would lead them, they would hunt down the warlocks and rescue Isleta. Taos agreed to lead them, but, as a medicine man, he first wanted to seek guidance.

He built a fire and tossed some green powder into it, while muttering magic words. He then waved his magic wand over the fire, and blue flames shot into the air. Taos closed his eyes for a few seconds as if in a trance. Then he raised his head and spoke to his tribesmen: "The Great Spirit has told me that the warlocks from Acoma did steal Isleta. He directs that these two good men from Acoma go with us as guides. We must hurry, for Isleta is in grave danger."

Taos told his braves that the mission was a very dangerous one, but that they should be no more afraid of the warlocks than of any other enemy. He told how he had fought with warlocks and witches many times before, and how his witch ladder* and magic wand had always helped him to overcome them. He reminded them that he, as a medicine man, not only could heal, but also inflict fatal maladies on his enemies.

The party hurried through the woods and over the cliffs. They didn't stop until they reached the enchanted mesa, for they were as tireless as the autumn wind. When they reached the mesa, Taos addressed his braves:

"Listen to the bird singing in yon bush. It is warning us of the great danger we face. It says to hurry for Isleta will be abused if she is not rescued soon."

---

* A special tool, used by witches, consisting of a string attached to thirteen feathers from a black crow.

As they began to climb up to the mesa, the warlocks heard the noise. They put Isleta to sleep and left her in the magic cave. They changed themselves into coyotes and crept to the other side of the mesa. Here, they changed back into men and shot at the invaders with poisoned arrows. But, they were too far away to hit them.

While the braves were fighting the warlocks, the Acoma Indians guided Taos into the magic cave. They picked up Isleta and carried her outside. Taos made a large circle on the ground and they placed the sleeping maiden in the middle of the circle. Taos pulled out his witch's ladder, waved it over her, said some magic words, and Isleta awakened. She told them she felt well, but couldn't remember how she got there.

Taos and the two Indians hurried Isleta down from the mesa, hoping to escape while the braves engaged the warlocks. The warlocks soon ran out of arrows and returned to the cave to get more. They were very angry when they found Isleta gone and realized she had been rescued by another warlock as powerful as they. They changed themselves into coyotes and followed the fleeing Taos and Isleta. After they had passed by, they turned themselves into men again and approached them, saying in a friendly tone, "We are looking for some lost burros."

But one of Taos' companions saw through their ruse. He wheeled and shot an arrow through the warlock's heart. The warlock fell to the ground dead, and his slayer said, "There is one of your burros."

At this, the second warlock jumped through his magic hoop, changed into a coyote, and loped away. He had not gotten very far when Taos' other companion shot an arrow which wounded him in the leg. As soon as the arrow struck him, he turned into a man again. He was bleeding so badly that he had to lie down and rest.

As it was now dusk, the Indians decided to camp on the spot and complete their journey to Laguna the next morning. During the night, the injured warlock managed to turn himself into a coyote once more and to limp away. But, in the morning his captors followed the trail of blood and caught him. Taos used his magic witch ladder to turn him back into a man.

The Indians decided the warlock must be destroyed by burning, so they built a hot fire. While they were roasting him, he cried out, "Why do you burn me when I am a man like you?"

"Because you are a warlock and must be killed," Taos answered.

So they burned him to ashes and returned Isleta to her grateful parents.

A MAN RIDES A WITCH

Flonnie Ann Killen, of Floyd County, Virginia, sat back on her rocker and began to talk:

"I've seen some of the gosh awfulest witch's doings' thet ever wuz. Some of 'em sound impossible, but they are the truth, so help me. I've forgot a lot of things I wuz told, but here's one I do recollect.

"Hit wuz about two grown-up brothers. One wuz a big strong man, and t'other wuzzen't big ner strong, but there wuzzen't nuthin' ailin' him till one summer he started a goin' down hill. He sed he wuz tired when he fust got up in the morning. Course, his folks thought right off thet he wuz jest lazy and didn't want to work, but afore long he started a lookin' peaked. His mammy started takin' notice thet he wuz eatin' less and less until finally he got so poor and skinny he hardly made a shadder. When she axt him whut wuz wrong, he'd say hit wuz nuthin', but she kept frettin' and stewin', and finally she had the idee of axting his brother Bill effen he'd try to git him to tell whut wuz wrong.

"One day, jest the two boys wuz outten the field a puttin' up hay. Lars got to pantin' for breath and wuz so frazzled thet he jest give up and laid down in the shade. Bill went over to him and axt, 'Lars, whut in the world is a pesterin' you? Where air you sick?'

"Lars laid real quiet for a while and didn't answer. Then, he sed, 'Bill, I hain't never told nobody whut's a killin' me. I wouldn't tell you now, but I know I hain't much longer for this world. Effen I take a few more trips, I know I'm a goin' to die.'

"Trips? Whut air you a talkin' 'bout, Lars? Air you outten yore mind? You hain't been on no trips. No, indeedy! You hain't been nowhere 'cept home sence we planted the crops way back in the spring.'

"Lars sed, 'Yep, I knowed you'd think I'm logy, but I reckon I hain't. Only the Good Lord knows why I hain't plum crazy. There air times when I wish I wuz a numbskull so's I wouldn't know nuthin' to tell.'

"Now Bill wuz flabbergasted, but he wuz ded set on findin' out whut wuz botherin' him, so he set down real clost to Lars and sed,

Collected by John W. Garrett, Floyd, Virginia, June 30, 1941. Told to him by Flossie Ann Killen, who was eighty-one years old. She had heard this story from her grandfather, I. S. Tingler, of Blue Springs, Virginia.

'Look here, Lars, I hain't a goin' ter down-face you, ner poke fun at you. I'm yore brother and you can tell me whut's ailin' you and I won't tell nobody nuthin' 'bout hit. But, I'll try to do somethin' to holp you.'

"I'm a doubtin', Bill, effen ennybody can holp me now. But I'm a tellin' you this kase when I die, I want you to know whut kilt me. Now, you know I never believed in witches, but I'm afeard a witch is a goin' to make a ghost outten me. Every night of my life for the past three months, a witch has come through the keyhole to my bed. She changes me into a horse, puts a bridle on me and leads me outside. Then, she puts her witch saddle on my neck, plaits my mane into stirrups, jumps on my neck and rides as hard as she can till nigh on to daylight. Then, she brings me back to bed all petered out, and I cain't do nuthin' 'bout hit. The fust time, I tried to fight her off, but she fought so hard thet she got the bridle and saddle on me in spite of all I could do. I've tried everythin' I know, but nuthin' works. Sometimes I think this is my last trip and I'll die afore we git back. Now I've told you, so when I'm kilt, you'll know I wuz rode to death by a witch.

"Lars stopped talkin' and laid very still for a while. Bill looked at his skinny, weak body, not knowin' 'zactly whut he orter do or say. At fust he wuz full of pity; then, he got mad and jest biled over. He sed, 'Lars, look here. Tonight you let me git in yore place in the bed. Then, jest let thet witch come and tackle me and I'll flail the livin' hell outten her. I'd jest like to see any witch thet could take this two-hundred pounds of flesh and muscle anywhere. Come on, let's go home now, Lars, but don't tell Maw whut you told me. Don't you worry no more. You jest go to bed and git some sleep and I'll handle thet witch.'

"As soon as dark come, Bill sed to Lars with a wink, 'Come on to bed now, Lars. I'm awful tired, and we've got a lot to do tomorrow.'

"So, they went early to bed and Lars, tired as a dog, went right off to sleep. Bill, all steamed up 'bout whut he hoped would happen, laid awake a waitin' for the fun. But, nuthin' happened, and he started to wonder if Lars 'ud been joshin' him. He got drowsy and wuz almost asleep when the clock struck twelve and in popped the old witch. Afore he knowed hit, he felt the bit of a bridle in his mouth. He reared up in bed and grabbed the skinny hand that held hit and started wrestlin' and tusslin' with her. Now Bill wuz big and strong, but fight as hard as he could, that infernal monster put the bridle on him and fastened hit. But, he still fought with all his might. 'I'll show you who you're foolin' with,' he sed. 'No witch is a goin' to take me through a keyhole nor ride me.'

"But, though Bill struggled and fought and kicked, afore he knowed whut wuz a happenin' he found himself outside the door. Then, the witch put her saddle on his neck and throwed the girdle over him. He wuz so mad, he jest about busted, and he sed, 'In the name of the Father, and the Son and the Holy Ghost, holp me to kill this witch.' He squirmed and he twisted and he fought till at last he got thet old witch by the arm and twisted hit and throwed her over his back. When she hit the ground, she turned into the purtiest white horse you ever seed. Bill grabbed the saddle, throwed hit over her, cinched the belly-band, climbed up on her and sed 'Gid-dup! Now Damn you, we'll see who does the riding tonight.'

"He recollected how she'd rode Lars hard all night, and he made up his mind thet she'd git a dose of her own medicine, so he rode thet white horse at full gallop till nigh daylight. When they got back to the cabin, she wuz in a lather of sweat and looked like the buzzards had picked her where she'd been through mud and brush. Bill got off, turned her loose and went to bed, where Lars wuz still asleep.

"Atter thet night, Lars and Bill wuz never bothered no more by the witch. Lars got his rest at night, started eatin' and puttin' on weight and got back to where he wuz as strong as he'd ever been."

WHY JUBAL DIDN'T GROW

When Hattie Sue Kitts married up with runty Hargis Helbert, the whole Kitts clan wuz agin hit. In the fust place, nobody else would have him, and in the next place, Tom Bale's oldest boy wuz a shinin' up to her, and he'd a been a right much better catch for her. Now, both Hattie Sue's mammy and Hargis' mammy wuz thought by some to be witches, and they didn't like each other one bit.

Sence none of the Kitts would have ennythin' to do with Hattie Sue atter she went to live in the Helbert's cabin, 'twas Granny Helbert who holped Jubal get borned when Hattie Sue's time had come. As she washed him and kivered him up, she 'lowed she mought a washed him in a leather noggin*, he wuz so little. She knowed right then thet she wuz a goin' to have to find some way to make him grow big and strong.

The puny little brat layed there on hit's pallet in the corner of the cabin and hit whined and cried and fretted, and hit didn't seem to grow one inch. So, Granny Helbert vowed to herself thet she'd see to hit thet hit growed up to be a big man, and strong enuf to whup wildcats. One dark, stormy night (the only time a conjure spell'll work) Granny lit out over the dark ridge to Buffalo Crick in the holler. She looked through the woods till she found some big cucumber trees which allus growed straighter and taller than t'other trees. She picked out the tallest and straightest one, and cut a long gash in the bark 'bout a yard from the ground. Then, she made a cross-cut at each end of the gash and, with the pint of her knife, she peeled the bark back a little. She put a few strands of Jubal's yaller hair agin the skinned part of the tree, put the bark back in place, and smoothed hit down. Then, almost in a whisper, she said:

> In the name of the Father and the Son
> And the Holy Speret, hear me:
>
> All tom, abem tim, fora abo,
> Git water, git food, git air and grow

Collected by Susan B. Morton, of Haymarket, Virginia, March 18, 1939. Told my Mildred Hopkins of Rockbridge County who had heard it as a little girl from her grandmother.

* A leather drinking cup which held about one-fourth of a pint of liquid.

Grow fast and straight and strong
And help little Jubal come along.

I cast a spell so you can
Make him grow to be a big, strong man.

She sneaked away from the tree and set down to rest for a spell. Hit 'ud been a long walk over the ridge and she wuzzen't as spry as she uster be, now thet she wuz a pushin' eighty. The storm wuz over and hit wuz real still so she could hear a rustle in the bushes. She got all flustered and nervous as a rattlesnake and wuz afeared she'd been spied on. She knowed the conjure spell wouldn't work effen she'd been watched by somebody who wuzzen't kindly disposed torge the baby and hit's mammy, and she wuz afeared thet hit wuz some of them Kitts and mebbe they 'ud try to harm her, so she slipped through the woods real quiet like back to the cabin.

Well, bless my soul, thet baby started a growin' and fer the next three years, hit growed like a pig. Hit's ma and paw and Granny all wuz plum proud of him. Then, all at onct, he stopped a growin'. Try as hard as they could, they jest couldn't get him to grow no more. He wouldn't eat, and his cheeks got all pale and his body got blue, and he wuz so puny, he could hardly move.

Right off, Granny Helbert knowed sumpthin' wuz outten kilter. She 'lowed mebbe sumpthin' 'ud happened to the cucumber tree, so she sneaked back up to Buffalo Crick and hunted up thet tree. Shore nuff, she found a big hole gouged outten the trunk of the tree right where she'd put the hank of Jubal's hair, and the hair wuz gone.

Now, Granny wuz afeared the jig wuz up, and 'lowed thet fust the tree 'ud die, then little Jubal 'ud die, too. Hit wuz too late to save the tree er the baby unless she could break the spell by castin' some on the Kitts. She got hoppin' mad, and vowed she'd git the best of them Melungion Kitts.

Well, 'twarn't no time 'tall till Jeff Kitts, Jubal's grandaddy, wuz kicked in the head by his horse and laid unconscious fer three days afore he died. Afore his grave wuz settled, Old Sal Kitts, Jubal's granny, fell and broke her hip and had to stay in bed the rest of her life. Then, lightnin' struck their barn and kilt their horses. Three times the Devil 'ud struck, and Granny Helbert 'lowed she wuz 'bout even with 'em. The cucumber tree died atter awhile, but the spell wuz broke and Jubal started a growin' agin and growed up to be a big strong man.

THE INVISIBLE WITCH

"Holp me! Stop that old woman with her head tied up from chasin' me and slappin' me! She's been beatin' me all the way from the kitchen. Please run her off!"

Maria, one of the young Negro servants in the house of Dr. McChesney, had run into the dining room just as the family was sitting down to its evening meal. Her light brown face was scarlet and her eyes bulged with fright. The McChesneys didn't see anybody chasing Maria, so they calmed her down and made her stay in the big house that night after her chores in the kitchen were over.

This happened in 1825, in August County, Virginia. Several days after this incident, Maria again complained that every time she was alone, an old hag with her head tied up chased her and beat her. And a few days later, as the family sat at their evening meal, Maria came running into the dining room screaming that the old woman was beating her again. Again, the family calmed her, but before they finished the meal, there was a noise on the roof and, upon investigation, it was found that rocks had been thrown up there.

After this, rocks would fall on the roof of the house at random times—sometimes in the day, but mostly at night. Some of them were as large as a man's fist, but some were too large to be thrown. And, sometimes the rocks were so hot they'd scorch the grass when they fell from the roof.

Stories about the falling stones spread through the community, and people came from miles around to see this strange happening. At times, the yard was full of people waiting for the stones to fall and determined to find out where they came from. But, nobody ever saw. They just appeared out of thin air. Meanwhile, Maria was still complaining that she was being beaten, and it was plain to everybody that witches were to blame and that they were after Maria.

Finally, Dr. McChesney decided that the best thing to do was to send Maria to stay with Mrs. Thomas Steele, his wife's sister, who lived a mile north of Newport. When Maria and her escort arrived at

Collected by I. M. Warren, Roanoke County, Virginia, May 7, 1939. This story was told by Mrs. Thomas Steele, Dr. McChesney's sister-in-law, and was handed down from grandmother to mother to daughter.

the Steele's, Mrs. Steele, her three children, a friend and a Negro servant were all out in the yard sitting under a tree. As Mrs. Steele greeted Maria, an awful racket arose inside the house. It sounded like a whole stable of horses were kicking and running around.

The whole company was frozen with surprise and fear, but, when they recovered a little, they went to the door and peered in. In the center of the large hall, all of the furniture and moveables in the house had been piled in a disorderly mess. As they stood there, rocks began to fall on the roof, and Maria started running and screaming that the old woman was beating her again. So, Mrs. Steele sent Maria back to the McChesneys, but rocks continued to fall on the house—and now in the house as well—breaking glasses, plates, windows, and scarring the furniture.

One night, the Steeles were visiting the McChesneys. They were sitting around the fire playing games and telling ghost stories and asking riddles. The doors and windows were all closed, as it was a cold night. Suddenly, a rock seemed to fall from the ceiling and it struck Mrs. Steele on the head. It seemed to cut off a lock of her hair and left a deep gash in her scalp which Dr. McChesney had to stitch up. The whole family was terrified, and Mr. Steele was boiling mad. He called whatever it was a white-livered coward to attack a helpless woman.

He sat down in front of the door and dared the durned thing to strike him. He started with surprise when he began to be hit by clods of dirt which seemed to come from inside the house. He sat there, as stubborn as a mule, while the dirt piled up around him. Finally, his family prevailed upon him to move, and the clods stopped.

The McChesneys were distraught and feared for their children's safety, so they were sent to their grandmother's, near Midway, and Maria went with them. But, the same shenanigans started here too: rocks fell on the house, the furniture was piled up in the hall, and Maria was still being beaten. One day, a large kitchen table started prancing around like a trotting horse. The children were amused by this, and young John Steele urged them to get on and ride. But, the table trotted and galloped so hard that they jumped off in alarm. John fainted.

So, the children and Maria returned to Steele's farm. The slaves there noticed that the tools and food they would carry to the fields would disappear and they'd find them later back at the house. And, Maria continued to complain about being beaten.

In desperation, Mrs. Steele determined to try all the things she'd ever been told were remedies to get rid of witches. She took Maria over her knees, hoisted her skirts, and took a thorn withe to beat off the invisible witch. She had Maria put salt and pepper in her shoes, and wrap cayenne pepper pods in brown paper packets and hang them over her door. But, none of these worked: Maria was still chased and beaten, and Mr. Steele said he could hear the sound of the witch's hand as it hit poor Maria's face.

As a last resort, Dr. McChesney sold Maria to a slave trader who took her farther South. When she left, she ceased to be bothered, and the house was again quiet.

After Maria had been gone for some time, a tobacco chewing old crone of the town described Maria to Dr. McChesney's neighbor as a fiesty, smart-aleck little nigger who'ud bad-mouthed her and threatened to kill her. The family came to the conclusion that this old woman was a witch who had harassed Maria as punishment and caused all the trouble.

PART THREE

HOW TO COUNTERACT WITCHCRAFT

INTRODUCTION

If someone thought that he was bewitched, something had to be done to break the spell. There was no shortage of procedures available to counteract the Devil's work.

The magic numbers, three, nine and thirteen played important parts in breaking spells. In one case, a door was removed and turned around three times before being replaced. In another case, the heart of a black rooster was removed, and thirteen pins were jabbed into it before it was burned. In "Grandpappy Breaks a Spell on His Rifle," Grandpappy stands on a stump and waves an ash twig over his head thirteen times. Billy Jack complains, in "Coffin Nails," that witches have already put eleven nails in his coffin, and if they put in two more, it will make thirteen, and he will die.

The superstition that a horseshoe brings good luck led many mountain people to hang one over their door to keep witches out. This idea was extended to include anything forked, such as a pitchfork, a pair of scissors, a stick, or a twig of mountain ash.

The early settlers had many superstitions about human hair. In "The Silver Bullet," Aunt Mellissa tells Lee Ann that her headaches were probably caused by birds carrying off her hair and using it to make nests. She also suggests that a witch had put some of her hair under the skin of a wild rabbit to cast a spell on her, and that the spell would not be broken until the rabbit is killed.

It was believed that a witch's spell could be broken by securing some of her hair and burning it. Alternatively, some hair and nail parings of the bewitched could be put in a bottle with three black pins and dropped in the fire. When the bottle was broken and the hair and nail parings consumed, the spell would be broken. In "Cornpone and a Witchball," some hairs from the victim's head are rolled into a witchball with henbane and mugwort leaves, and put under the doorstep to keep the witch out of the house.

The colors of white, black and red were important in breaking spells. White and black were associated with good and evil. The Devil was seen as black with fiery red eyes, and hell was a place of darkness with the only light present coming from the red glow of the fire. The black cat was the symbol of bad luck, since it was a witch's familiar. In "Lige Hall's Bewitched Rifle," Lige is advised by a white witch to slay a black goat and roast its shoulder in order to break the spell. In "Old Bowdy," the breastbone of a black hen is buried to break a spell, and in "The Witch of Cenescu," the heart of a black rooster is cut out and used to counteract a spell.

The color red was used in various ways to break spells. Red pepper was a favorite ingredient of the foul mixtures used by both black and white witches. In "The Bell Witch of Tennessee," red pepper is used in this way. In "Betsy, Beans and the Pitchfork," both red pepper and a red cloth are used to tie around a mare's neck to break a spell. Lige Hall mixes red corn with other ingredients when he breaks the spell on his rifle in "Lige Hall's Bewitched Rifle."

It was believed that if one could get some blood from a witch, this would break her spell. As a result, it was often suggested that a witch suspected of bewitching a person be brought to his bedside so that the victim could scratch the witch and draw blood. In "The Witch of Cenescu," Eutiquio cuts a small cross on the forehead of the witch, and, as it starts to bleed, she falls to the floor helpless, and her spell over him is broken.

Beating a witch or even threatening to do so was often an effective way to break a spell. Very often, witches were beaten "sympathetically" by striking the object or person who was bewitched. A bundle of thorns known as "the Devil's club" was used for this purpose. In one case, the thorns were used to whip bewitched milk from a hog trough.

One of the most widely used methods of breaking witch spells and punishing witches was to burn them sympathetically. This was done by burning, roasting or boiling objects which had been bewitched. In "A Doll and a Bag of Money," Aunt Nan Miller cups her hands together, fills them with bewitched milk and throws it on the fire, saying, she hopes it will burn the old witch who put a spell on her churn. And, in "Roasted Mutton," Jeb Paul builds a fire and bakes a sheep's shoulder slowly, causing the witch to cry out that he was burning her to death.

Because of the fundamentalist religious beliefs of these people, it is not surprising to find that they used the Bible to counteract witches. A white witch advised John Bell to sleep with his Bible under his pillow so as to prevent a witch from bothering him at night in "The Bell Witch of Tennessee." This was also thought to keep the devil away. Invoking the Holy Trinity or the sacred names of Mary and Jesus, making the sign of the cross, and taking communion were all used to counteract witches and take off their spells. Granny Sexton in "Betsy, Beans and Pitchforks," burns her bewitched hog to ashes while she reverently prays, "In the name of the Father, and the Son and the Holy Spirit, head off the witch's spell and drive it away." In "Lige Hall's Bewitched Rifle," Lige prays, "In the name of the Father, and the Son and the Holy Ghost, break the spell on my gun."

An idea carried over from Europe was that a witch would stop to count each grain of sand or rice in front of a door. This would delay her until sun-up when the crow of the cock would remind her to disappear. This practice was modified slightly in America to include all kinds of small objects that might be difficult to count. Maria Williams uses this idea in "The Scissors, Tablefork and Sifter," when she ties her flour sifter over the door knob, thinking it will surely take a witch until dawn to count all the holes.

Just as black witches prepared all sorts of noxious brews and potions to bewitch people and animals, white witches used many of the same ingredients to counteract these spells. Red pepper, asafoetida, dog fennel, sulfur, sage, ginseng, sassafras and mugwort were all used. Vera Bell's witchball in "A Cornpone and a Witchball" contains dried sassafras, ginseng roots, mugwort and henbane leaves.

Effigies, pictures and rag dolls were commonly made, and were used to cast spells as well as to break them. In breaking a spell, the image of the witch was shot with a silver bullet. These bullets were usually made by melting down a silver coin.

When a witch found out that someone was trying to break the spell she had cast on a person, she tried to obtain something from that person by begging or borrowing. In "Roasted Mutton," we find the witch persistently trying to borrow something—even just a glass of drinking water. In another case, a witch feigns illness and tries to get the bewitched person to give her medicines. When black witches were unable to beg or borrow something, they resorted to stealing it, and white witches advised their followers to do the same.

THE BELL WITCH OF TENNESSEE

Around 1885, John Bell moved his family from Turkey Knob, North Carolina, to the Red River section of Tennessee. The country was still a wilderness of huge oak, beech and hickory forests filled with panther, black bear, and wild pigeons. John Bell had been a large landowner in North Carolina and he had grants for large tracts in Tennessee and was soon buying more.

As soon as the Bells arrived on their new land, they cleared the trees and built the finest house in the community. Not too far away, they built a schoolhouse, since John and Lucy Bell had nine children—seven boys and two girls. They were all industrious, pious folks, and soon John was a leader in the Baptist church as well as in the larger community. He made money and bought more land with it.

He bought one parcel of land from an old widow named Kate Batts. She was reputed to be a witch, but John dickered with her until she came down to the price he wanted to pay. Later, old Kate got to brooding on the deal and she concluded she'd come out at the little end of the horn. She told her neighbors she'd get even with him, come hell or high water.

John had hired a young man by the name of Richard Powell as their schoolmaster when he had come to the community seeking a job. He was taken into the Bell home to live with the family, and he and young Betsy Bell were soon sweet on each other.

Soon, strange things began to happen in the Bell home. They began to hear noises in the walls of the house—tappings, scratchings and whisperings a little like beetles would make. Then, the children complained that they could see eerie lights around their beds at night. They also said that the covers were snatched from their beds, and something dumped them out of bed and they awakened in the middle of the floor. The noises grew louder day by day, and the harrassment of the children worse every night.

One night, the family was gathered around the fireplace while John read aloud from the Bible. A noise began which sounded like a boy just learning to whistle through his teeth. The noise then

Based on a story by Frank Oates of Knoxville, Tennessee told in April, 1925. It was later published in *God Bless The Devil*, W. P. A. Project, by the University of North Carolina Press, Chapel Hill, North Carolina, 1940.

changed to a kitten's meow, and then to a soft whisper before dying away. Then, a raspy woman's voice began to read the same passage of scripture which John had just read. It said, "John Bell, who was the last poor widow you cheated out of her land? You had better go tomorrow and make it up to her for that swindle."

Well, John shook like a dog in a wet sack, but he wasn't scared enough to part from his money, so he told the family to say nothing about what had happened, and he'd see if he could put a stop to the witchings. Of course, he had recognized the voice as that of Kate Batts.

But, as such things will, word soon got around the community about the strange noises and voices in the Bell home and neighbors took to spending evenings with them hoping to hear them. They were usually rewarded by a voice cutting into the conversation with abuse of John, calling him names that would have put a sailor to shame. After this, people came in crowds to hear the voice. Some of them were so scared that they took off across the fields like scared rabbits.

The harassment of the family grew worse: the children were kicked, and pinched and their hair was pulled. Dishes, pots and pans were thrown at John and his daughter Betsy. Cream was skimmed off the milk so that they couldn't make any butter. To say the least, John was very upset.

One of their neighbors confirmed John's opinion that the witch causing all the trouble was Kate Batts. He suggested that John consult Sid Moore, a white witch who lived up in the hills. He warned John that Sid's price would be high, but John was in such a state that he thought any price would be cheap, so he went to see Sid. For twenty-five dollars, he was given complete instructions to stop the witch's harassments, and a plan to get her out of the community for good.

Sid's instructions were that the breast bone of a black hen should be buried in front of the doorstep to keep the witch from entering the house. But, in case she did, John was to sleep with his Bible under his pillow to prevent the witch from bothering him. Further, each child was to wear a cloth containing the dried toe of a toad around his neck, and, when they went to bed at night, they were to turn their stockings wrong side out. If any of them should meet the witch, they were to double their thumbs inside their hands. If they wanted to get rid of Kate Batts at once and for all time, the last Bell child who had been christened would have to leave a branch of mountain ash where Kate would have to touch it. She would then be marked as the next victim the Devil was to carry off.

John didn't really believe in witches and witchcraft. He thought these suggestions were crazy and that he had been robbed of his twenty-five dollars. Upon reflection, however, he decided that there would be no harm in trying these things, so he gathered his family around and told them what they must do. As he was speaking, they heard a sound like the buzzing of a swarm of bees. The doors burst open and then closed and the windows rose and fell. The light from the fire and the candles faded away, and out of the darkness came a raspy voice saying, "John Bell, I'll hound you as long as I live, and when I die, I'll come back to this earth and haunt you."

After this, the Bell family lost no time in putting Sid's instructions into practice. The next day, the children went to the woods to hunt toads to get a toad's toe for each of them. Mr. and Mrs. Bell began sleeping with their Bibles under their pillow. Cemantha, their cook, stewed a black hen, took out the breastbone, and Mrs. Bell buried it in front of the door. Then, Cemantha cooked a large chocolate cake which Betsy took over to Kate Batts. She was instructed to borrow a pod of red pepper and to leave a branch of mountain ash inside the door where Kate would have to pick it up.

These methods of thwarting Old Kate seemed to work, because the Bell family was not bothered any more. But, Kate didn't leave the community—perhaps she swept the branch of mountain ash out instead of picking it up. She did, however, suddenly get religion, and became accepted in the community as a good Christian woman. The next winter, both the Methodists and the Baptists held revival meetings at the same time. Kate was a glutton for preaching, so she would go to the first half of the Baptist meeting and the last half of the Methodist. But, the hellfire of the Methodists and the water of the Baptists got her so confused that she backslid and lost all her religion.

She went out on the mountain to John Garnett's still, bought a jug of tanglefoot, and got drunker than a pig at a stillhouse. She went by John Bell's house and told him he hadn't seen the last of her and that she'd dog him to his grave. Furthermore, she'd make it hot for that little smart-aleck Betsy who had left the mountain ash branch in her house. She cussed and rared* and picked up some dirt and threw it in John's face. Then, she went home, drank some more and passed out. It was a cold night and she had let the fire go out, so

*A corruption of "reared," used in the sense of "quarreling" or "talking loudly."

she caught a fever and, in a few days, Old Kate was dead. This was a relief to the Bell family.

It wasn't long before all hell broke loose in the Bell household. They heard Old Kate scream. She whacked John and Betsy black and blue. She stuck them with invisible pins, and snatched food from the table and threw it in their faces. None of Sid's charms would work on a ghost, and the Bells decided to move to another state. But, the voice of Old Kate warned them she'd follow wherever they went, so the Bells resigned themselves and kept on praying.

By now, Betsy Bell was a beautiful blonde, blue-eyed young woman, and schoolmaster Powell wanted to marry her, but she had many suitors and favored young Josh Carter. Josh had cursed Old Kate when she was alive, so one night her ghost appeared to Betsy and warned, "Don't marry Josh Carter. If you do, you'll forever be sorry."

Whenever Betsy would go out with Josh, Kate tried to prevent it by filling her hair with a tangle of burrs, ripping her dress, or gouging her eyes until Betsy would give in and stay home. Whenever she went out with any other boy, she had no trouble at all.

Well, the news about the Bell's witch spread far and wide. President Andrew Jackson heard about the witch and her ghost that visited the Bells, and he and some friends decided to go and see for themselves. Well, the moment Jackson's carriage crossed the county line near the Bell home, the wheels locked. The driver whipped the horses and cursed them, but nothing happened. President Jackson poked his head out to speak to the driver and a voice above his head said, "You can go now. I'll see you tonight, General." And, the carriage began to move.

Sure enough, Old Kate kept her word. That night Busby, General Jackson's companion, heard her say, "All right, you coward, you threatened to shoot me. Here I am: shoot and be damned."

Busby pulled out his gun, loaded it with a silver bullet, aimed it in the direction from which the voice had come, and pulled the trigger. The hammer clicked, but the gun didn't go off. Then, Busby began to squirm and twist and in a few minutes he went hopping and yelling about the room. He moved as if someone were leading him by the nose. The door flew open and, with a loud thump, he went sprawling down the steps. As soon as he hit the bottom step, he got up and took off for the woods, yelling at the top of his voice. Right then and there, President Jackson got up and headed for home.

One morning about a year later, John Bell was found dead in his room. He was sitting in his chair with a bottle of poison beside him. Nobody knew how it got there, but, of course, the family was convinced that Old Kate had done this evil deed. The ghost did seem to be gone, however.

Some months after this, Betsy Bell and Josh Carter went to a picnic where they intended to announce their engagement. When Josh stood up to make the announcement, a loud voice said, "Well, well, here we are. I've come back to make sure that fly-up-the-creek Betsy don't marry Josh Carter. If you do, Betsy, I'll make your lives a hell on earth just like old John Bell's was." Then, the voice faded away.

In the confusion as people scattered and fled, the announcement was never made, and Betsy gave John's ring back to him. Later, she and Professor Powell were married. They stayed in the community and raised a large family, and were never again bothered by the Bell witch-ghost.

THE OLD MAN AND HIS TOAD

Way up in the mountains, in Patrick County, Virginia, before the Civil War, there were a lot of witches roaming through the woods. If a member of a family became a witch, she would leave home and live in a cave or abandoned cabin. Everybody in those times believed in witchcraft. There were many good witches (known as *white witches* or *witch doctors*) who helped people who were sick or in trouble. Sometimes, people would lose faith in a good witch, and then she would change into an evil one, or *black witch*. Jenny Shultz used to tell this story about one witch to whom this happened:

"My grandmother wuz born way up in the mountains of Patrick County, Virginia, but she spent the last years of her life in my father's home in Pittsylvania County. When I wuz a little young'un, she told me a story 'bout an old witch who uster live in the mountains nigh her home during her mother's lifetime.

"Now, in them days, witches roamed the woods. Effen a woman got to be a witch, she'd run away from home, live in caves er huts, and spend her time bewitching folks. Hit 'peared like in them days most everybody believed in witches. Sum wuz good witches who helped people outten trubbel. Sum wuz mean, spiteful and done things to hurt folks. Sometimes folks 'ud lose faith in a good witch, then she'd change into a black witch.

"Durin' Granny's early life, the mountain folks of Patrick County made a lot of illegal likker. Moonshiners, as they wuz called, lived like outlaws. Every man carried a gun and he'd shoot a person at the drap of a hat effen he thought the person 'ud tell 'bout his still. These folks 'ud give little young'uns likker and let 'em smoke er chew terbacker.

"There wuz a widder, Gussie Proffit, who lived with her fifteen-year old son outten the top of the highest mountain. She kept her cabin much cleaner and neater than most other folks. Her flowers bloomed so purty thet they made her little cabin the brightest spot on the mountain. She wuz a granny doctor, and brewed

Collected by Raymond T. Sloan, Rocky Mount, Virginia, May 10, 1940. Told to him by Jenny Schultz, of Patrick County. The event was said to have taken place near Big Reed Island, in Grayson County, in the late 1800's.

mountain yarbs into simples* to treat all kinds of sickness. She wuz a kind and good old woman, allus a tryin' to holp folks who wuz sick or in trubbel. She told some people thet she had visions while settin' at her spinnin' wheel and dreams at night thet showed her who needed her holp and whut to do fer 'em. She tried to get people to turn away from their wickedness by warning 'em of turrible things thet 'ud happen to 'em effen they didn't. Most of the mountain folks loved and respected her.

"One fall, the weather turned bad and there wuz a turrible hurricane. The whoopin' wind blowed down trees and barns and kilt folks' animals. Then, there wuz a long wet spell thet brung on a big flood. The small branches and cricks turned into big rivers and run all over creation, washing away many stills, cabins and barns. Never before had such awful things happened to these people, and a lot of 'em were frightened and tried to find the cause of such happenings.

"People got to talkin' 'bout all these trubbels comin' all at onct, and one of the moonshiners, Old Lige Askew, who wuz a cruel and wicked old man, sed he figgered hit musta been Old Gussie Profitt outten the top of the mountain who wuz a causin' all of their trubbels. So, he started to pass the word along thet she wuz an evil night-witch and thet she had caused the storm. Some folks got the jim jams, and they got angry at the old woman. Then, one night, Old Lige rounded up a bunch of men and they went outten Gussie's place, kilt her son, drove Bessie outten the cabin, and burnt hit to the ground with everythin' she had in hit.

"Now, Gussie had no place to go, so she jest roamed 'round and lived in the woods. Atter this, she never went clost to nobody. Sometimes folks 'ud ketch a quick glance at her, feeble and bent over and walkin' slow leanin' heavy on a big stick. Allus atter this, she wuz knowed as the 'Old Witch Woman,' and she got blamed for ennythin' bad thet happened for miles around. Folks believed thet she could vanish into thin air like a puff of smoke effen she seed ennybody watchin' her. 'Twarn't long afore fear and hatred of the 'Old Witch Woman' spread all through the mountains.

"Late one evenin' in December, three men wuz out a huntin' on a cold day when they got kotched in a blizzard, and they went to an empty cabin to git outten the storm. There wuz Steve Carter, an old codger with a weather-beaten and wrinkled face; Herb Hill, who wuz tall and skinny as a fence rail, and didn't have but one eye; and Old Lige Askew, the bully thet had led the mob who burned

*See note on page 67.

down Gussie's cabin and kilt her son and who wuz a strong, red-faced old man with beady black eyes and a turrible temper.

"The cabin had one winder with no coverin' cept a blind which kept out some of the rain but not much cold air. They built a big fire in the fireplace and moved the table and a bench near hit, put their gallon jug of red-eye likker in the middle of the table and began to play cards.

"Steve Carter wuz so nervous thet he jumped outten his seat every time hit thundered. 'This is a helluva night,' whined Steve. 'Jest the night fer sperets to be a roamin' and witches to be a ridin'. Enny time we git thunder and lightnin' on a cold night like this, hit's a shore sign thet sumpthin' awful's a goin' to happen. I've got a feelin' deep down in my bones thet bad luck is a comin' tonight. They do say thet the Old Witch Woman wuz a prowlin' round in the woods early this mornin'.'

"Old Lige interrupted Steve by sayin', 'Jest you let me see her, and I'll fix her onct and fer all. Now old man, you shet up and give your tongue a rest and wet your whistle with some more of thet red-eye.'

Steve followed Old Lige's advice and tuk a long, gurglin' drink from the jug, but he wuz too nervous to keep his trap shut. He sed, 'All of you know 'bout the toad thet old witch-woman's a carryin' round with her. Some say hit's her imp, and thet someday hit'll take her soul off to the witchworld. Then, hit'll change into a devil and come back to earth to tote off to hell the souls of them whut's bothered her here on earth. You know thet toad goes along in front of her and leads her to them thet would harm her.'

"Again, Old Lige interrupted and sed, 'She cain't skeer me with a puny little toadfrog. I'll jest dowse her and her little old warty toad in thet jug of moonshine, and see effen they can hop their way outten hit.'

"Steve sed, 'You'd better mind whut you're a sayin, Lige, and not rile thet old witch-woman. You know a witch can hear ennythin folks sez, and they know everythin' they're thinkin, too.'

"Annudder flash of lightnin' lighted up the whole cabin, and hit wuz follered by a deafenin' crack of thunder. All three men were skeered and shaking in their boots, and they all made a lunge fer the likker jug at the same time. Each one gulped down a big hootern of the stuff.

"Then, Herb Hill, who up to now was too skeered to say a word, got up and turned around and his face got as white as a sheet. He froze in his tracks and stared straight ahead, jest like he'd been turned to stone. Lige and Steve turned to see whut had happened, and they spied the Old Witch Woman a leanin' on her big stick with her toad beside her.

"When Herb got holt of hisself enuf to axt, 'Lawd a massey! How in the world did you git in here?' hit wuz Steve who sed, 'They musta come in through thet latch hole. There hain't no other place they could a come in.'

"Then, thet toad hopped right up on the table beside thet jug of likker. Hit spoke right up and sed, 'You must give us food and warmth.'

"Old Lige started torge thet toad and hollered loud enuf to wake the daid, 'Git outten here afore I burn you up. Git out, I say!' And, he grabbed at the toad to throw hit into the fire. But, afore he could tetch hit, thet toad started to rise up and hit turned into a big red devil. Hit reached over and tuk the big stick outten the Old Witch Woman's hand, and hit turned into a pitchfork.

"Old Lige started a shakin' like a dog in a wet sack. He wuz too skeered to speak. Then he tuk a long, gurglin' swig of likker and staggered torge the Old Witch Woman and sed, 'I've allus heard thet you carried a lot of money in thet old bonnet of your'n. I'm a goin' to snatch hit off, git yore money, and slap your old wrinkled jaws real good.'

"As he started torge her, Steve hollered, 'Lige, don't you tech her! Don't rile her!'

"As Lige's boney hand reached torge her, the toad-devil cotch him with the pitchfork and pinned him agin the wall. Then, the Witch Woman sed to Lige, 'Now, this time you're under my power. I knowed in your evil mind you'd decided to burn the toad and to bury me alive. But, tonight I ride the clouds, not you, and I'll leave you to a worse fate than bein' roasted er buried alive.'

"Then, she hollered, 'I'm a comin, I'm a comin. I'll be ridin' tonight,' and right before their unbelieving eyes, she went up the chimney like a puff of smoke.

"Annuder loud crash of thunder made two of the men dive under the table. Steve mumbled, 'She's gone, but where's her toad?'

"Then, Old Lige, who betweenwhiles 'ud fallen agin the door and slid to the floor, hollered, 'I see him, I see him!'

"Whut do you see?' axt Herb.

"Old Lige replied, 'I'm witched. I see the devil and all his wicked angels right there in hell. I see the sperets of all the folks thet I've ever done a wrong. The skies have opened up into this roarin' furnace, and all of hell is a roarin' past my ears. I see the clouds a openin' up and a carryin' the Old Witch Woman up outten the chimney torge hell. Look! She's left the toad!"

"The cabin door suddenly blew open, and the toad hopped torge hit. Lige hollered, 'Hit's a goin' and I've got to go too,' and he follered the toad out into the storm.

"Then, Herb Hill and Steve Carter fell to the floor as daid as a doornail.

"Allus atter thet, insted of seeing the Old Witch Woman a prowlin' in the woods, folks seed a bent old man a follerin' a frog and mutterin, 'I'm witched, I'm witched.'

"Atter thet, all the mountain moonshine likker made by them folks on the mountain wuz witched. Thet's why ennybody thet drinks red-eye moonshine allus ends up a seein' big red devils."

THE LAME HORSE AND THE LAME WITCH

For more than an hour, Jerry Ritton and his old woman had been darting in and out of their little cabin doing the morning chores of feeding the chickens and ducks and milking the cows. While Susie took care of the milk, Jerry entered the barn to feed and water his prized mare. He was flabbergasted to find that she had gone lame during the night, and wouldn't leave the stall. While he was bending over attending to her, he heard a voice over his shoulder which said, "Your horse is lame." When he looked up, there stood Old Lana Hutton of Cobleskill.

"How do you know he's lame?" asked Jerry.

"Why, he's so lame, he can hardly stand on three legs, she answered with a triumphant smile on her wrinkled face.

"You confounded old witch, how do you know he's lame?" Jerry asked again.

She didn't answer, but took off down the road. Abe Smith was sitting on his porch as she passed by so she stopped and said, "Ritton's horse is lame, Abe."

Abe came right over and told Jerry, Lana had told him about his lame horse. "I'd like to know how she knew it," fumed Jerry, "but she wouldn't tell me."

"I'll tell you how. She's a witch," Abe answered. "And you can prove it by heating a flat-iron red-hot and dropping it in a pail of water. You'll hear her yell, I'll bet!"

So, Jerry heated the iron, fetched it to the back yard, and dropped it in a pail of water. Just as the steam hissed, he heard the old witch let out a terrible scream. She hobbled around with a bandaged foot for the next three weeks, but Jerry's horse was well the next day.

A black colt appeared and was seen grazing in the field near Old Lana's house. No one knew how it got there or to whom it belonged. The feeling grew in the community that the colt was Lana herself.

If this were really so, Jerry Ritton saw his chance to get even

Based on a story told by Hal Jones, age sixty-nine, of Utica, New York, July 10, 1948. He heard this story from an old school teacher when he was a child.

with her. One evening late, he sneaked into the field and caught the colt. He took it to the blacksmith shop where he had it shod and turned it loose again in the field.

The next day, Lana Hutton was seen with her hands bandaged, and she walked as if her feet were paining her. No one could induce her to tell them what ailed her. However, years afterward, people saw scars on her hands which looked as if they had been made by nails.

THE WITCH-CAT

One blustery March day, back in 1850, a handsome young man showed up in the Bold Creek community, bought a piece of land, cut some logs and had a houseraising to build him a cabin. He cleared a few acres of land, put in some crops, got him some chickens, a horse and a cow and settled down to hard work. That man was Ron Nock Dye. Helen Skeen, of Cootes Store, Virginia, picks up the story:

"Ron Nock Dye, my grandpappy, wuz a handsome, smart young man when he come to the mountains. He fell in love with Effie McConnell and they got married and set up housekeeping near Bold Camp. They worked hard and wuz savin' so they done well.

"Everybody got to know 'em on the mountain, liked 'em, and give 'em help and encouragement 'cept old Denice Jane Pilynor. She wuz a stooped, haggard old woman who lived by herself not far from Ron and Effie, but she wouldn't have ennythin' to do with 'em. This made 'em suspicious and afeard of her, and they had a feelin' thet she had bad-mouthed and down-faced them to all of the neighbors. Some of the folks faulted Old Denice as bein' a witch, but Effie and Ron didn't believe in witches and such like, and they paid no mind to this.

"In due time, Effie brought a big bouncin' boy into the world, and Effie and Ron wuz both pleased as bumblebees in a clover field. They'd spend hours a playin' with the young'un, and each 'ud brag 'bout how he looked like t'other. They 'lowed they could see him grow and change every day. They had fixed a little bed for him and put hit not far from their own.

"When the boy wuz 'bout two months old, they wuz woke one night by a low cat yowl. Effie wuz startled, cause she remembered she'd put their cat out before they'd gone to bed. Then, she leaped out of bed torge the young'un's bed. On the bed wuz a whoppin' big black cat with one white paw. Hit hissed at her and whined and jest seemed to fade away. Course, Effie'd heard 'bout cat suckin' a young'un's breath and killin' 'em, but, she didn't believe in sech

Collected by Lelia Branch Bess, of Potts Creek, Virginia, June 9, 1939. Told to her by Helen Skeen, a seventy year old resident of Cootes Store, Virginia.

things. But, when she looked at her young'un, hit wuz stone daid. Her and Ron 'zamined hit real good, but they found nary a scratch, ner cut, ner bruise. Course, Effie and Ron wuz outdone, and powerful sad thet they'd lost their first young'un.

"In time, Effie brung annuder young'un into the world, and this time hit wuz a girl. When hit wuz nigh unto three months old, they wuz woke agin by the same cat-cry. This time, Ron wuz on his feet and beside the young'un's bed quick as think. There wuz the same black cat a stranglin' the young'un with hits long white claw. He tried to get at the cat, but a spell wuz on him and he couldn't move his hands nor his feet. The black cat seemed to vanish like light, but the young'un wuz daid. Ron and Effie wuz skeered and shaken, but they felt as helpless as a new-born squirrel, and didn't know what to do.

"The next year, Effie born annuder young'un. Ron sed, 'Effie, I'm afeard this young'un'll be kilt jest like t'others. I've been a tryin' to set my mind 'bout whut to do. Let's go and see a witch doctor, sence mebbe hit's a witch thet's a pesterin' us.'

"Effie agreed, and they went nigh Witch Mountain, where there's a lot of witches and witch doctors. They talked to Zeus Finklin who wuz a well-known white witch. He told Ron and Effie whut to do, but he made 'em promise they'd not tell ennybody 'bout their plans.

"Ron got his big huntin' knife and whetted hit as sharp as a briar. He kept hit under his piller where he could reach hit easy. Then, he got him a little bottle and went out and cotched him a black spider, a snail, and got the toes offen the left foot of a tree toad. He cut a little piece offen a bat's wing, and wropt these things in a little red rag and squeezed 'em all into the bottle. He tied a string to the bottle and hung hit aside the young'un's bed. Zeus had told him this 'ud keep the witches from a spellin' him so he could fight effen they come back.

"From thet time on, Ron slept with one eye on the young'un's bed. He kept the sharp knife under his piller, but weeks passed and nothin' happened, then months. Ron and Effie started to think mebbe the witch doctor 'ud skeered the witches away. Then, one pitch-black night, they heard the cat-scream agin. Ron grabbed his knife and, in one single leap, wuz at the young'un's bed side. He landed betwixt the black cat and the young'un jest as the cat stretched out hit's white paw torge hit. Ron wuz a shakin' in his legs and wuz afeard he couldn't move, but he shot out his long arm and cotched the cat's paw and squeezed hit real hard. Then, he whacked hit off with one swipe of his sharp knife. Agin, the cat jest faded into the air and wuz gone, but hit hadn't touched the young'un.

"Course, Effie and Ron didn't sleep no more thet night. Ron 'lowed hit wuz a witch-cat, and hit wuz the same one whut kilt their other young'uns. He hoped he'd broke the spell.

"When hit got light, they looked 'round to find the cat's paw. But, lo and behold, whut they found wuzzen't no cat's paw 'tall, but the hand and lower arm of an old woman. Right there and then, Ron swore he wuz a goin' to see Old Denice Pilymor, kase he knowed she wuz the witch who'd kilt his young'uns.

"He hurried over to Denice's place, and later told Effie 'bout hit: 'Honey, I found thet witch, all right. Old Denice didn't want to let me in, but I forced open the door. She wuz a holdin' her right arm behind her back, so I tried to get her to shake hands with me, but she wouldn't. I axt her whut wuz wrong with her right hand, but she didn't answer me. So I jest held out thet hand offen the cat and axt her effen she ever seed hit afore. She turned as white as snow, and 'most passed out. She screamed, 'Now, you give thet to me.'

"She grabbed thet hand from me, pushed me outten the cabin door, and bolted hit behind me. I thought 'bout settin' the cabin afire and burnin' the old devil up. Then I 'lowed they'd send me to the pen fer killin' the old hellion, and I knowed you and the young'un needed me worser than I needed to kill her. Besides, I'm a goin' to see Zeus and tell him whut happened and axt him effen this has broke the spell.

"So, Ron went to see Zeus, and he told Ron thet the spell wuz broke for good. But, Ron slept with the knife under his piller till thet young'un was most two years old, but the cat didn't come no more."

BROTHER, HE LEFT IT ALL

A whole caboodle of witches lived way back on the Hurricane, in Wise County, near old Louis Gray's place. Old Louis was so greedy and tight that he wouldn't let people pass through his land. He had it all posted and took some people to court and had them fined for trespassing. Now, folks in the mountains didn't like this because they couldn't get to the witches to clean them out, and a lot of them 'lowed that old Louis was either in cahoots with them or was spelled by them. But, let Joe Atkins tell it:

"Old Louis Gray wuz a skinflint, and his stinginess sometimes caused him to do dishonest deeds. He wuz knowed as 'Chinch Gray' kase he wuz as tight as the skin on a chinch's belly atter hit 'ud had its fill. He wuz so stingy he wouldn't let people walk through his land, but had hit posted and took folks to court for trespassin' effen they cut acrost hit.

"Now, a whole caboodle of witches lived way back nigh Old Louie's place, and folks couldn't get to 'em to clean 'em out kase Old Louie wouldn't let them acrost his land, so folks 'lowed he wuz in cahoots with them witches and wuz protectin' 'em.

"Onct, Old Louie went outten the mountain and moved the stone which marked the line betwixt his land and Gus Quillen's so's he could have a few more feet of land. Course, he figgered nobody'd ever notice hit, and 'pears thet nobody did.

"'Twarn't more'n a month of Sundays atter he'd moved thet marker thet Old Chinch Gray knew he wuz on his last legs. He knew he'd soon have to face his Maker, and he got to worryin' 'bout movin' thet marker. But, thet little scrap of land meant a lot to him, and he found hit hard to put hit back. Then, he thought effen hit wuz found out thet he'd moved the marker, Old Gus 'ud bring him into court and hit 'ud cost him a heap of money, so he had to make a hangman's choice. One night he decided he'd better go out and move hit back, but the witches musta stopped him and kilt him. He wuz found in the wood daid as a hammer. When they laid him out and 'zamined him, they didn't find nuthin' wrong 'ceptin a big blue spot jest under his heart. Hit looked like a witch ball'd hit him.

Collected by James Taylor Adams, Big Laurel, Virginia, June 30, 1939. He was told this story by Joe Atkins, then seventy-seven years old, who had heard it from his mother, who in turn had heard it from her mother.

"They had a wake at his place, and the next day tuk him to the church for a big funeral. A lot of folks wuzzen't shore whether to be sorry er glad bout him dyin, but they come from far and wide to his buryin'.

> The day wuz as cold as a witch's smile
> When they buried Old Chinch Gray;
> His friends (he didn't have many) gathered to talk
> Afore they put him away.
>
> He wuz a moughty rich man, an old codger sed,
> He hardly spent ennything t'all;
> I wonder how much he left, ennyhow?
> His friend sed, 'Brother, he left hit all.'"

"'Twarn't long atter Old Chinch Gray wuz buried thet folks started a seein' his spittin' image a standin' nigh the line betwixt his place and Gus Quillen's holding a stone high above hit's head. Hit wuz a sayin, 'Where must I put hit?'"

"Then, Gus Quillen's widder smelt a mouse and went to the court house and looked at the deeds to find where the line markers should be. She went outten the line and found thet the marker 'ud been moved. So, one night, she went outten the ridge to watch, and shore enuf, 'round midnight, Old Chinch Gray showed up. He had thet big stone marker lifted above his haid, and when he passed the widder, he axt, 'Where must I put hit?'

"The widder said, 'Put hit back pimeblank where you tuk hit from.'

"He put hit back where hit belonged, and as he passed the widder, the wind blew her apron 'gainst thet stone and burnt a big hole in hit. And, nobody ever saw Old Chinch Gray's ghost no more."

THE CAT WIFE

The pale December evening spread a slanting curtain of darkness through the woods as I trudged over the rough wagon road up the creek and over Adair Ridge to Big Lick Mountain, on my way to John Mack Rose's cabin. The heavy fog and piercing cold urged me along a little faster than I normally would walk. Long before I reached the cabin, the barking of John Mack's dog had announced my arrival, and he was peering through the door into the dusk.

"Hi, John Mack," I called, using my friendliest tone to dispel his fears. "Don't you remember the woman who came to swap yarns with you last summer?"

"Sure as shootin, effen hit hain't Sallie Beth Smith," he said with obvious relief on his leathery face. "Yep, I'm tickled pink to see you. Indeedy, my old woman jest sed this very day she'd be pleased effen you'd come back to see us. She's been poorly lately, and you stayin' a spell'll holp perk her up. Now, you mustn't think nuthin' 'bout me not knowin' at fust who you wuz, hit bein' such a dampish and early night. Then besides, we've been 'spectin' to see some revenooers sence they allus show up jest afore Christmas. Come in the house; Lindy Jane'll be moughty proud to see you."

The cabin was a two-room log structure with a small porch and a large rock chimney at one end. The fire-room was typically mountaineer, with a large log fire providing both heat and light. Festoons of red peppers, dried beans, small bunches of onions and strings of dried apples hung against the mud-pointed log walls. Clothes hung against the walls on wooden pegs, and a few postal cards and calendars with bright pictures provided the decoration.

Aunt Lindy Jane Rose had lived in this house all her life. She was known as the best story teller in the hills. She had folded her skinny frame into a rocking chair before the fire, and her one-piece black dress gave her figure more substance than it really had. As she puckered her friendly mouth into a smile of welcome, she bared her few remaining teeth. Her pallid face, wrinkled like a withered apple, radiated joy. Aunt Lindy greeted me in her wispy voice: "Why didn't you come back sooner, Miss Smith? I've been poorly

Collected by Raymond T. Sloan, Rocky Mount, Virginia, June 8, 1939. He was told this story by Sallie Beth Smith, who heard it from Mrs. John Mack Rose. The natives of the community call the story "The Cathole."

with the rhumatis* ever sence the cold weather set in, and this wet spell had made my rhumatis act up worsen ever. Pull up a cheer and set a spell."

Her crooked hickory walking stick leaned crazily against the stone chimney near a big sleek tomcat who was snoozing in front of the fire. Her clay pipe rested on a nearby table, and she took it up, filled and lighted it as I made myself comfortable. She sat there silently smoking for some moments, the puffs of blue smoke curling over her snow-white head. She stared into the fire in deep thought. I broke the silence by asking, "Granny, do you believe in witches?"

The old woman struggled to her feet as fast as her stiff joints would let her, as if I had unloosed a dangerous animal in the room. She clutched the walking stick in her boney hand and her alert blue eyes sparkled with fear and excitement as she declared, "Witches, did you say? Yes, chile, they'se witches. They're everywhere. They'se human witches, they'se cat witches and kittens, er whutever else kind of varmint they want to be. They bloodies cow's milk, blasts crops, rides folks like they're hosses, rides 'round on brooms, and causes folks to fight and quarrel with one annuder."

After her long soliliquy on witches, Aunt Lindy slowly folded her stooping frame back into her rocking chair. She spat in the fire and re-lit her pipe. She was trembling and the quiver of her lips exaggerated the movement of her pipe.

As if on cue, the big tomcat roused, arched his back and bristled, gave a low wail, and vanished through the cat-hole in the door. "Now, jest look at thet cat," Aunt Lindy said. "Hain't no tellin, mebbe he's a witch hisself er else is witched right now."

In the meantime, John Mack had joined us before the fire and said, "Speakin' of cats, Lindy Jane, cain't ye tell Miss Smith thet crazy tale 'bout the cat wife?"

"Ah, John Mack, you know Miss Smith didn't traipse through these rough hollers and over these steep ridges jest to hear a prattlin' old woman tell wild tales like thet. Ennyhow, she's a larned woman and she wouldn't believe sech stories. You don't want to hear sech rigamaroles, do you, Miss Smith?"

"Aunt Lindy Jane, besides wanting to visit with you and John Mack, that is part of the reason I came up here. You're such a wonderful storyteller, please do tell me that story. I haven't heard it, and it doesn't matter whether I believe them or not," I urged.

Lindy Jane tapped her clay pipe lightly against the hearthstone

* The common mountain expression for rheumatism.

to dislodge some ashes. Then, she filled it, lighted it from a hot ember, and sat back, puffing hard to get it going. She began: "Well, hit wuz nigh onto a hundred years ago, accordin' to my mammy, when a very fine young man by the name of Lonnie Abb Dixon come to the County, nobody knew from where ner why. He'd saved his yearnings, so he bought a parcel of good land from Old Skinflint Carter and his neighbors had a big house raising for him and holped him build a smoke house and barn besides. Soon, he had stocked the place with hosses, sheep, cows, chickens and hogs, and put out a big plantin' and raised some good crops. He lived by hisself, and done his own cooking and housework and 'peared to git along moughty well, though hit wuz lonesome-like.

"Then, one blustery winter night he wuz a settin' by his fire-place, downfaced and lone-some, when a purty spotted cat came though the cat hole in his door. Hit meowed and purred and rubbed hitself agin Lonnie's laig fer a whet, but when he reached down to rub hit, hit ran fast as the wind for the cat hole and vanished. After thet, most every night thet cat 'ud come into the cabin and run off agin afore Lonnie could tech hit. Now, Lonnie's cat had been kilt by a panther, and he wanted this 'un for company, so the next time the cat come, he stopped up the cat hole. Then he kotched the cat and started a rubbin' hit's back.

"Well, bless my soul, effen all of a sudden thet spotted cat didn't turn into the purtiest young woman you ever laid your eyes on. She stood there by his side, looking down into his face and smilin'. Nacherely, bein' a single man and so handsome, he started a buckin' up to her right then and there. Nobody ever knowed how long this went on, but atter a while hit wuz norated 'round thet Lonnie wuz a goin' to marry up with a purty woman."

Lindy Jane paused, puffed on her pipe, shifted her boney frame in the chair, and continued: "He left his place and wuz gone fer a short spell, and when he come back, he had married up with this purty woman and brought her back with him. They wuz moughty happy, and in time she brought two young'uns into the world. They worked hard a makin' crops and the young'uns kept 'em busy, so nobody seed much of 'em.

"But, one dark night afore Christmas, when hit wuz too cold to work outside, a whole passel of young folks had a gatherin' at Lonnie's place. They talked, guessed riddles, told stories, played games and drunk cherry bounce, persimmon beer and moonshine 'til hit wuz time to go home. But, an awful winter storm come up, with the cold wind whistlin' through the bare trees and screechin' round the cabin like all the hants from the graveyard and all the witches of hell wuz yellin' at onct. The cabin trembled, and hit set in a snowin. And, in a short spell, hit had snowed so much thet the're all afeard to try to go home. So, they jest 'lowed the'd set up and talk by the fire all night. They wuz havin' sech a good time a drinkin' and swappin' yarns and some of 'em had too much tongue and got to swappin' yarns 'bout how each of 'em found, sparked and married their mates.

"Atter they'd all gabbed 'bout their courtin' days and bragged 'bout their infairs, hit come time for Lonnie to tell his story. They wuz all curious sence they didn't know ennythin' 'bout Lonnie, so they listened real hard. Now, Lonnie wuz 'bout three sheets in the wind, so he started by sayin', thet the way he'd found his woman made him call her 'pussycat.' When he sed this, his old woman gathered their two young'uns clost to her, and squirmed and twisted and made funny faces to get Lonnie's 'tenshun, and shook her haid at him to git him to shet up. But, Lonnie Abb paid her no mind, but tuk annudder swig of persimmon beer and went on with his yarn.

"He got up and staggered to the door to show 'em how the cat 'ud come in through the cat hole. A moughty blast of wind hit the cabin and rocked hit like hit wuz a cradle and skeered the livin' daylights outten everybody. The wind howled so loud thet nobody heard Lonnie's last words, but a purty yaller and white spotted cat and two kittens darted outten the hole. Lonnie Abb's wife and young'uns wuz never seed nor heard of agin atter thet."

BETSY, BEANS AND PITCHFORKS

I wuz a little shaver, bout knee high to a duck, when I went to spend a while with my Granny Callie Lou Sexton one fall. Her old log cabin, built in the early 1800's, clung like a loose button to the hillside at the head of Cedar Springs Crick in Patrick County, Virginia.

Granny had just picked her fall crop of beans and had strung, pickled and dried all that were fit to be preserved. She had about a half-bushel of October beans left over that were too ripe to string, so she'd laid them aside to be shelled later. She said to me, "Effie, honey chile, you jest set down on the floor in front of the fireplace and shell these beans for me. I'll go fasten up the chickens and fetch the aggs afore hit gits so pitch dark I cain't see the aggs."

So, I got a pan from the shelf to hold the shelled beans and a basket to hold the strings and hulls and a candle. I lighted the candle and set it on the floor beside me, poured out the beans and began to shell them. These were the prettiest Octobers* I'd ever laid my eyes on.

I hadn't shelled many when Granny got back from the barnlot. She raised her hands in the air in horror and hollered, "Young'un, don't you know better'n that? Hain't you got no sense at'all? Put out thet light right now. Mebbe hit's already too late. Don't you know thet you cain't have no lights up here in the holler atter the sun falls down? When hit gits dark, them pesky witches'll come a snoopin' round where's a light. The light from them burnin' logs'll give you all the light you need to shell them beans."

So, I sat on the fire and shelled beans by firelight while Granny told me stories 'bout the witches that lived here in the mountains and how they'd spell folks and varmints and how the witch doctors 'ud help folks to break these spells. We went to bed fairly early.

In the early morning, Granny sent me to the barn to feed the

Collected by James Taylor Adams, Big Laurel, Virginia, August 12, 1941. Told to him by Patrick Addington, who had heard it from Eliza Seymour, who, in turn, heard it from her grandmother. The events are said to have happened around 1800.

* Large beans whose mature speckled red and white shells split when they are being strung. They ripen late in October and early November and are cooked in the hull. Most of these beans will separate from the hulls when cooked.

horse and the chickens. I noticed that Old Betsy, the black mare, looked mighty droopy and didn't touch anything I put in her trough, so I told Granny when I went back to the cabin that I thought Betsy was sick.

"Laws a massey, chile, there's no two ways 'bout hit, them witches wuz 'round here last night."

She was all worked up to a lather, and she chunked the fire and got a pinch of sulfur and sprinkled it over the burning logs, mumbling some words I'd never heard before. When she had done this, she made a bee-line for the barn to see for herself about Old Betsy. When she got back, she was mad as a wet hen. She took a dab of asafoetida from a little black box she kept on the mantle, and put it in a little piece of red flannel. She added a dash of sulfur and some dog fennel leaves to it and rolled it all up in a little poke. She tied a long string to it and ran out to the barn to hang this bag 'round old Betsy's neck. As soon as she did, Betsy started to get better, and she started eating and fidgeting in her stall.

Soon after this, it was hog-killing time, but one of Granny's big fat hogs got all logy and pined away and died. Granny boiled over at this, said something about "them onery witches," and swore she'd get the upper hand of them. She sent me to the woodpile to get a big pile of chips and wood. We hoisted the dead hog on top of it and set it afire. When it was burning, Granny lifted her hands and head towards Heaven and said, "In the name of the Father, and the Son, and the Holy Speret, head off the witch spell and drive these witches away."

Then, she grabbed her bonnet, smacked it on her head and set off over the ridge to Jed Lay's place. Jed was a witch doctor, and he told her what to do to break the spell on her animals. She was to go to the buryin' ground at the dark of the moon and catch a rabbit. She had to skin the rabbit and dry the skin, wrap a new knife in it, and sleep with the package under her pillow.

But, Granny told Jed she was afraid of graveyards at night, and asked if there wasn't something else she could do. Jed told her, "Folks 'round here have knowed fer a long time thet witches air afeard of forked sticks, so they put forked sticks up over their cabin and barn doors to keep them away. Some of 'em even have forked sticks on their gates and bars. When the witches come along and see them sticks, they allus turn back."

Granny laughed in old Jed's face, and she felt he'd fleeced, foxed, and skinned her. But, the witches kept on devilin' her, so one day she walked over the ridge to talk to Sue Proffit who used forked sticks, and Sue said they shorely did work for her. So, Granny decided she'd try one. But, before she got 'round to cutting some forked sticks, she went to a store over at the county seat and saw some new-fangled forks made of iron. They called 'em pitch-forks, and Granny 'lowed they had more'n one fork and ought to be better than a forked stick. So, she bought two of them and put one over the cabin door and the other over the barn door. And, if it didn't work. Granny was never again bothered with witches.

ROASTED MUTTON

The Powell Valley, in the Cumberlands, and the many small valleys leading into it were flat, fertile and serviced with abundant rainfall to make the natural grasses flourish. As the settlers cut out the timber and removed the brush, great quantities of land suitable for grazing became available.

Most of the mountaineers made good use of hides and skins in making their own clothing, but good wool was a necessity for making the linsey-woolsey cloth which was their chief clothing material. Wool was also used for knitting headgear, stockings, sweaters, mittens and warm bed covers. Sheep raising soon became a very important part of their self-sufficient economy. Stories about sheep raising quickly developed. Mrs. William Adams of Big Laurel, Wise County, Virginia, tells this story:

"When I wuz 'bout ankle high to a cricket, my Mammy told me this witch story. Hit happened when she wuz jest a little girl, and I'm nigh on to eighty-six, so hit wuz a long time ago.

"When folks fust come to the mountains from eastern Virginia and North Carolina and settled here in the Cumberlands, a man by the name of Jeb Paul Wolf got him a moughty big parcel of land and stocked hit with a bunch of fine sheep. Everythin' went along smooth as shootin' fer quite a spell till, all of a sudden, Jeb Paul's sheep started a dyin' fer no reason t'all as fur as he could see. He watched them sheep real close, and, when he'd see one keel over suddenly and die whilst hit was a feedin', he'd 'zamine hit but couldn't find nuthin' wrong. So, the best he could make out, them sheep wuz witched.

"He hot-footed hit up Skunk Crick and over to Sunray Ridge to see Old Jake Collins, who wuz knowed as a witch docktor. Old Jake told him jest whut to do to break the spell, but he warned him not to tell ennybody why he wuz a doin' hit. He told Jeb Paul to be certain not to lend ennything to ennybody, ner even to give ennybody a drink of water till the spell wuz broke.

"So, Jeb Paul come back home and done jest as we wuz told. Fust, he skinned the shoulder outten the next sheep thet died and

Collected by James Taylor Adams, Big Laurel, Virginia, June 6, 1941. Told to him by his mother, Mrs. William Green Adams, whose grandfather was the chief character.

had his old woman put hit in the oven and bake hit real slow. He knowed 'twould be 'most two hours afore thet shoulder 'ud be roasted good, so he went outten the wood pile to chop more firewood, and to the barn to feed his critters. Now, Jeb Paul hadn't 'splained to his old woman why he wanted thet shoulder of sheep roasted, but Connie wuz as smart as a whip and had made out fur herself whut wuz up.

"Jest as thet shoulder started to bake, Connie looked down the path and seed one of her neighbors, Julia Turpin, a comin' torge the cabin a puffin' and pantin' along as fast as her old legs 'ud carry her. She come right up to the door and would've come into the cabin effen Connie hadn't been in her way. She wuz a shakin' like a dog in a wet sack and her face wuz as white as an egg. She fidgeted like a hen on a hot roof and axt Connie to borrer some meal. But, Connie knowed jest whut to do, and she sed she didn't have no meal. Then, Julia axt fer a drink of water, but Connie sed, 'There hain't no water up, and you passed right by the spring. You orter git a drink on your way back home.'

"Well, Julia moseyed off down the path with a hang'dog look on her face, but in two shakes of a sheep's tail she wuz right back at the door. This time, she wuz a wheezin' more than afore, and wuz all unstrung. She told Connie she had to have some salt, but Connie told her she didn't have none. Then, she axt fer a glass of buttermilk, but Connie told her she didn't have thet neither.

"Now, Julia had smelled thet roast and she axt Connie whut she wuz a cookin'. When Connie told her hit wuz mutton, Julia pushed her way through the door in spite of Connie and dashed torge the fire. She grabbed the oven lid and tried to git thet roast outten hit. But 'bout this time, Jeb Paul come in, and old Julia made a beeline fur the door. She tucked her scraggy old head and toddled slowly back down the path.

"In no time t'all, she wuz headed fer the cabin agin, a trottin' along as fast as a skeered rabbit. She lunged into the cabin and hollered, 'Fer Gawd's sake, Jeb Paul, git thet oven offen the fire. You're burnin' me to death. Look here!' She ripped the top of her dress offen her shoulder and hit wuz a crisp brown jest like the sheep shoulder in the oven.

"Well, thet burn did get well, but thet old woman had a blistered and festered shoulder fer a long while. If she ever practiced her witchin' ennymore, hit wuzzen't 'round here. No more of Jeb Paul's sheep died suddenly and nobody seed ennythin' more of Julia atter she wuz well agin."

LIGE HALL'S BEWITCHED RIFLE-GUN

Grandpappy Vance told this story:

"Old Lige Hall, from outten Bear Crick, in Buckeye Cove, wuz a crack shot with his rifle-gun. Onct, he trudged through the woods over the ridge from Wes Steele's place at the shank of a raw April day, and, in the half-light of dusk, he run smack dab into a big wildcat a stalkin' his young heifer calf. Old Lige, wily as a fox, sneaked behindst a big tree, tuk dead aim at the varmint with his rifle-gun and cut loose. Lo and behold, thet bloomin' wildcat never moved a whisker. Now, thet kinda shook old Lige up, but he edged through the bushes a little closer, leaned against a tree, tuk aim and cut loose a second time. This time, he missed hit a country mile. Now, this made Lige mad as a wet hen, so he jumped from behindst thet tree, lambasted the bushes, and skeered thet critter 'most outten his skin.

"When Lige got home, he told Liz, his old woman, and me, who wuz livin' with 'em, how he'd missed thet stinkin' wildcat twict at close range. Now, hit's a serious matter to a mountaineer effen his gun won't work right, kase part of his livin' comes from huntin, and he needs hit to pertect his family and critters from Indians, bears, panthers, and other sech varmints.

"Liz 'lowed to Old Lige thet mebbe his rifle-gun 'ud been witched so hit wouldn't shoot straight. She figgered thet she'd feel a lot safer effen he go over to Roarin' Fork and git Eulis Salyer, a witch doctor, to break the spell on his gun. So, Lige lit out the next day, and Eulis told him whut to do to break the spell.

"When Lige come back home, he cotch him a black goat, cut hit's throat and bled hit good. Then, he biled thet brute till all the meat come offen the bones. Then, he washed the right shoulder blade without touchin' hit with his finger er a knife and wropt hit in a black cloth. He got a red ear of corn and shelled hit. Then, he tuk his rifle-gun, the wropt shoulder blade, and the grains of corn outten the woods and found him a big stump. He laid his rifle-gun on the stump, the bone on top of hit, and crost the shoulder bone

Collected by James Taylor Adams, Big Laurel, Virginia, May 19, 1941. Told to him by Patrick Addington, who heard it from Clint Sexton. The people in this section referred to their muzzle-loading rifles as rifle-guns. They believed that guns could be "spelled."

and rifle-gun with them red grains of corn.

"Three days atter this, he went back and found thet all of the corn'ud been stole by wild varmints, so he tuk the bone and buried hit in a little grave nigh the stump. He drawed a ring 'round the stump and the grave, then stood with one foot inside and one foot outside the ring and said, 'In the name of the Father, and the Son and the Holy Speret, break the spell on my rifle-gun.'

"Now, Lige 'ud done jest as Eulis had told him, but when he tried to shoot a squirrel at eyeball range, he missed hit jest as he'd missed thet wildcat. Course, he figgured the gun wuz still witched, so he went back to the cabin and told Liz whut had happened. She recollected thet Sal Riner, a witch doctor who lived in Whitewood Holler, wuz beholden to 'em sence they'd given her a calf and Lige had holped her git in her crops last fall when her old man had been sent to the pen for shootin' a revenoor. Liz 'lowed Sal could shorely break the spell, sence she'd broke one on Ned Harless' mules some time back.

"So, Lige went to see Sal Riner, and, like Eulis Salyer, she warned him to do 'zactly as she sed and not to tell ennybody whut he's a doin. He promised, so on the thirteenth of the month, at 'zactly midnight, he went over to a place betwixt Jess Gross and Tim Tatum's places where they's an Indian graveyard. He dug down into one of the graves and found an Indian jawbone and fetched hit home. He scraped some of hit off, mixed hit with his gun powder, put in a pinch of sulfur, and loaded hit into his rifle-gun. Then, he went out on Greasy Crick and found a black gum tree and shot thet bullet into hit. The next day, he stalked thet wildcat and kilt hit with his fust shot.

"Old Lige wuz tickled pink thet the spell on his rifle-gun wuz broke, and he 'lowed he mought need thet Indian jawbone agin, so he put hit in his loft. Thet night, when he wuz in bed, hit wuz so quiet his pulse agin the piller sounded like a drumbeat. All of a sudden, there wuz a cold breeze in the room, and Lige had a feelin' thet there wuz somethin' in the room clost to him. He heard an awful cry from the loft, and sumthin' went 'C-o-o, W-o-o, B-a-n-g.' Then, there wuz a terrible noise thet sounded like a millrock 'ud fell on the floor of the loft.

"Now, Old Lige wuz a man who wuzzen't afeard of thunder and lightnin' ner man ner beast, so he jumped up and looked 'round, but he didn't find nuthin. The next night, the same noises woke him, and kept up for five nights in a row. There jest wuz no rest fer his body ner his soul.

"Lige had a notion whut wuz a causin' the ruckus, so he climbed up in thet loft, fetched down thet Indian jawbone, and tuk hit back to where he'd dug hit up and buried hit again. He never heard the noises no more."

THE WEDDING PICTURE AND THE CONJURE MAN

Barry Holbrook was reminiscing one night when he got around to his courtship.

"There's no two ways 'bout hit, Herman Foltz wuz down-hearted when I beat his time and married up with Rachael Watts. She wuz purty as all git out, and all the fellers fer miles 'round 'ud a give their eye tooth to have her. Course, nobody stayed away from the infare* on account of how they felt 'bout losin' her to me. There wuz a lot of drinkin' and some jowerin' and fist fights, and the dance lasted till midnight. 'Bout a month later me and Rachael went to spend a night with her folks out on the Hurricane. When we got back home, Rachael noticed right off thet the weddin' picture wuzzen't thar on the mantle shelf.

"Rachael sed, 'Barry, I'll lay a bet thet whoever tuk thet picture toted hit to Nick Ison, the conjure man. Silas Calder over at Bull Run told me onct thet effen a witch dipped a weddin' picture into magic water, the next day the married pair 'ud both go outten their minds. I believe thet, kase Silas is a moughty smart conjure man hisself. Mebbe we orter hustle over and git Silas to put a spell on old Nick Isom afore he does us in.'

" 'Yep, Rachael, you're right,' I sed, and we tuk off like a house afire torge Bull Run and wuz there afore daylight. 'Silas,' I sed, 'peers like Herman Foltz has stole our wedding picture. We figger he's a aimin' to tote hit over to Old Nick Ison to git him to bewitch hit. We want you to holp us git hit back to head off enny witch spell.'

"Silas listened, then smiled and sed, 'I know 'zactly whut to do, but I 'low we've got to work fast as lightnin' effen Nick's already got thet picture.'

"So, Silas and me and Rachael tuk off a high tailin' hit through the woods torge old Nick's place on Crane's Nest Gap. Silas knowed a lot of short-cuts, so twarn't long afore we wuz in sight of the cabin.

Collected by Emory L. Hamilton, Wise, Virginia, July 8, 1939. Told to him by Bernie Holbrook of Big Laurel, who said that this story had been handed down in their family for generations.

* See note on page 22.

Then, Silas crept quiet-like down through the cornfield jest like a fox a smellin' a chicken house until he got clost to the cabin and could hear Herman Foltz and Old Nick a talkin'. Then, he jumped up and sprung his gun right on 'em. 'Give me thet wedding picture er I'll blow yore head offen yore shoulders,' he ordered.

They give him thet picture quick as a wink. Then, he made 'em set down on the floor. With Rachael and me beside him, he told 'em straight out thet they'se a goin' to let these young folks alone now and forever. Then, he told Rachael to git a cup from the cupboard and fill hit with water. He dipped the picture into hit, made Herman Foltz take a sip of hit, and Old Nick drink every last drop whut was left. Then, he give the picture back to Rachael.

"Silas wouldn't take nuthin' for holpin' us, but sed when we had our fust boy young'un, we could name hit for him. Then he went home, and we came back to our cabin.

"Three days atter this, Herman Foltz left to jine the army. Not long atter this, Old Nick Ison wuz found dead out on Moccasin Crick. They 'lowed a rattlesnake 'ud stung him.

"Me and Rachael never had no more trubble with witches, and now young Silas Calder's old enuf to holp me make a livin' for our t'other nine young'uns."

OLD SUTTON'S HIDDEN TREASURE

The two-wheeled cart stacked high with plunder and farm tools rattled and jerked along the rocky bed of Indian Creek which was the only road in these parts. Mize Hunter, barefooted and with his linsey-woolsey pants rolled up to his knees, waded the cold water and led his horse. The four other newcomers trudged over the path that skirted the little stream for nearly a mile from Wildcat Valley to the head of Tomahawk Cove. Finally, they came to a sudden halt where the stream began in a gushing spring at the foot of a cliff. Nearby was their new home.

The three-room log cabin, with its huge outside stone chimney built back in the 1840's, had stood empty for over a year. It was said that witches had taken it over as their meeting place. Mize Hunter bought it and moved in with his wife, two children and his mother-in-law, Granny Sue Dunst.

Granny Dunst insisted on putting her bed near the fireplace where it was warmer and where she could watch the flickering shadows on the wall after she retired. She said this helped her go to sleep. But, things didn't work out that way. The first night they spent in the house, at exactly midnight, Granny's bed jumped right out of the corner and landed in the middle of the room. Granny was shaken up, and, although she wasn't white-livered nor chicken, she left the bed where it was. She trembled and allowed that the witches had done this because the family had taken over their meeting place.

The next morning, Granny moved her rocking chair to the corner where her bed had been. At midnight that night, Granny was again awakened by a terrible noise, and, when she looked about, there was her rocking chair jumping about. It, too, landed in the middle of the floor.

The next day, she put her spinning wheel in that corner, but was awakened that night by another racket. This time, her spinning wheel jumped around and landed in the middle of the floor.

When their neighbors learned of Granny's experiences, they were not surprised. Most of them attributed these happenings to the disturbed witches. Then, someone remembered that, many

Based on two stories, "Hidden Money," and "Old Sutton," published in *The Tennessee Folklore Society Bulletin,* Volume 9, Number 2, May, 1943.

years ago, Sutton Spencer, a rich, eccentric and miserly old man, had lived in that house by himself. Indians had raided the house, and old Sutton had not been seen since. It was assumed that he had been carried away by the Indians and his supposed treasure with him.

The next family to live in the house had moved because they thought it was haunted. That was why it was empty when Mize bought it. The Hunters didn't believe in ghosts, but, after they heard this tale, they began to call that corner where furniture wouldn't stay put "Old Sutton's corner."

Of course, Granny Dunst wasn't afraid of ghosts, witches, nor the Devil, so, when the weather got cold again, she insisted that her bed be moved back to the corner. Mize told her that Old Sutton would get her, but he moved it back.

That night, it was very cold and began to snow. The family, except for Granny had gone over the ridge to a neighbor's house before the snow began to fall, and it was midnight before it let up and the Hunter family started home. The ground was covered with several inches of snow as they waded over the last ridge and could see their house. To their horror, it was engulfed in flames. The blaze rose high above the roof, and flames were spewing from the windows. They ran toward the house, apprehensive about what had happened to Granny.

But, to their intense surprise, when they came to the fence around the yard, the fire seemed to have gone out. The snow on the roof had not melted, and there was no sign whatever of a fire. When they entered the house, there sat a terrified Granny in her bed in the middle of the floor. She was trembling and insisted that her bed be moved to another room at once. She said she was never going to sleep in the room with Old Sutton again.

But, Old Sutton must have gotten lonesome without Granny to pester. Before long, nightly at midnight they began to smell a putrid odor which would penetrate the entire house and make them sneeze, cough and make their eyes water. Then, the windows and doors would open, and the odor would be blown out by a brisk breeze. This would be followed by a noise in Old Sutton's room which sounded like rocks from the chimney were bouncing on the floor. When they entered the room, the noise would stop. The clock on the mantle would always stop at three minutes after twelve.

After about three nights of this, the family decided they had had enough and couldn't live there any more. Mize took his family over to the Cumberlands and left them with his people. Then, he came back, rounded up some neighbors to cut logs, had a house-raising, and built a new house about a hundred yards from the old one. This was a large four-room house with a chimney at each end.

The men ran out of rocks for the two chimneys, so they decided to get some from the old chimney, and they tore the old house down. When they removed the rocks from the fireplace, they found a human skeleton underneath the hearth. Beside the skeleton was an earthenware pot filled with gold coins.

Old Sutton never visited the Hunters' new house.

THE SILVER BULLET

Lee Anne Robinson could tell by the evening sun's rays through the cabin window that it was time for John to come in from the field, a hungry man anxious for his victuals. She dished up greens from the iron pot, laid a slab of salt meat on them, took out some cornpone from the oven, and then went to the springhouse to fetch a crock of buttermilk. When this was all on the table, she looked out to see if her husband was in sight. He wasn't to be seen. She wondered what was keeping him. It was not like him to be late for his supper. After waiting for about fifteen minutes, Lee Anne put the cornpone in the warming oven and the buttermilk back in the bucket.

Lee Anne wished that John would hurry, as she could feel one of her headaches coming on and nothing would relieve it except to sleep it off. When the sun had set, she put the rest of the food away. Her head was getting worse, and she wet a cloth in cold water and wrapped it around her forehead. She promised herself that in the morning she would go see Old Melissa Ward to get some herbs for these headaches. Between the throbs in her head, she wondered why John hadn't come home, but finally she went to bed and to sleep.

Next morning, she found that John had come home and left again without disturbing her. She started to Aunt Melissa Ward's place and, as she was passing, saw Stacy Yopher standing in her doorway. Stacy was a beautiful woman with sparkling black eyes and was very attractive to the men of the community.

"Howdy, Lee Anne," she greeted. "Where air you a goin' so fast?"

"Hello Stacy. I'm going over to see Aunt Melissa to see if she can give me something for the bad headaches I've been having lately."

Stacy strolled down to the fence, and Lee Anne notice a new red ribbon in her dark hair. "Laws a massey, Lee Anne, Melissa can't cure your headache. Her old yarbs hain't worth nothing. I've got something that's much better. Wait a spell and I'll fetch hit."

She returned with something tied up in a small white rag and

Based on the story "The Silver Bullet," by Mildred Harris, published in the *Tennessee Folklore Society Journal*, volume 3, number 3, 1937.

tossed it to Lee Anne. "Here, put these powders in your next drink and they'll cure you."

Lee Anne dropped the rag in her pocket. "Thank you, Stacy. Since I'm this near, I reckon I might as well go see Aunt Melissa."

"Well, child, don't you pay no heed to what she says. Hit's the naked truth, she's an old fool," Stacy sneered. As Lee Anne moved on, she called, "Remember me to John."

Aunt Melissa was sitting on the porch of her little cabin when Lee Anne entered the gate. "Howdy, child," she called. "Come up on the porch. What in the world is the matter with you? Your face is as white as a sheet."

"I've got a miserable headache, Aunt Melissa. I've been having them for some time. Effen you'll give me a drink of water, I'd be obliged so I can take these powders Stacy gave me. She said they'd cure me."

Aunt Melissa snatched the package from her hand and asked, "Stacy give you this?"

She untied the knot, opened the cloth, spread out the powder and sniffed it very cautiously. "Lord help you, child, effen you'd a taken this, you'd be worser off than you air. 'Pon my honor, that Stacy Yopher hain't no good t'all. Here, swallow this pill. Hit'll cure your headache effen it can be cured. Hit hain't pizzen like this stuff."

Lee Anne took the pill and was about to put it in her mouth, but at these last words of Aunt Melissa, her hand froze in the air. Her eyes widened with horror and she whispered, "Pizzen?"

"Hit shore is, child. I reckon hit wouldn't kill you right off, but hit 'ud shore make you awful sick."

"But, Aunt Melissa, why would Stacy want to give me pizzen?"

"Now, you listen to me, Lee Anne," Aunt Melissa began. "Stacy Yopher is after your man. Hit's the truth. Sister Becky was over here t'other day and told me she saw John going in there taking Stacy a box of snuff and some apples in a poke. Then, I seed him with my own eyes a sneaking in Stacy's back door, and I seed him more than onct. Tell me, honey, what do you do with your hair thet comes out in the comb?"

Lee Anne sank down in a chair, nearly overcome with this terrible news and bewildered by Aunt Melissa's abrupt change of subject. "I don't recollect," she said, "Sometimes I put it on the fire and sometimes I just throw it outside."

"You're crazy, girl," Aunt Melissa said, very much agitated.

"Them headaches of yourn are likely caused by birds carrying your hair away. Then again, hit's more likely that Stacy's got holt of some of hit, put hit under the skin of a wild rabbit and turned hit loose. If she did, till that rabbit has been kilt, you'll have no rest. Lee Anne, from now on, do your hair up in a ball when you take hit outten the comb and hide hit somewhere thet Stacy can't get hit. And, you be careful, cause that Stacy's a witch. Her ma was one, and she taught Stacy to be one, too."

"Ah! Aunt Melissa, there hain't no sich thing as witches," Lee Anne scoffed. "They're jest like Santa Claus. Folks jest make up tales about 'em."

"You'll think they're not jest made up before Stacy Yopher gets through with you," Aunt Melissa predicted.

Lee Anne was silent for a few minutes, staring into space as if in deep thought. Then, she asked, "Aunt Melissa, how can I keep Stacy from getting John?"

Aunt Melissa didn't reply but got up and went into the cabin. She returned in a minute with a small package in her hand which she handed to Lee Anne. "Here, honey, make a strong tea from sassafras roots and put some of this powder in it. Give it to John for breakfast, and hit'll keep him a thinking about you all day long."

"Can you kill a witch, Aunt Melissa?" Lee Anne inquired.

"There hain't but one sure way," she answered. "Take a board and draw a witch's picture on hit and shoot through hit with a silver bullet. That'll kill any witch."

From bits of gossip which came to her ears from time to time, Lee Anne knew she was losing John. Her headaches came more often and stayed longer. She neglected her housework. And John began to grumble about the housework and the poor meals. At times, he'd shove his plate back and get up and leave without eating. She suspected he was going to Stacy's for a meal.

As John was at home less and less, and as her headaches grew worse, Lee Anne thought about what Melissa had told her about Stacy being a witch. She didn't want to believe in witches, but still she knew that Stacy's mother had been reputed to be one. Could Aunt Melissa be right?

One afternoon, Lee Anne was weeding her garden in an effort to forget about her headache. As she stooped over to pull up a jimson weed, she heard a faint crack as if a bone in her neck had slipped back into place. Suddenly, the pain in her head was gone. She felt clear-headed, with no dizziness, no throb. She was cured at last! She was so relieved that she started singing aloud.

"Hi, there, Lee Anne. You're a mighty happy girl today. What's the good news?" inquired a voice. Lee Anne straightened up to see Hughes Wayburn, gun in hand, leaning against the fence.

"Well," said Lee Anne, "I am feeling right peart because for onct in a month of Sundays, I don't have a headache. Who air you a gunning for?"

"I've been shooting some varmints what's been a chewing up my cabbages. Here's one of 'em." He swung a large grayish-brown rabbit from a string across his back. "I kilt him over there about ten minutes ago."

"Ten minutes ago!" Lee Anne thought. It was just about ten minutes ago that she had heard the crack and felt the pain leave her head. Was the crack of the gun what she'd heard and thought it was her neck bone? "You won't have no relief from them headaches till that rabbit is kilt," had been Aunt Melissa's words. Now the rabbit was dead, and her headache was gone! Aunt Melissa was right about the spell!

"Wait a minute, Hughes," she cried, hurrying toward the woodshed. When she returned, she was carrying a pine shingle and a piece of charred wood she had picked up from the ashes under her wash kettle. She drew the crude outline of a woman on the shingle with the charcoal and showed it to Hughes.

"I want to see how good you can shoot. John's always bragging that you're the best shot in Tennessee. I'll set this picture on a stump. Try to hit her in the left leg."

"TRY to hit her!" exclaimed Hughes. I can hit her in the left foot. I could even hit her eyebrow effen you'd draw one."

"I reckon," Lee Anne mocked. "Shoot first and then brag."

Hughes raised his gun to his shoulder and pulled the trigger. Lee Anne rushed to the shingle, and there was a clean hole through the leg of the woman. "Why, Lord, Hughes, you really did hit it in the leg. I never thought you could."

"Maybe after this you won't be such a doubter," said Hughes as he shouldered his gun. "Well, I've got to be going. You and John come over and set a spell."

Lee Anne picked up the shingle and took it with her to the house, where she tucked it between two pieces of wood on the hearth.

From that day, Lee Anne's headaches ceased to bother her, and she no longer moped about. She began to keep the house clean and neat and cooked good meals again. She became her old laughing, gay self, and John began staying home again.

One evening, there was a knock on the door and Lee Anne opened it to see Mag Nipper standing there in the dusk.

"Law*, Lee Anne, I didn't want to pull you away from the supper table," she apologized, "but I was passing and thought I'd stop by to borrow your new quilt pattern."

"Glad you stopped, Mag; come in and eat some supper with us," Lee Anne replied.

"That cornpone and them beans is mighty tempting, Lee Anne, but I eat over at Stacy's house. I've been over setting with her. You knowed she's sick and bedfast, didn't you?"

"No," replied Lee Anne, I didn't know. What ails her?"

"Nobody knows exactly. About three weeks ago, she was took with bad cramps in her left leg, and she's getting worser by the day. She jest seems to be withering away. You ought to go and see her, Lee Anne, cause she's shore not long for this world."

Lee Anne had been hunting for the pattern while she talked to Mag, but now she stopped and went to the hearth and felt for the shingle she had put there and forgotten. She felt a surge of horror at the news that Stacy was dying, and from a pain in her left leg! She, Lee Anne Robinson, was a murderer! The very thought almost overwhelmed her, and she swayed dizzily.

Meantime, John poured some milk for Mag and said, "Here, Mag, have some milk and one of Lee Anne's good fried apple pies."

"I don't mind effen I do," said Mag, as she sat down at the table.

John and Mag's voices made Lee Anne come to her senses and she resumed her search for the pattern. She found it, and was somehow able to talk to Mag pleasantly until she left an hour later.

A few days later, Stacy Yopher died. John began to notice a change in Lee Anne after this. Her housekeeping and meals were still good but she was restless, always doing something. She weeded the garden over and over, although it didn't need it. She tossed restlessly at night. John didn't like it, and Lee Anne could see him watching her. But, her ever-present thought was that she had killed Stacy Yopher.

One day, Aunt Melissa showed up. "What's wrong with you, Lee Anne?" she demanded.

"Nothing," Lee Anne replied, wiping her hands on her apron. "Why?"

"There's something a pestering you, Lee Anne. You've got something on your mind, and you'd better jest tell me and get it

* Lord.

straight."

Lee Anne couldn't contain her misery and guilt any longer, and her confession poured from her lips. "Oh, Aunt Melissa, I'm a killer," Lee Anne moaned. "I'll go straight to hell for this."

"I knowed something was wrong when John came to see me yesterday and told me how you'd been acting. I told him I'd come to see you. Now, child, what kind of a bullet did Hughes use?"

"Jest a regular bullet, I guess, jest like the one he kilt the rabbit with," replied Lee Anne.

"Now, you listen to me, honey," said Aunt Melissa, "Stacy had come down with a fever about a week before she was took with her leg. None of the family could sleep for her moaning and groaning, and her brother George said that he thought a witch had put a spell on her. So, he drawed the picture of a woman and shot hit with a silver bullet. So, you see, child, George Yopher kilt his own sister, not you. I told you that it takes a silver bullet to kill a witch, and you ought to have remembered that."

As soon as Aunt Melissa had gone, Lee Anne rushed to the hearth, took the shingle with the woman's picture on it, broke it up and put it on the fire. John must never know what she had tried to do. As she watched the flames devour the pieces of pine, Lee Anne reflected that Aunt Melissa certainly knowed what she was talking about when it came to witches.

THE SCISSORS, TABLE FORK AND SIFTER

One day Pearl Morissett, of Danville, Virginia, asked Maria Williams, a former slave, a question: "Why do you have your scissors and a table fork on your window sill near your bed?"

Maria, a little flustered, looked Pearl in the face and vowed, "Effen you sleeps wid a fork and a pair of scissors under yore piller, hit'll sho' keep them witches and ghosts and nightmares away. I'll tell you what a witch done to me onct, and that wuz enuf fer me."

"Please do tell me about it, Maria," Pearl begged.

"Well, hit wuz like dis: I wuz livin' in a little old shack behind some white folk's house on Main Street. I shore did like them folks, 'cause they were plum good to me, but dat house wuz the worstest one I ever seed er lived in on account of witches, and my little house wuz hanted too. I wuz afeared to stay dere by myself, so I tole the woman in the big house I wuz movin' out. She axt me how come, and I ups and tells her about the witches and hants. She shore did laugh at me, but I knowed whut I'd heerd and seed, and I moved."

"Please Maria, tell me what kind of witches bothered you," Pearl begged.

" 'Pon my soul, Miss Morissett, sumtimes, when I'd be sleepin', hit wuz like sumbody had dere hands a pressin' agin' me in the back. But, I couldn't see nobody ner nuthin'. Dey jest 'ud bar down on me and shake me, and I'd wake up myself a sayin', Ugh, Ugh, Ugh. I'll swear, t'was ebery night. So I talked to sum of the folks over at the terbaccker factory where I worked, and one of 'em told me whut to do, and I done it."

"What did you do?" Pearl persisted.

"Well, you jes orter seed me. Fust, I tied the flour sifter ober the door knob. Den, I puts a pair of scissors and a fork under my piller ebery night. You see, when dat witch done come to the door, it had to stop and count all dem holes in the sifter, and this took till daylight. When daylight comes, dem witches hafter go back where dey come from, and dey don't have no time to bother me. So dese things worked and kept 'em comin' after that. I cud sleep all night 'thout bein' pesterd.

Collected by Mrs. Pearl Morrissett, Danville, Virginia, October 23, 1940. Told to her by Maria Williams, of Danville, as a true experience.

"Where I lives now, I don't have to use a sifter, kase it's got gravels in front of the doorstep and dem witches have to stop and count dem gravels. But, I still sleeps with the fork and the scissors jest in case sum of 'em finds annuder way to git into the house."

THE HUNTER'S WITCH

Most poor folks in the mountains kept one or more horses to do their plowing, hauling and to provide transportation to town or to the mill. But, some of the mountaineers had a love for fine riding horse in their blood, and sometimes they bought one even if they couldn't afford it. These horses generally came from the neighboring counties of Pulaski and Wythe where they were raised on the fertile grazing lands.

Tad Dolen tells this story about his grandfather.

"My Grandpappy, Billy Jo Dolen, had a fine roan mare named Bonnie. She wuz a dandy saddler, could trot, pace, canter and do other steps. She wuz a high-spereted brute, fat and sleek as a butterball. Now, an old woman, Fannie Funk, who lived nigh Grandpappy, tuk a fancy to thet mare, and bantered Grandpappy to sell her. But, Grandpappy thought a lot of thet hoss, and he knowed Old Fannie didn't treat enny of her critters right, so he wouldn't sell her.

"Twarn't long atter he refused Fannie's offer thet Billy Jo 'lowed he heard Bonnie a kickin' and a whinin' and a goin' on in the barn like sumpthin' wuz a pesterin' her. He went out to see 'bout her, but he didn't see nuthin' ner nobody. But, sumpthin' wuz botherin' her every night atter thet, till she got so pore and droopy thet she lost all her speret. Billy Joe 'ud go outten the barn in the mornin' and find her mane all tied up in tangles so tight he'd have to cut the hair offen her to git shet of the tangles. Atter a whet, she looked jest like a sheared mule.

Now, Billy Jo 'lowed mebbe she wuz a goin' to lose thet mare, so he went over to Witch Mountain to talk to Hans Schleissen 'bout hit. Old Hans wuz knowed as a witch doctor and he like to show how smart he wuz, so he told Billy Joe a whole passel of things he could do to break the spell. But, he figgered the best way wuz to git a dab of asafoetida, a pinch of ginseng root, a mess of dog fennel leaves and a dash of sulfur, and wrop all this in a little red bag and tie a string to hit and swing hit 'round the mare's neck. Effen this don't work—he 'splained thet sometimes the spell wuz so powerful thet hit 'ud take more'n one thing to break hit—then he said to take

Collected by John W. Garrett, Floyd, Virginia, July 3, 1940. Told to him by Tad Dolan who heard it from his grandfather, Bill Dolan.

one of the old shoes offen the mare and nail hit over the barn door.

"Grandpappy Billy Joe sed he done 'zactly as he wuz told. He tuk thet bag of stuff and hung hit 'round the mare's neck and waited three days to see whut would happen, but hit didn't do no good. Then, he got one of Bonnie's shoes and hung hit over the barn door. Atter this, he didn't hear her enny more at night, and her mane and tail wuzzen't tangled enny more. In no time t'all, thet mare started to gettin' peart and a eatin', and she got back her sperets. So, the witches didn't bother her no more kase they're afeard to go under a hoss shoe.

"One mornin', soon atter he'd broke the spell on Bonnie, Billy Joe and three of his friends went a huntin'. As they went by Fannie Funk's place, she come out and sez, 'Hit won't do no good fer you to go a huntin' today, kase you hain't a goin' to kill nuthin'. You'll mebbe skeer up a deer, but, effen you shoot at hit, you won't kill hit.'

"Course, they didn't pay her no mind, and went along into the woods. Afore long, the dawgs skeered up a deer and hit run by 'em chased by the dawgs, and they all tuk a crack at hit, but nobody got clost to hit. The varmint come by more'n onct, and they shot up a storm, but, fer the life of 'em, they jest couldn't hit thet deer.

"Then, Grandpappy remembered one of the things thet Hans Schleissen 'ud told him. He'd made a silver bullet and had toted hit with him. So, he loaded his rifle-gun with hit, and cut loose at thet deer the next time hit come 'round. His gun seemed to 'most jump outten his hands when he fired hit, and, instead of hittin' thet deer square betwixt the eyes as he knowed he could, he jest grazed hit's shoulder, and hit run off.

"Now, jest as Fannie sed, they didn't git no game t'all. As they come back by her place, they heard the gosh awfullest groanin' and moanin' a comin' from the cabin. When they went in, they found her on the bed a bleedin' from the shoulder jest 'bout where Grandpappy'd hit thet deer. Now, they didn't git no deer on thet trip, but I figger they got 'em a witch. Atter thet, Grandpappy had no more trubbel with Fannie Funk."

POTHOOKS AND TERBACCKER SEEDS

Already the spring sun had made fires in the mountain cabins unnecessary, but a thick column of blue wood smoke curled out of the chimney of Jim Tom Bond's cabin. The cabin was out on the point of Chestnut Ridge, near Coeburn, Virginia. Grandpappy Patrick Addington was trudging along the narrow rocky trail along Greasy Creek on his way to Jim Tom's place when he began to reminisce.

"Onct when I wuz a shirt-tail boy 'bout ten years old, old Jim Tom tried to break a witch spell. I went down to his place a aimin' to borrer some terbaccker seeds, and when I looked in the door, there wuz old Jim Tom all hunkered down afore the fireplace. He wuz a holding' one end of his pothooks in his hand and had t'other end rammed agin' the coals in the forestick. When he heered me, he looked up and wuz startled to see me a standin' in the door. He got nervous as a rattlesnake and started hollerin' and blusterin', 'Howdy Pat! Don't you come in here till I've finished a tryin' out this scheme. I've got an inklin' hit ain't you, but atter all of the signs, hit shore does pint in yore direction.'

"I thought the old codger musta cracked his bean or be in cahoots with the Old Scratch hisself, but I stopped where I wuz. I axt Jim Tom what in thunderation wuz a devilin' him. Then, he 'lowed: 'Now, Pat, you can come in. I can make out hit wuz somebody else who's a witchin' my milk. Hit's been witched for nigh onto three weeks now. Hit jest won't turn t'all, er effen hit does, hit wouldn't give no butter.'

"Now, I wuz bent on findin' out how to break the spell, so I went over to Guess Station and talked to Herman Hunsaker, who's knowed to be a good witch doctor. He told me lots of ways to git shet of witches and break their spells. He 'lowed thet effen I knowed who the witch wuz, hit 'ud be easy, but I told him I didn't rightly know who hit wuz, and sence there wuz a whole caboodle of folks who wuz a devilin' us with their evil doin's, I didn't want to bark up the wrong tree.

"Then, Herman sed sence I didn't know who hit wuz, I could

Collected by James Taylor Adams, Big Laurel, Virginia, September 11, 1940. Told by Raymond Addington of Coeburn, Virginia, whose grandfather—the chief character in the story—told it to him.

take my pothooks and hold 'em in the fire. He sed when they got real hot, they'd burn the witch, and he'd come to the cabin ter borrer sumpthin' er axt for a drink of water. He sed effen I lent the witch sumpthin' er gave hit a drink of water, then I would't break the spell.

"Now, Jim Tom wuz a heatin' them pothooks when I come to the door, so naturally, he suspicioned I wuz the witch who'd been witchin' his milk. Deedy, I did come to borrer some terbaccker seeds, and I wuz moughty thirsty atter my walk, but atter whut Jim Tom told me 'bout the witches, I left real quick and come on home without 'em. I knowed effen he really 'lowed I wuz the witch, he'd try to whup the livin' daylights outten me, kase he wuz a caution to wildcats when he wuz riled."

BUTTER, WITCHES AND THORNS

Mandy Jane Patton, like most folks in this mountain community, depended upon selling their surplus butter, eggs and chickens, along with some ginseng and other mountain herbs, to provide the money to buy salt, soda, store-bought clothes, tools, and to pay their taxes. Every home had several cows and usually a big spring-house for keeping milk and butter cool. The cows roamed free in the woods and hollows with little expense to the owners. *Usually*, the work was routine.

Mandy Jane Orr lifted the corner of her blue and white checked apron to wipe the sweat from her red face. "No, indeedy, I hain't never been so whupped in all my born days," she sighed as she saw her neighbor, Ella Anne Carter, coming toward the springhouse.

"Wherever air you, Mandy Jane?" called Ella Anne before she saw her half hidden by the springhouse door.

"Right here in front of yore eyes; right where I've been fer the last two hours er more a churnin' and a churnin'. I cain't git this butter to come to save my life. This wuz the purtiest yaller cream thet you ever seed, and allus afore hit tuk jest half an hour to churn. Whatever in tarnation is the matter is past my knowin'. Whut's more, this is the day fer the men from town to come to buy my butter and eggs, and now hit 'pears like they'll git no butter here. Likely as not, I'll lose their trade kase of this."

Ella Anne, who was older than Mandy Jane, asked, "Can I take a look at thet cream? Air you shore hit hain't too cold er too hot, Mandy Jane?"

"Mercy me no, hit hain't neither. I 'lowed hit mought be too cold, so I poured bilin' water in hit, but hit didn't do a speck of good. Hit jest weakened my buttermilk and hit jest foamed and run over worser than ever. No, bein' too cold er hot ain't whut ails hit. I know hit's as right as hit's ever been."

Mandy Jane stood up, fanning her hot, tired face with her apron as Ella Anne washed her hands, then tilted the lid of the

Collected by I. M. Warren, Roanoke, Virginia, June 24, 1939. Told by Boyd A. Rhudy, Elk Creek, Virginia, who heard this story from Mrs. Jane Suter. The story happened many years ago in an isolated section of Grayson County.

seven-gallon churn to the side. The thick yellow cream had swollen up near the top, and small flecks of butter floated aimlessly about in the milk, but there was no sign of any butter gathering in a lump as it was supposed to do. Ella Anne moved the churn dasher slowly around and said, "I b'lieve hit's 'bout done, Mandy Jane. A few more turns 'll do hit. Lemme me churn fer a spell. I know you air plum petered out atter churnin' fer two hours."

So, she reset the lid and started churning, turning the dasher a little bit with each stroke. She watched for particles of butter to form on the dasher as a sign that butter was forming.

Mandy Jane said, "This shore does look awful, me a standin' here a holdin' my hands and you churnin' away, but effen you're hell bent on churnin' I'll go in and git my dinner on to cook. I'm hongry enuf to eat a horse, and I know you'll be ready to eat when you git through there."

"Go ahead, I'll soon have this butter ready fer the print," Ella Anne promised, and Mandy Jane disappeared inside the cabin. She hustled about with the vegetables and put them on the wood stove in the small dark cook room. She finished several other jobs she'd abandoned to get to the churning and was startled when the clock struck.

"Geemany! I didn't know I'd been in here thet long," she said to herself. "Wonder whut Ella Anne's a doin' all this time? I didn't mean fer her to print thet butter, too. Churnin's enuf, 'thought printin' and cleanin' the churn and things."

Mandy Jane scampered out of the cabin and hurried towards the springhouse. She found Ella Anne still patiently lifting the dasher up and down, letting it turn slightly each time. Her face was flushed and she was sweating. A tired frown revealed that she was weary enough to drop in her tracks.

"Goodness gracious alive, Ella Anne! Why didn't you yell fer me? I clean forgot how long I wuz in the cabin, but I 'lowed you wuz done a churnin' by now."

Ella Anne's jarring laugh removed any doubt of her serious concern as she answered, "I cain't fer the life of me make out whut's wrong with this cream. I've churned many a turn of cream, but I declare, this milk hain't a bit nigher done than hit wuz when l started."

She stood aside so Mandy Jane could look in the churn. Just as she lifted the lid, an old woman appeared in the door and asked, "Whut in tarnation air you'uns a doin' out here a churnin' at this time of day? Sakes alive, I got my churnin' done afore seven this mornin. I shore had a good turn of butter, too. Hit's all printed, rolled up in cloth and ready fer the butter-en-egg man."

Mandy Jane, taken aback by her sudden and unexpected visitor, said, "Howdy, Miss Alice, I'm tickled pink to see you. Mebbe you can tell me why my butter won't come. I've churned fer two hours, and Ella Anne's been at hit fer over an hour, and hit ain't a mite closer to bein' done than hit wuz atter the first half hour. I know hit ain't too hot ner too cold, but whut is the matter, I don't know."

Alice Wolfe peered down at the cream, stood back, put her hands on her hips and said, "Good gracious alive, Mandy Jane, this churnin' hain't a goin' to turn out no butter t'all. You can churn till doomsday and you won't git no butter from this cream."

"Geemany! Miss Alice, whut do you mean?" demanded Mandy Jane. "I know there's butter in thet cream kase I can see hit. Hain't I been a churnin' two pounds and sometimes three with this same amount of cream?"

"Well, whether er no you've been a makin' a lot of butter, you hain't a goin' ter git none outten this milk. I don't doubt thet the butter's there, but Holy Moses, thet milk is witched!"

"Witched?" Mandy Jane and Ella Anne asked in surprise.

"Yep, thet's whut's wrong, and you hain't a goin' to git no more butter ever effen you don't git shet of them witches whut cast their spell on this churn. I'll bet my buttons she hain't fur away this very minnit. Mebbe she's a watchin' you and a sniggerin' fit to kill," Alice explained.

"Whut can I do 'bout hit? Do you mean thet somebody can keep the butter from gatherin? Laws a Massey! I won't have none ter sell," she sighed.

"Thet's 'zactly the way hit is, Mandy Jane, but they'se a way to git shet of the witch, but you'll have to pour this cream out."

"Waste hit all?" Mandy Jane sighed. She walked silently over to the churn in deep thought and examined the milk again. "Whut must I do, Alice? Jest tell me and I'll do hit."

"Have you got a trough in thet empty hog lot over there?" Alice inquired.

"Yep," said Mandy Jane in wonder.

"Well," Alice instructed, "Git your ax and cut you a good thick thorn bush with plenty of limbs and thorns on hit. Then, tote this cream outten the lot and pour hit in the trough. When you've done thet, you light in with thet thorn bush and whup hit with all your might till you whup every drap outten the trough. By the time you've done thet, the witch'll be here, and she'll want to borrer sumpthin' frum you. Thet's how you'll know she's a witch. But, mind my word, don't you lend her nary a thing, kase effen you do, you'll be a churnin' all day agin and never git no butter. Effen you do 'zactly as I've told you, thet witch'll be dead as a hammer."

"Dead!" Ella Anne and Mandy Jane repeated together in a horrified tone. "We wouldn't want to kill nobody," Mandy Jane said.

"I don't mean she'll be wropped in a shroud and put in a grave," Alice hastened to explain. "But her power to witch will be dead, and she cain't never do you no more devilment. But, effen you don't kill her evil magic, she'll jest keep on a pesterin' you till you'll have no peace t'all."

Right there and then, Mandy Jane set to work all by herself, as Alice explained she had to do, since it was her churn. She poured the cream from the churn into buckets and emptied them in the hog trough. And, she did everything else that Alice told her to do. She was so angry at losing all that cream, that she took up her thorn withe and whipped it with a will.

When she'd finished, she turned around and there was an old crone who asked Mandy Jane to lend her a butter print. Of course, she refused and told her to get off the place or she'd sick the dog on her.

After this, Mandy Jane had no more trouble with her butter coming.

THE BEGGAR-THIEF

Darkness embraced the small inn nestled under giant live oaks on the meandering bayou of La Fourche, in Louisiana, when there came a faint knock on the door. The innkeeper opened it to find a shivering beggar on the doorstep. His miserable, dirty rags were soaked with rain and his hands were red from cold. All of his worldly belongings were in a cloth bag suspended on a stick over his shoulder. His plea for lodging was granted, although there was not a spare bed in the house. He was put on a mat in front of the kitchen fire, but he told the innkeeper he was happy with this and felt very lucky to be inside on such a night.

Soon after he was admitted, everybody went to bed except Olla, the cook. She was very much agitated by having her kitchen occupied by a dirty beggar, for she distrusted people who had no job. So, from her room back of the kitchen, she watched him through a peephole.

As soon as the inn was quiet, the beggar rose from the floor and seated himself at the table. He extracted from his cloth bag a dried, brown and withered human hand. He set this "hand of glory"* upright in a candlestick, removed some grease** from a small box, melted it, and anointed his fingers with it. He applied the candle flame to his greasy fingers and they began to burn with an eerie greenish-blue flame.

This gruesome activity filled Olla with apprehension, so, with trembling steps, she crept up the backstairs to alert her master. But, she couldn't rouse him or anyone else. They seemed to be in a charmed sleep. Very much frightened now, Olla nevertheless

Based on a story told by Grayson Hayes, age seventy-four, of Thibodaux, Louisiana, March, 1951. He heard the story as a child from his grandmother.

* The hand of glory is made from the right hand of a man who has been hanged for murder. The hand is cut off at the wrist, wrapped in a piece of winding sheet, and drawn very tightly so as to squeeze out any blood that may remain. It is then placed in an earthenware jar, covered with water, and saturated with salt, pepper, and saltpeter. It is left in this mixture for two weeks until it is pickled, afterwhich it is dried in the sun until it is completely dry.

** Grease or candle is used by witches in conjunction with the hand of glory. The mixture is made from the fat of a hung man, a little fat from the corpse of a suckling child which has not yet been christened, and virgin wax.

sneaked quietly downstairs and posted herself at the peephole. All the ghastly fingers were flaming except the thumb. This was a sign that someone in the house was awake, but the beggar seemed unconcerned.

Olla watched as he collected all of the items that were of any value and placed them on the table. Then, he went into the next room to look for some more loot. Olla rushed out and shut and barred the door to the room, shutting the beggar inside. Then, she tried to extinguish the flames on the hand of glory, but this was not easy. When she blew on them, they burned brighter. She poured dishwater on them to no avail. Then, she tried milk, but it burned like oil. In desperation, she dumped a pot of black Cajun coffee* on the flames, and this extinguished them.

Only then did Olla let out a shriek loud and terrifying enough to curl the French Beard [Spanish moss] of the live oaks up and down the bayou. The whole household was aroused; the thief was taken and turned over to the law; and the hand of glory was buried in the mud of the bayou.

* A black coffee brewed by the Creoles of Louisiana, who consider this coffee to be "as sweet as love, and as strong as death."

THE WITCH GETS SCORCHED

Mrs. James W. Thompson, of Big Stone Gap, Virginia, tells this story: "My Paw, Sam Tipton, had a blaze-faced sorrel mare thet wuz the purtiest thing you ever laid yore two eyes on. But, all of a sudden, she got sick nigh unto death. She laid down in the barn, rolled her big eyes and paid no heed to a soul. 'Twarn't no ifs ands ner buts, she wuz a dyin'.

"Now, hit warn't long afore this thet Paw had locked horns with Old Millie Gay Ison, a neighbor, 'bout her hawgs a gittin' out and ruinin' his corn patch. Millie wuz mean as the Old Scratch when somebody got her dander up, and a lot of folks figgered she wuz a witch. So, Paw put two and two together and 'lowed thet mebbe Millie 'ud witched his mare. He sent young Tod over to Sudie Mae Larkin's to find out whut to do. Old Sudie wuz a good conjure docktor fer brutes, and she knowed how to get the upper hand of witches.

"Sudie couldn't come, but she told Tod whut Paw should do. He wuz to go over to Millie Gay Ison's place afore the sun fell down and borrer some meal. Then, he wuz to scorch thet meal and rub hit on his mare's nose jest as the sun inched over the ridge.

"Now, Sam Tipton really did believe in Sudie's magic, so he done jest whut she told him ter do. Then, afore he bedded down, he went outten the barn and found thet mare a standin' up. The very next day, she wuz as peart as a cricket, and, in a day er two, he hitched her to the plow.

"Not too long atter this, folks noticed thet Millie'd started a wearin' a big sun bonnet all the time. She kept it tucked down over her left ear and her neck. In a few weeks, she moved away to a mining camp, but afore she got away, one of her neighbors vowed she'd seen Millie onct when her bonnet wuz blowed off by the wind. She swore thet Millie's left ear and the left side of her neck wuz a dark brown color jest like hit'd been scorched. Hit musta been kase Paw 'ud scorched thet meal he'd borrered from Millie."

Collected by James N. Hilton, Wise, Virginia, May 3, 1942. Told to him by Mrs. James W. Thompson, of Big Stone Gap.

A DOLL AND A BAG OF MONEY

Strange things were always happening to Aunt Nan Miller. This is how she tells it:

"Onct, a strange voice jabbered to me all day long. Torge the end of the day, as I wuz a gettin' ready to go a milkin', hit whispered, 'Would you like to find some money?' Of course, I answered, 'Yes.'

"Well, I'll swanny, on my way to the milk gap, I seed a piece of money on the ground a shinin' in the sun. When I bent over to pick hit up, I couldn't believe my eyes, kase there wuz a bag of money right aside thet coin. Then, thet voice told me, 'No matter whut you find in thet bag, you mustn't tell nobody 'bout findin' hit, ner how much is in hit. Don't ever spend all of hit, kase effen you keep some, hit'll allus git you out of trubbel.'

"When I opened thet bag, I found hit filled with silver and gold pieces. I spent some of hit to buy me a wood stove, a new plow and some other things I'd been a needin' fer some time. But, I kept thet bag and some of the coins. One of them coins shore did git me outten a pack of trubbel.

"Jim, my old man, and me wuz both a pushin' eighty, so we argued a niece, Dora Hall, to come and live with us. Soon atter Dora got settled down, she wuz a churnin' one day, and she churned and she churned, but she couldn't git no butter t'all.

"So I sed, 'Dora, this milk 'pears to be spelled by a witch. She's been a doin' this to me fer moughty nigh a year now, and I'm a gittin' sick and tired of her shenanigans. I'm a goin' to git shet of this old crone onct and fer all.'

"I raised the lid of the churn, cupped my two hands together, dipped 'em down into the churn and come up with both hands full of cream. Then, I made a beeline fer the fire and dumped thet cream into hit. When hit spewed up, I sed, 'Effen this milk is witched, I hope hit'll burn the old witch who cast the spell on hit.'

"Now, old Nita Cutler who lived back in the woods with her yaller feiss dog and a black cat, wuz a quare, snaggled-tooth old woman who wuz norated to be a witch. So help me, effen the very next day Old Nita didn't show up at the door and beg to borrer some

Collected by I.M. Warren, Roanoke County, Virginia, April 12, 1939. Told by Iva J. Geary, about an aunt and an uncle, James P. Snider and his wife, who lived on a farm on Bridle Creek, Grayson County, around 1800.

meal. She had her left hand all tied up in a rag, and when I axt her 'bout hit, she wuz all of a flutter and sed thet she'd been a pickin' a chicken yestiddy and scalded her hand. Now, I knowed she wuz lyin' kase she didn't have no chickens. So 'twas plain as the nose on my face thet Old Nita wuz the witch thet 'ud spelled my milk. When I put thet milk in the fire, hit 'ud burnt Old Nita.

"Course, I allus try to be a good woman, and 'cordin' to my old man, my heart has allus been too big fer my own good, so I give Old Nita some meal. Then, right atter this, Dora started a havin' a wastin' sickness. When she'd git up in the mornin', she'd complain thet she wuz all wore out and wuz sore and tired. She told me she'd been turned into a horse durin' the nights by a witch and rode sech a fur piece thet she wuz wore out. She 'lowed hit mought be Old Nita Cutler. Some mornings Dora 'ud get up with knots in her hair where Old Nita 'ud tied 'em in the horse's mane fer stirrups.

"Now, onct a witch doctor had told me how to get shet of witches. So, I got my old man, Jim, to holp me and we set out to git shet of Nita's witchin'. I give him a silver coin outten thet bag and he melted hit down and moulded hit into a silver bullet. Whilst he wuz a doin' thet, Dora and me made a rag doll thet wuz the spittin' image of Old Nita Cutler. Then, Jim fastened thet doll onto a broomstick and tuk hit outten the woods and stuck hit into the ground. He loaded his rifle-gun with thet silver bullet, backed up seven steps, tuk dead aim, and fired at thet doll. Now, Jim wuz one of the best squirrel shots in these parts, and he hit thet doll smack dab betwixt the eyes. Hit rolled over in the grass.

"Me and Dora and Jim all laughed loud enuf to wake the daid at the way thet doll looked. Jim sed, 'Now, we won't be bothered no more by thet witch 'round here.'

"Well, hit's the truth effen I ever told hit, Dora soon got over her wastin' sickness. She lived with us and tuk care of both of us right on atter this."

OLD BOWDY

Old Phoebe Ward appeared in Northampton County, North Carolina, just like a robin in the spring. Nobody knew where she came from, nor anything about her past life. She had neither home nor family, but lived first with one family and then another, and begged for a living. Most people thought "Old Bowdy," as they called her, was a witch, and they were all afraid to refuse her anything. When she found a family who would take her in and be kind to her, she would begin to abuse their kindness before too long. Some families consulted a white witch to find out how to keep her away without offending her.

They were given a variety of methods. Some nailed a cross of ash, a horseshoe or a twig of hackberry [bird-cherry] over their doors. Others buried the breast bone of a black hen in front of their door; hung a sieve over it; or put holly leaves just inside it. Some scattered pebbles or grain in front of the door which she would have to stop and count before she could come in. A few turned their stockings wrong side out at night or slept with a Bible under their pillow.

Those not otherwise protected would often stick pins in their chair bottoms when they saw Old Bowdy approaching. They would offer her such a chair, but she always seemed to know which ones had pins in them, and never sat in one. Some people waited until she was in the house, then tossed red pepper pods on the fire. She would leave as soon as she smelled the burning pepper.

One of Old Bowdy's favorite pastimes was to turn people into horses and ride them at night. One man who had been so ridden said that she could make them jump across a river like it was a narrow ditch. Another man said she had turned him into a bull and ridden him over to Roanoke Rapids, and described the evening.

"When she came to the Roanoke River, she said,
'Through thick and thin we ride,
Now jump to the other side.'

"As I was about halfway over, she said, that was a damned good jump.

Published in the *Journal of American Folklore*, volume 22, number 9, 1909, under the title "The Story of Phoebe Ward."

"Down came the bull—me—splashing down right in the middle of the river. I almost drowned. You see, a witch is not supposed to speak while she is crossing a stream."

Once, Old Bowdy almost got buried before her time came. John Siever had just moved into a new house, and hadn't had time to put anything over the door or in front of it to keep witches out. So Old Bowdy had moved into the house with the family.

The Sievers were going to give a housewarming, and the most successful ones in North Carolina are held over a brandy barrel. So, John Siever bought a barrel of apple brandy, and it was soon surrounded. As the brandy flowed, spirits rose, tongues were loosened, and the devil got into them. They started looking about for ways to have some fun.

One man looked into a back room and discovered Old Bowdy there fast asleep. With the brandy doing the thinking, he decided she was dead, so he carried her into the front room to give her a proper wake. She was shrouded in the sheet, and laid out on the floor in the corner.

The brandy barrel had now been refilled with cherry bounce and the men were sampling it when there came a squeaky voice from the enshrouded corpse, "Give me a little of that. It's cold over here."

All those big, brave men took to their heels and cleared out of the room like a wisp of smoke. That is, everybody but Old Uncle Dave Helig, who was too drunk to run. After a few minutes, Old Bowdy repeated her request, but Old Dave just said, "Ah! shut up, you damned old witch. We're going to bury you when daylight comes."

The other men were afraid to return to the house until daylight, but when they did, they found Uncle Dave and Old Bowdy sitting in front of the fire, contentedly warming their shins and drinking cherry bounce.

Uncle Dave took a shine to Old Bowdy and took her home with him. She lived the rest of her life as a member of his family.

DIVINATION BY CARDS

The Reverend Mack Arthur served his first charge at Harrisonburg, Virginia. In time, he moved on to another church, but several years later, he was again invited to the Harrisonburg church. Friends advised him not to return, since a pastor often has difficulties when they come back to a charge they have held before. But Reverend Arthur said that, since he had been called there, he didn't think it would be right not to heed the call.

Shortly after his return to Harrisonburg, his church held a Sunday evening picnic. At the picnic Reverend Mack paid particular attention to one young lady, a Miss Holly Mae Groud. Lucy Gordon, with whom the Reverend had kept company during his first period of service at the church, was also there and helped to serve the food.

On Monday morning, Reverend Arthur was a very sick man. A doctor was called who left some medicine, but it didn't seem to do any good. Then, he consulted a second doctor, and then a third . . . but, none of them seemed to be able to find out what was wrong with him. Finally, they all gave up. As Reverend Mack was too ill to continue his work, he gave up his pastorate and moved back to his home at Spring Mill. There, he tried a local yarb doctor, but she didn't help him either, so in desperation he took someone's advice and went to see Liz Gootchin, an old conjure woman.

Now, Reverend Mack Arthur, being an educated man and having been out in the world, didn't want folks to think that he believed in witch doctors, so he tried to keep his contacts with the conjure woman a secret. He felt that he wasn't long for this world and was ready to try anything.

He told Liz about his past life, his work and his education, but he made no mention of the two women whom he had courted. Old Liz looked him straight in the eyes and seemed to be studying him. She asked him to sit in a chair in her back yard, and went in the house to get a deck of cards. She sat down on the ground in front of the Reverend and began to turn some cards over and stare at them.

After a while, she said, "Reverend Mack Arthur, I see some wimmin in yore life. One of 'em is not too fur back, but t'other goes

Collected by Roscoe Lewis, Elizabeth City County, Hampton, Virginia, May 15, 1939. Told by the Reverend P.L. Harvey, who was a seminary classmate of the Reverend Mack Arthur, the chief character in the story.

way back. Now, you didn't tell me nuthin' 'bout yore girl friends. It 'pears thet the fust girl is still sweet on you, but you haven't cared much for her and have give her the mitten.*"

Now, Reverend Mack thought of Lucy Gordon, who'd set her cap for him when he was at the Harrisonburg pastorate the first time. He had't paid her much mind, and had forgotten all about her after he'd left. When he returned, he started going with another girl. Old Liz told him that his trouble was connected with these two girls.

After Liz had gone through the cards three times, she picked up the deuce of spades, looked him in the face and said, "Young man, hit 'pears like you've been pizzened real bad." She said Lucy had no doubt sneaked some poison in the food she served him at the church picnic.

"Effen you'd come to me two er three months ago, mebbe I could've straightened you out, but now hit 'pears like all I can do is give you some medicine thet'll keep you up and going. But, hit's not likely to cure you atter all this time. Take this, and when you run outten hit, come back to me fer more."

Mack paid Liz well for her services and for the bottle of medicine. He was really shaken by what Liz had told him, but he took the medicine and in a few days began to feel much better. He took four bottles of it, and then was feeling so well that he decided he didn't need to take any more.

Within a week after he ceased to take the medicine, he came down with the skitters. He was very ill, and before his family could get any more of Liz's medicine, he was dead.

---

* To refuse someone as a lover. If someone asked a girl to marry him, he asked for her hand. If refused, he got only the mitten. The term also refers to a woman who does not succeed in getting a proposal out of a man whom she is after.

THE BLACK WOODSMAN

There's an old Indian fort a few miles outside of Boston in the middle of a grove of oak trees. Legend has it that Captain Kidd buried his treasure under one of these trees and left it to the guardianship of the devil.

In the early 1700's, Tom Walker lived near this oak grove. He was a money-grubbing old man, and his wife was equally close-fisted. In fact, they were so much alike they often haggled with each other and had many bitter quarrels about things which should have been common property.

One day, Tom went to Boston and, on his way back home, took a shortcut through the woods near the grove of oaks. The place was dark even in the day, and there were quagmires into which a person might fall. Tom sat down to rest on a rotting log, heard a noise, and looked up to see a huge black man standing before him. He had an ax on his shoulder, curly black hair, and his face looked as if it had been smeared with soot.

"Who are you?" asked Tom.

"I go by many different names," he answered. "Some call me the Wild Huntsman, others call me Old Scratch. Still others call me Satan. Here I am known as the Black Woodsman."

The Black Woodsman offered to show Tom where Captain Kidd's treasure was buried, provided he promised to use it as he directed. Tom, being greedy, could not resist the temptation, so he agreed. The Black Woodsman said Tom could use the money for the rest of his life if he would pay the Woodsman one-half of the profits he made with it, and promise to accompany the Black Woodsman when he was through with the money. Tom agreed to all of this.

They dug up the treasure, and Tom opened a broker's office with it. He lent money at high interest rates, foreclosed mortgages on those who couldn't pay, and drove many people into bankruptcy. He would pretend to be a friend to people until he got all their money, then turn away when they needed him. He was a genius at this kind of business, so he prospered and made a lot of money.

As Tom grew older, the thrill of making money became less

Based on "Selling the Soul to the Devil," by Gayle Parr, Bloomington, Indiana, November 26, 1945. Published in *Hoosier Folklore from Egypt*, Folklore Society of Indiana Journal, volume 4, number 4, 1945.

exciting. He recalled the many good things life had provided him, and he yearned to continue such a life after death. He joined the church, attended regularly, and read his Bible in all his spare moments. All the while he tried to plan some way to get out of the bargain he had made with the Black Woodsman.

One summer morning, Tom was about to foreclose a mortgage which would ruin a man. The man begged and pleaded with him to give him just one more day to raise the money, saying, "Tom, you've made so much money from me, you should be willing to wait for just a little while longer."

At this, Tom forgot his piety, lost his temper and became abusive. He said angrily, "May the devil take my soul right now if I've made a red cent off of you."

At that very moment there was a loud knock at the door. When Tom opened it, there stood the Black Woodsman holding the reins of a beautiful black horse. He put Tom on the horse, climbed up behind him, and they galloped down the road toward the oak grove. Nobody ever saw Tom or the Black Woodsman again.

A man who lived near the grove said that on the night Tom disappeared, a lightning bolt had struck a tree in the grove and had set all the trees on fire. When his executors started to settle his estate, they found ashes in his vaults instead of money. What had once been horses in his stable were only skeletons. Shortly thereafter, his home was struck by lightining and his wife killed in the ensuing fire.

HE GAVE HER THE MITTEN

Mrs. Belle Kilgore of Esserville, Virginia, told this story from her childhood:

"My Granny, Anna Rose Ramey, had been sick fer a long time. She couldn't sleep, and she'd twist and squirm and dream all night long, and she 'lowed she'd been witched.

"My Grandpappy, Ben Boone Ramey, 'ud move her bed frum place to place in the room. Allus, the fust night atter she'd been moved, she'd sleep like the daid, but atter thet, she couldn't sleep a wink. Atter a whet, she told Ben thet an old crone 'ud come and stand over her bed and devil her so she couldn't sleep.

"So, Grandpappy made up his mind thet he'd sleep in Granny's bed one night. He tuk a hammer to bed with him, and swore effen thet witch did come, he'd bust her haid with thet hammer. Granny begged him not to do thet, but he wuz hard-headed and paid her no mind. He put Granny in his bed and got into Granny's with his hammer.

"He'd started to doze off when he had a feelin' thet somebody wuz a watchin' him. When he opened his eyes, there wuz the worst lookin' old hag he'd ever seed standin' there with an ugly frown. She had snitched his hammer and had hit drawed back in both hands jest like she wuz a goin' to whack his brains out. Ben's blood'most turned to ice, and he cringed back agin the wall. Then, he lunged outten bed, snatched the hammer outten the old hag's hand, and she turned and run. Grandpappy threw thet hammer at her with all his might, but she bobbed her haid to one side and the hammer hit the wall. Hit bounced off and hit her on the heel, making sparks fly when it hit. Then, the old hag started to draw up and she got littler and littler until she wuz jest a shadder. She floated right through the keyhole outten the cabin.

"The next mornin', Grandpappy had to go over to Paw Paw Grove to work one of his fields, but, afore he left, he told his family not to lend nuthin' to ennybody, kase effen they did, hit 'ud give the witch magic power to spell 'em all.

"Lo and behold! He'd hardly got outten sight in the woods afore Kate Keen's young 'un come to the cabin and axt to borrer

Collected by Emory L. Hamilton, Wise, Virginia, April 6, 1940. Told to him by Mrs. Belle Kilgore, who heard it from her grandmother when she was a child.

some linament. She said a horse'd kicked her mammy on the leg and hit wuz swole and red and she wuz in a bad way.

"Now, my Mammy wuz jest a little girl, but she told thet young'un she couldn't borrer nuthin' from her and for her to git. Then, the youn'un started a bawlin' and she sed, 'Thenia, how can you refuse me a little thing like some liniment when my Mammy's a dyin? Hit jest mought happen sometime to yore Mammy. Then, the shoe 'ud be on t'other foot.'

"My Mammy blurted out, 'looka here, my Mammy's in a worse fix right now than yore'n, and hit's yore Mammy's fault. Now you make tracks up thet road, er I'll sick the dawgs on you.'

"All day long, fust one and then annuder of them Keens 'ud come to borrer sumpthin. Kate Keen's old man come to beg fer a bit of Pine Tar salve and a little rag to tie up the bruise on her leg. He sed hit wuz all busted to pieces and her whole leg 'ud swole plum up to her thigh. He pleaded, 'Please, let me have sumpthin', kase hit don't look like Kate's a goin' to live till sundown.'

"All this beggin' done no good 'tall, kase Granny recollected whut Ben 'ud sed, and she didn't let none of 'em have a smidgen of nuthin'. Grandpappy got back to the cabin whilest Kate's old man wuz still there, and he told him he couldn't git a spoonful of nuthin' from there. He sed, 'Let Old Kate die; then she won't be a pesterin' folks 'round here.'

"Bless my soul, effen thet old man didn't beg so hard and pitiful and even offered to work fer Grandpappy a whole day effen he'd jest let him have sumpthin' fer Kate's leg. So, Grandpappy figgered thet he wouldn't be lendin' him ennything effen he worked fer hit, and he got soft-hearted and knuckled under and sed, 'Well, I'll take a rag, some string, linament and salve over there and fix her up myself.'

"When Grandpappy went into the Keens' dirty shanty, there wuz no doubt that Kate Keen wuz the same old crone he'd seed a standin' by his bed. So, afore he done ennything fer her, he made her promise thet she'd never bother Anna Rose ner none of his family no more as long as she lived.

"The old crone wuz so racked with pain, she'd a done en-nythin' to git shet of hit, so she broke down and told Grandpappy why she wuz a pesterin' his old woman. She sed, 'When I wuz a striplin' of a girl, I fell in love with you, but you paid me no mind 'tall. You went on and got married up with Anna Rose. Right there and then I made up my mind thet I'd let her rest no more as long as she lived with you. So, I got myself made into a witch, and larned to do magic, and I hain't let Anna Rose have much peace sence.'

"Grandpappy fixt up Kate's wounded heel with linament, put some salve on hit and bound hit up. Then, she told him, 'Ben, I ort not to have told you I'm a witch er whut I've been a doin'. The Devil allus punishes witches fer tattlin' any of their secrets, and he'll kill me fer this. He told me I would die three months atter I told ennybody 'bout being a witch. I'll die jest afore sunset, and I'll sweat blood afore I die.'

"She made Grandpappy promise he wouldn't tell ennybody whut she'd told him. She axt him to promise thet, when she died, he'd see thet nobody undressed her to git her ready to bury, but jest to bury her in the long black witch dress she wore. Now, Grandpappy knowed Kate wuz still a witch, so he wuz afeard not to do 'zactly as she axt.

"Hit wuz 'zactly three months to the day atter this when there come a big thunder and lightnin' storm. Kate sent her young'un over to git Grandpappy, and he hurried over to her place. She told him she wuz feelin' moughty poorly, and she tuk to her bed right away. She started a sweatin' and they wiped hit off with a towel. The sweat wuz pink and then red. Jest as the thunder and lightnin' stopped, she stretched out on the bed and slipped away. Grandpappy saw to hit thet she wuz buried in her black dress withoutten hit bein' tuk off.

"Now, everybody 'ud been so skeered of Kate whilst she wuz alive thet they hadn't talked 'bout the things she'd done, but they got to talkin' at the wake. Some of the neighbors sed they'd seed her turn her young'uns into grasshoppers, flies and June bugs, and make 'em go through the keyhole. Grandpappy sed she told him, when she confessed to bein' a witch, thet she'd holped the Devil to kill one of her young'uns and bile hit in the witches' stew when they wuz a makin' witch balls. There wuz other bad things said, and there wuzn't no one a sorry to see Kate daid."   .

PART FOUR

WITCHCRAFT FOR MONEY
AND MISCHIEF

INTRODUCTION

Black witches carried on their evil business for many reasons including spite, jealousy, romantic entanglements and efforts to outwit the devil to whom they had pledged their souls in exchange for their magic powers. Most of them sold their services as a means of earning a livelihood, but some used their magic merely to deceive or hurt someone. Of course, white witches also sold their services as doctors and honestly attempted to help the sick counteract the spells of the black witches.

In "The Disappearing Witch," a witch changes herself into a black cat in order to enter a man's home and rob him. Later, she robs his store as well. Another witch, in "The Witch and Her Dwarfed Daughters," uses her magic to steal the necessities of life. In "Mont and Duck," a couple makes a living by intimidating and blackmailing their neighbors into giving them what they need, although they pretend to use their magic powers to heal. In another case, a witch uses her powers to steal milk from her neighbors.

Witchcraft was also used by some to protect property rights. In "Can't Steal," magic power is used to protect a man's mill from theft. The ability to cast spells is used in other stories as a means of protecting hunting areas and hunted animals.

In "Cured from a Distance," the Reverend Ben Cordle uses his ability to faith-heal Ebb Bond without charging for his services, but he lets it be known that he would be pleased to receive a pound of ginseng as an honorarium. In "The Finder and the Charm Doctor," the conjure man performs his services for a friend, and neither expects nor receives any kind of remuneration.

Witchcraft was often used for spite and as a means of striking back at an enemy. In "A Cornpone and a Witchball," Mattie Lou uses her magic powers against her former friend, Granny Sturgis, because they could not resolve a misunderstanding. In another story, witchcraft is used to harass an innocent person, and to drive him from the community. On the other hand, Old Nan Feeney, in "The Burning Mill," carries on her evil work because she honestly feels her victim was depriving her of something which was rightfully due her.

Sometimes, witchcraft played a prominent role in trying to solve problems of the heart. In "The Bewitched Wives," Rija, the youngest and most beautiful wife of the arrowmaker, arouses the jealousies of his other wives, one of whom strikes at her through witchcraft.

And sometimes, witchcraft was used against people simply for malice. On occasion, the intended party suffered. On other occasions, the scheme backfired and the witches suffered more than their targets.

A LIZARD IN THE LEG

Annaise Duly, of Coleman Falls, Virginia, came from a family with generations of experiences with witches. Here is her story:

"All the folks 'round us b'lieved in witches and conjurin'. When I wuz a young'un, Grandpappy told me 'bout Old Ned Hogston who lived way back on Turkey Branch, nigh Grandpappy's place. Everybody knowed he wuz a witch doctor who could drive out devils, break magic spells, and cure folks who'd been witched.

"One day, Hilda Riner and Sudie Ricks had a fallin' out 'bout some wool cards, and they give one annuder a tongue lashin' worse'n all get out. Lo and behold, thet Sudie Ricks wuz a witch, and she put a witch ball under Hilda's doorstep. 'Course, Hilda didn't know thet witch ball wuz there, so twarn't long afore she stepped over hit. Right there and then she got an awful pain in her leg.

"Hilda sent for Granny Clay, who'se a yarb doctor, to come and see her. Granny rubbed some foxglove ointment dissolved in rattlesnake oil on her leg every day fera week, but hit didn't do nary a bit of good. Then, she burned some sulfur in the house, and tied a poultice of potato leaves, sassafras roots and sage 'round Hilda's leg. This didn't do no good neither, so, atter a week, she give up.

"Then, Hilda sent for Old Ned Hogston to come and see her. He 'zamined her leg and told her she'd been 'spelled.' He sed more'n likely she had a snake er a lizard er sumpthin' like thet in her leg, and he could get hit out fer five dollars. 'Course, Hilda Riner wuz a poor woman. She wuz keerful with her pennies, and she'd saved a little. She got out her money bag and counted hit, but there's only three dollars and eighty-nine cents. She axt Ned effen he'd doctor her fer thet, but Ned sed he didn't rightly know effen he could cut his price, kase effen he did, and folks found out 'bout hit, he'd be ruint.

"Then, Hilda told Ned that come Saturday, she'd take some eggs and butter to the store to sell, and hit orter bring enuf to make

Collected by Isaiah Volley, Lynchburg, Virginia, April 3, 1940. Told to him by Annaise Duly. This story, which was supposed to have happened to a member of their family, had been handed down to her from her maternal grandparents.

the five dollars. But, Ned sed she'd have to git the money Friday, sence his magic wouldn't work effen hit wuzzen't done on Friday night.

"So, Hilda went to the store on Friday, and made enuf to rake together the five dollars. Thet night, Ned come back, and sed fust thing he'd have to have the five dollars. Atter Hilda 'ud give him the money, he got down on his knees and started to rub her leg and to quote frum the Bible. He sed, 'And the Lord said, even the Devils air subject to us through Thy name. . . . He commanded the unclean speret to come outten the man and he drove the Devil into the wilderness. . . .'

"Atter a while, Ned reached up his sleeve and pulled out a big red bandana and started to rub her leg with hit. Then, he sed, 'Fer unclean sperets cryin' with loud voices come outten many thet wuz possessed by the Devil and many took palsies and them thet wuz crippled wuz healt.'

"Then, he rubbed real hard and sed, 'Then, I seed three unclean sperets like frogs, one come outten the mouth of the dragon, annuder outten the mouth of the beast, and the third one come outten the mouth of the false prophet.'

"Atter he'd rubbed her leg seven times with the red bandana, a little lizard crawled acrost the floor. Ned kotched hit and sed, 'In the name of the Father, and the Son and the Holy Speret, thar hit is. That's the lizard thet wuz in your leg.'

"Then, Ned sed real sad like, 'Thar's a big hole in the back of your leg where thet lizard bored hit's way out. Now, I've got some special ointment thet'll make the hole git well so quick hit won't even be sore. I gits two dollars fer a can of hit.'

"Hilda sed, 'But I don't have no more money. I give you the last cent I had.'

"Then, Ned sed, 'Sence you've had sech a hard time a gittin' five dollars, I'm a goin' to rub thet ointment on your leg to heal hit, and I hain't a goin' to charge you one red cent fer hit.'

"Well, hit's the truth effen I ever told hit. Ned sure pulled thet trick on Hilda slick as a whistle. She never found out thet Ned had brung thet lizard with him in thet red bandana and thet the magic ointment he'd used on her leg wuz nuthin' but Cloverine Salve thet you could buy ennywhere fer a dime a can."

THE DEVIL WOULDN'T HAVE HIM

The little one-room log blacksmith shop with its big outside shed was a necessity for all mountain communities. It was a beehive of activity, yielding an incessant stream of sounds. From daylight to dusk, the clang of the smithy's hammer against the anvil, his husky voice hurling curses at frightened horses he was trying to shoe, and the sizzling of the hot iron being tempered in a pail of water could be heard for a long distance. His hours were long, his work dirty, and his pay meager—often in the form of meat, corn or wool.

Late one Saturday evening, Pat was ready to close his shop and go home when a stranger entered. They began talking, and soon Pat was telling him of his difficult situation. The stranger listened attentively and expressed sympathy. He offered to make a bargain with him which would forever do away with all his financial worries. He said that if Pat would promise to go away with him at the end of a year, he would promise that every time Pat would put his right hand in his right pocket he would find gold, and every time he would put his left hand in his left pocket, he would find silver. Pat agreed to this, and the stranger smote him on the shoulder to seal the bargain.

Pat couldn't believe his good luck, and invited the stranger home with him to spend the night. The guest was entertained as lavishly as Pat's meager resources would permit. The guest was pleased and said he wanted to reward such a hospitable host by granting Pat any three wishes he cared to make. Pat made the wishes.

A strange priest suddenly appeared, and Pat told him about the bargain he had made with his guest, and about the three wishes he had been invited to make. The priest then asked Pat if he had noticed anything unusual about his guest. "No," Pat replied, "I was much too excited about the wonderful bargain to notice him very closely." The priest then pointed out his guest had feet with hooves like a mule's and that he had small horns above his ears. Pat looked closely at his guest and saw that these things were true. He

This story was told by William Crowley, Conway, Arkansas, January 15, 1938, who heard it from his grandfather when he was a little boy.

163

realized that he had been dealing with the Devil. He had already bargained away his soul. Now he would have to find a way to outwit Old Satan.

The Devil insisted that he had to hurry along. He told Pat to make his three wishes known to the priest, who could vouch for their truth when he later wanted to use them. Then, both the Devil and the priest left. Pat spent the remainder of that Sunday pulling gold and silver coins from his pockets and laying them away in piles for the future.

During the following year, Pat and his family lived in luxury, at the same time hoarding great piles of gold and silver for the future. At the end of the year, the Devil reappeared and inquired if Pat were ready to leave with him. Pat assured him that he was, but would he give him just a few more minutes. He was working on a scythe for a neighbor and had promised to finish it today. Would the Devil be so kind as to hammer it into shape while he turned it for him? The Devil consented and picked up the jack-hammer. When the hammer struck the anvil, it stuck and the Devil couldn't remove it.

Then, the strange priest reappeared. When the Devil demanded an explanation, Pat told him that he had merely used one of his wishes. The priest verified this, and said that Pat wished that, when anyone used his jack-hammer, it would stick to his hands and the anvil, and the anvil to the floor so that the person couldn't move until Pat gave the order.

Of course, the Devil was furious that he had been tricked. He ranted and raved and threatened to stick Pat with hot pitchforks when he got him down in hell. But, Pat didn't give in to his threats, and made him promise to give him one more year on earth as a condition for his release. Then, Pat told him he could move, and both he and the priest disappeared.

During the second year, Pat and his family really enjoyed all the things money could buy. The year passed happily but speedily, and, at the end, the Devil reappeared. He told Pat that this time he would tolerate no trickery. Pat assured him that he wasn't planning any and he was ready to go. He asked only that he be allowed to go home to tell his family good-bye. The Devil agreed, and when they entered the house, Pat pulled up an easy chair and invited the Devil to sit down while he made ready to go. The Devil sat down and Pat left the room.

In a few minutes, the priest appeared in the living room. The Devil attempted to rise to greet him, but found he could not get out of the chair. The priest explained that Pat's second wish had been that anyone who sat in one of his chairs would not be able to get out until Pat gave the order. Again the Devil cursed and threatened Pat with all kinds of torture when he got him in hell, but it got him nowhere. He had to promise Pat another year on earth before Pat would release him. When Pat ordered him to get up, both he and the priest disappeared.

The third year was a hectic one for Pat and his family. There wasn't too much more for them to experience, but they tried so hard that they were all much dissipated by the end of the year when the Devil appeared once again.

"This time your tricks will do you no good. You're going with me whether you like it or not," vowed the Devil. Pat was frightened by this, and when the priest appeared, he asked for his blessing. The priest advised him to go along with the Devil without any more tricks. He reminded him that he had only one more wish, and he suggested Pat keep it, for he was sure to need it in hell.

Pat seemed to agree, and said they would have a drink on it. He felt in his pocket but didn't find a coin. So, he blurted out: "I wish I had a silver coin to buy us all a drink."

When Pat said, "I wish," the Devil changed into a silver coin which Pat put in his purse. His third wish was that if he put a coin in his purse, it could not be removed until he wanted it to be. But, Pat had no peace with the Devil in his purse because he grunted and groaned and cursed and squirmed and demanded to be let out. Pat was almost driven out of his mind, and it was clear that he must rid himself of this nuisance in some way. He decided to pound the purse and the coin to dust with his jack-hammer. With the help of the priest, and the accompaniment of the screams and groans of the Devil, this was done. The temporary tenant of the purse went up the chimney in smoke and flame.

Pat never saw his hoofed and horned guest again, nor the strange priest. He asked about in the community for the priest, but no one had ever seen him. Pat thought that the priest must have been one of the Devil's cohorts.

But, the Devil quickly had his revenge on Pat: the piles of gold and silver he had laid up for the future turned into piles of horse and cow dung. With his money gone, Pat's family deserted him. He fell on his anvil and injured himself so badly that he couldn't work. He was forced to beg from door to door, but his neighbors, envious of his former good fortune, refused to help him. He became weak and emaciated and a fever soon carried him away. Finally, he was buried in a pauper's grave.

Knowing that it would be of no use to apply to Heaven, Pat went directly to hell and knocked on the door. One of the little imps peeped through a hole at him, and announced to his father that Patrick J. Duffy, a blacksmith from the Ozarks, had arrived and was seeking admittance. The Devil called through the peephole, 'Ah! At last, you miserable liar, cheat and crook, you've come to me of your own accord."

Pat replied that it wasn't quite that simple, but he did want to get in. But, the Devil answered, "I wouldn't admit you to hell under any conditions! There's never been, and never will be, the likes of you down here. I order you to return to earth and wander up and down it until Judgement Day. You'll never have a moment's rest or peace by day or night. The Devil then gave an order and the strange priest appeared and

> Trundled him in a sack, and
> Lugged the wicked blacksmith back.

Now, where Pat's blacksmith shop once stood, there is an ever-present stench of corruption. A phantom has been seen distinctly near the spot, and many people say it is the restless spirit of Pat Duffy roaming around and still trying to outwit the Devil.

A CORNPONE AND A WITCHBALL

It was extremely difficult to raise turkeys in the mountains, and losses were heavy. Eagles and turkey buzzards swooped down and picked up young turkeys that strayed from the mother hen and foxes stalked them. If the turkeys were hatched in the wild, and this happened quite often since domesticated turkeys would hide their nests in the woods, the young turkeys would often revert to the wild state. Most mountaineers knew of these hazards and didn't try to raise them. However, Mattie Lou Looney was an exception. As Aunt Bessie Beaton tells it:

"My Granny, Julia Fay Sturgis, onct had a neighbor, Mattie Lou Looney, thet she liked a whole heap. They wuz allus a borrowin' and a lendin' things with one annuder. Then, Granny sold Mattie Lou some young turkeys and them turkeys jest wouldn't stay with Mattie Lou. They'd come back to Granny's place every time Mattie Lou 'ud let 'em loose, and she'd have to come and fetch 'em. Onct, when them turkeys wuz loose and come over to Granny's place, hit 'peared like a fox had kotched some of 'em, and when Mattie Lou come for 'em, some wuz a missing. She faulted Granny for stealin' her turkeys, and they had a big ruckus and sed some mean things to one annuder. Atter this, Mattie Lou got to actin' quare like and stayin' to herself and a lot of folks sed she wuz a witch.

"Twarn't long atter this when Granny Sturgis tuk to her bed and wuz porely for a long spell. She wouldn't talk to nobody ner answer when they axt her things. Three yarb doctors give Granny brews, made poultices for her, and tried all their simples, but none of 'em done her nary a bit of good. They give up on her, and her folks wuz a feelin' moughty downfaced and gloomy. Then, Grandpappy paid a city doctor to come and he 'zamined her and axt her a lot of questions. But, she didn't answer. He sed he didn't know whut 'ud come over her, and he give up, too. He sed sence she wudden't talk, she wuz dumb, and he remembered sumpthin' 'bout a dumb girl in the Bible who had to have devils drove outten her afore she could talk.

Collected by James N. Hilton, Wise, Virginia, June 3, 1939. Told to him by Bessie Beaton, of the Pound section of Wise County, who heard this story from her grandmother when she was a child.

167

"Now, this put an idee into Grandpappy's haid and right away he set off to talk with the Reverend Elijah Jones, a hardshell Baptist preacher. Reverend Jones told l im to 'Seek God's holp.'

"After that advice, Grandpappy read him a passage from the Bible which sed, 'She sought Him that He would cast the Devil outten his daughter.'

"Reverend Jones 'lowed Grandpappy should git Vera Bell Simmons to come and drive out Julia Mae's devils and break the spell. But, Grandpappy couldn't make outten this, kase he knowed 'cordin' to the Bible thet witches wuz wicked. He 'lowed castin' spells and drivin' out evil sperets wuz the work of the Devil and his helpers. But, Reverend Jones 'splained by readin' from the Bible where hit says in Luke 11:14, 'He wuz castin' out a Devil and she wuz dumb, and when the Devil wuz gone out, she spoke.'

"Then, he sed, 'Effen the Devil is put in by Beelzebub and a Devil's helper cast 'em out, then 'He is divided against hisself, so how shall his kingdom stand?' Effen Vera Bell is the Devil's helper, and she drives the devils outten Julia May, then Vera Bell must be on the side of the Lord.'

"Atter Reverend Jones 'splained this to Grandpappy, he wuz flabbergasted. But, sence Julia May wuz a gittin' skinnier and skinnier and wuz jest a bag of bones already, he figgered he'd be smart to give Vera Bell a chance. So, he went over to Trimble Crick and fetched Vera Bell back with him. She axt Julia Mae some things and, when she wudden't answer, she 'lowed Julia Mae'd been spelled and she would cast her own spell. She got her a little dab of sulfur, a pinch of asafetida, a mite of sage, a smidgen of cayenne pepper and a few mustard seeds and wropt 'em all together in a dried toad's skin. Then, she burnt this in the fireplace so Julia Mae could smell hit.

"Atter this, she axt Julia Mae some questions, and she started a talking. She told Vera Bell thet every night a witch 'ud come and change her into a horse. Then, she'd plait her mane into stirrups and ride her all night long. In the mornin', she'd be pegged out and nigh a goner. She 'splained thet witches didn't ride people like you would ride a horse. The witch put the saddle on the horse's neck and she didn't talk to the horse like people do. 'Sted of sayin' "Giddup" er "Come on, horsey" the witch 'ud say, "Up! Up! Go horsey, go horsey, go!"'

"Vera Bell wuz sartin Julia Mae wuz a tellin' the truth, kase everybody 'ud seen them tangles in her hair. Now, Vera Bell wuz clearheaded and kerful, so she studied on what Julia Mae 'ud told her for a spell. Then, she figgered outten a plan to get rid of the witch for good.

"She told Julia Mae's old man to go out and dig some sang and sassafras roots and dry 'em. Then, she axt him to git some mugwort and henbane* leaves and dry 'em. Then all this dry stuff had to be ground into a powder and rolled into a ball with a few hairs from the crown of Julia Mae's haid, using molasses to stick hit all together. Then, he had to hide the ball under the door step. She 'lowed thet three days atter they'd done this, the witch 'ud come to the cabin to borrer sumpthin'. She sed to give her three hooters of meal mixed with the rest of the powdered stuff. Sence they wuz hellbent on gittin' shet of the witch, they done jest as Vera Bell told 'em.

"Well, I'll be hanged effen in jest three days here comes Mattie Lou Looney a blusterin' to the door. She axt Julia Mae's mother how Julia Mae wuz a doin' and her Maw told her Julia Mae wuz still porely. Julia Mae's mother axt Mattie Lou to come in to see Julia Mae, but Mattie Lou sed she wuz in a hurry and had jest come to borrer a little flour. 'Course, Julia Mae's Maw wuz ready for her, so she sed, 'I hain't got no flour, but I do have some moughty good meal, and you're welcome to some of hit.'

"Now, hit 'peared like Mattie Lou smelled a mouse, kase she frowned and sed mebbe the meal 'ud do, but she wuz moughty fed up on cornpone. But, she tuk hit, kase she 'lowed she'd borrowed sumpthin and she 'ud still hold a spell over Julia Mae.

"Old Vera Bell shore knowed whut she wuz a doin'. Hit wuzzen't long afore Julia Mae started a talkin' up a storm and she got outten the bed and walked around for the fust time in a long spell. She wuz shore feelin' moughty good, and got well in no time t'all.

"Then, Old Mattie Lou Looney got moughty porely from thet mess of stuff in thet meal she borrered. Hit mighty nigh made a ghost outten her, but, atter a while, she got peart agin. But, she never wuz able to cast enny more witch spells."

*See note on page 67.

THE WITCH AND THE PLOW POINT

The noisy waters of Big Island Creek flow along the foot of a rock bluff deep in the Blue Ridge Mountains, near Hillsville, in Carroll County, Virginia. The sun never seems to shine on the peak of the mountain. Tall pines cast dark shadows over its rocky sides, and their protruding arm-like branches helped give this area the name of Witch Mountain. A hundred years ago, this was supposed to be the abode of many witches who roamed the countryside harassing people with their evil deeds.

Ginny Sayler, who lived near Witch Mountain and was a grand-niece of Jeffry and Nancy Bobbit, had said that Aunt Nancy had no doubt whatever that there were witches. She told how she could recite tale after tale to prove it. This is one of Aunt Nancy's stories:

"Onct, Uncle Jeff's ewes lambed early, and one of 'em died and left two nursing lambs. We put 'em with other ewes, but, for some reason, one of the ewes wudden't have nuthin' to do with the lamb we give to her, so I fetched hit to the cabin to try to raise hit by hand. Workin' with thet purty little helpless baby, I got to thinkin' a sight of hit.

"Well, one mornin' thet lamb wudden't tech a bit of hit's food, so I put hit outside, 'lowin' thet he'd forage for hisself. I'll swanny, effen hit didn't jest run 'round and 'round like a chicken with hit's haid cut off, a buttin' into things like hit wuz blind. I brung hit inside and dregged hit good with yarb tea and simples, but, in spite of all thet, thet lamb got no better. My sperets wuz low when Victor Largin come by to borrer Jeff's adze. Now, Vic wuz knowed as a good witch doctor, so I axt him effen he thought thet mebbe thet lamb wuz spelled. Well, right off, he 'lowed hit wuz. Then, he told me how to break the spell, but he warned me hit wudden't work effen I didn't do 'zactly like he sed. I promised him I'd do hit jest thet a way.

"Fust, I went into the woods and hunted a holler stump and got me a jugfull of stump water. Then, I hunted some henbane leaves and biled 'em in vinegar and mixed hit with the stump water and a

Collected by Raymond H. Sloan, Rocky Mount, Virginia, August 3, 1939. This story was told to him by Boyd A. Rhudy, who heard it from Steve Ward, grandfather of Ginny Salyer, of Witch Mountain.

few red pepper seeds. I got Jeff to cut some locust logs fur my fire and built a big fire in the fireplace. When the fire wuz a burnin' real good, I axt Jeff to fetch me a broke plow pint. I put the pint in the hot ashes, lit my pipe, and set back in my rocking cheer to see effen whut Vic 'ud told me would happen.

"Well, bless my soul, in no time, 'tall, there wuz aloud knockin' and, when I opened the door, there wuz old Kate Lipps, who lived 'bout three miles up alongside Witch Mountain. She sed, 'Howdy, Nan. I've come to git the lend of your wood cards.'*

"Now, Vic 'ud told me whatever I done not to lend nuthin' to nobody till the spell wuz broke er the witch'd have the power to witch me, so I sez, 'Nope, Kate, hit's already lent ter Bell Martin.'

"Now, I hain't fergot my manners, even effen I'm a messin' with a witch, so I axt her to come in the house and set by the fire to warm herself.

"She come in and set by the fire, and afore long she axt me fer a drink of water, as she wuz feelin' porely. I told her I didn't have a drap in the house, and this made her so mad thet she ups and storms outten the house a sight faster'n she'd come in.

"Atter she'd gone, the fire got real hot and I pulled thet plow pint outten the ashes and poured thet stump water and yarb mess onto hit. The steam from thet mess stunk up the house sumpthin' awful.

"Well, hit's the truth effen I ever told hit, thet lamb got as peart as ennythin' right away. But, hit did make me feel gloomy not long atter this when they found Old Kate Lipps all drawed up in a knot a layin' in the path outten Horse Chestnut Ridge, on Witch Mountain, daid as a doornail. I got to worryin; thet mebbe I didn't take thet plow pint outten the fire as soon as I orter, or mebbe I biled them henbane leaves a mite too long."

*See note on page 18.

A WITCH AND HER DWARF DAUGHTERS

Many years ago, a dilapidated, weather-beaten old house stood on the outskirts of a mountain village in southern West Virginia. This house appeared quite different on the inside. It was furnished with good furniture, and filled with shiny new gadgets. An old woman, Clytie Babb, and her two dwarf daughters, Nettie and Bittie, lived in the house. It was widely believed in the community that Clytie was a witch and her two daughters were her helpers, yet there was no proof that they had ever done any witching. Old Clytie had no means of making a living, but she and her strange daughters seemed to live well. People suspected that they lived on goods and money stolen from the nearby village of Welch.

Late one very cold evening, two men, travelling on foot from a distant mining camp, approached the house. The sun had set, and it was almost dark. They inquired of Clytie if she could spare them a bed for the night, as it was getting dark and they were too tired to continue their journey. Clytie told them they were welcome to what she had to offer, but that she was a poor woman with no husband.

Clytie showed them the room which they agreed was quite comfortable. She then introduced them to her weird daughters and asked them to sit down and make themselves comfortable while a meal was prepared.

As they waited for dinner, the two men—Eli Johnson and Jake Keller—wandered around the living room, astonished to find so many new and expensive items inside this shabby house. The meal they were served of vegetables, fruits and drinks had obviously come from a store. It was delicious and they ate heartily.

The two men were tired from their journey, excused themselves early and went to bed. Very soon Jake was snoring in a deep sleep. But, Eli had a queasy stomach and couldn't go to sleep. He tossed and turned, but sleep just wouldn't come. After some time, Jake ceased to snore, and a thick silence enveloped the room. Eli felt distinctly uneasy, and began to feel that the room was charged with something.

The clock struck twelve, and, through his open door, Eli saw

Based on the story "The Six Witches," published in the *Journal of American Folklore*, volume 32, number 3, 1919.

the three women appear in front of the fireplace in the living room. Clytie reached up the chimney and pulled out a large gourd. She took something out of it which Eli thought looked like a green frog skin. She unfolded this and removed a pinch of white powder which she sprinkled over each of their heads. She then refolded the skin, put it back in the gourd, and replaced the gourd in the chimney.

Clytie tossed her head back at a haughty angle and said in her wispy little voice, "Cum-tu, vo-si, to-vay, up and away." Up the chimney she went! Then, Nettie and Bittie repeated these words and followed their mother up the chimney.

By this time, Eli was trembling like a leaf in a breeze. His eyes bulged and his hair stood on end. He had never seen witches at work before. He wondered what would happen if he did the same things they had done. Now that they were gone and Jake was asleep, it wouldn't hurt to try. So, he got up, dressed, went to the chimney, and retrieved the gourd. He took a pinch of the white powder from the green skin, returned the gourd to its place, and sprinkled the powder on his head. Then, he said, "Cum-tu, vo-si, to-vay, up and away" just as the women had done. Up the chimney he flew!

When Eli landed, he was in a store in the village. He looked around and saw the three women. He went up to Clytie and asked her how they had gotten there and what they were doing. She ignored him and the three turned away without a word. Then, they mumbled some strange words which sounded like "Ga-tha, mo-go, ri-vitch," and out they all went, leaving Eli alone in the store.

Now, Eli had been so excited at finding them in the store that he had not listened very closely to the magic words they had uttered, and he wasn't sure whether the last word was "bi-vitch, vi-vitch, or wi-vitch." He tried "bi-vitch" first, soared to the ceiling, bumped his head and fell to the floor. He tried what he thought were the other two words, but had no better luck with them.

Eli was in a panic when daylight appeared. He was sure he would be arrested as a thief when the owner came to open the store. When the storekeeper did appear, he thought that Eli had hidden in the store before it had closed the night before. "I've been missing things from the store for a long time now, and I've caught you at last," said the storekeeper with satisfaction.

"Oh, no, it wasn't me. Give me a chance to explain," pleaded Eli. And he told the owner the whole fantastic tale of the night's happenings. Of course, he didn't believe a word of it, and, when Eli insisted it was the truth, he thought he was crazy and called the sheriff in.

Eli of course told the same story to the officers and they hooted at it and took him to jail. Finally, Eli was able to persuade them to go to Clytie's house and tell Jake where he was and what had happened. The storekeeper accompanied the sheriff to Clytie's, where he recognized many articles as having come from his store. He was positive he had never sold any of them to Clytie. Perhaps Eli had been telling the truth.

Clytie and her daughters were arrested and Eli was freed, with the proviso that he would testify at the trial. They were tried and convicted of being witches, of breaking and entering, and of theft.

Before the judge passed sentence on them, he asked if they had anything to say. Clytie asked permission to sing a song, which was granted. The three women sang about ten verses of "The Farmer's Curst Wife," then started again at the beginning. As they sang, they began to rise from the floor, out the door, higher and higher in the air until they could scarcely be seen. They sailed over the ridge and disappeared.

Each deputy who had been detailed to guard them immediately began to quarrel as to why the other one had not prevented this escape. They started to shoot into the air after the escaping witches, but the judge interceded and stopped them, lest they shoot each other or somebody else.

He ordered the sheriff to retrieve all the stolen goods from Clytie's house and return them to their owners. And, to prevent the witches from returning, he ordered them to set fire to the house and see that it was burned to the ground.

MORNING SICKNESS AND
PICKLED BEANS

Mountaineers who believed firmly in witchcraft thought that any old, wrinkled woman was a wicked witch who had sold her soul to the devil in exchange for magic powers with which to inflict disabling illnesses sudden death and a host of other misfortunes. These women often served as a convenient scapegoat. Polly Johnson tells of one such case:

"Old Sallie Sue Weyland wuz a strange kinda person, and some of the things she done made a lot of folks think thet she wuz a witch. You know, witches have to keep their magic spell on sumpthin' er somebody all the time to keep their powers. Now, Sallie Sue warn't really old, but folks called all witches 'old' so and so. Onct, when I went over to see Sallie Sue, she wuz a settin' with one young'un on one knee and t'other on t'other knee a goin' 'tum, tum, tum.' She wuz sorta trottin' em up and down on her knee and them young'uns wuz a goin' 'wheeny, wheeny, wheeny! sorta quare like. They wuzzen't 'zactly cryin, but jest a whindlin', you know.

"Now, I wuz curious 'bout them young'uns, so I axt Old Sal whut wuz the matter with 'em and whut she wuz a doin'. Sal told me, 'Oh, nuthin, Granny.' But, bless my corn shuckin' soul, the very next mornin', them two young'uns wuz both daid as doornails.

"Onct, one of Sallie's neighbors, Sadie Coggin, wuz big with her fust child. She got mornin' sickness so bad thet she spent a lot of time in bed, helpless. Most every time she wuz in bed, Old Sallie Sue 'ud come right up to her bed and pop her dirty finger in Sadie's eyes and nearly gouge 'em outten her haid.

"Well, Sadie's old man, Jonathan, got sick and tired of these monkey shines, so one day he made out like he's a goin' away off somers. Then, he snuck back to his place, and thet night he tuk Sadie's place in the bed. All at onct, Sallie Sue popped right down the chimney and outten the hearth and made a bee-line torge the bed and started to gouge her eyes. But, Jonathan jest grabbed Sallie

Collected by Emory L. Hamilton, Wise, Virginia, October 30, 1940. This story was told to him by Mrs. Polly Johnson, of Wise.

Sue's finger in his mouth and moughty nigh bit hit clean off. She hollered loud enuf to wake the daid, and tuk off right up thet chimney.

"In a few days, there wuz a workin'* up the holler at a neighbor's place and Jonathan and Sadie both went. Ever since she'd got big with the young'un, Sadie 'ud been a longin' fer some pickled beans,** and Jonathan knowed thet these folks 'ud have 'em fer dinner.

"When dinner time come, bless my soul, who should pop up but Sallie Sue Weyland. When she come into the room, she had her finger all tied up with a rag. Jonathan axt, 'Sallie, whut's wrong with your finger?'

"She sed, 'Oh, I wuz a cuttin' some cabbage and I made a mislick and cut hit.'

"'Cabbage, hell,' Jonathan exploded, lookin' her straight in the eye. 'You know damned well thet I nearly chawed thet finger off t'other night when you come to my house to pester Sadie.'

"Sallie Sue wuz flabbergasted and didn't know whut to say, so she didn't answer Jonathan. When they went to the table, Jonathan got the dish of pickled beans and set 'em down by Sadie's plate and sed, 'Now, here, you jest eat every one of them effen you want to.'

"But, Old Sallie Sue seed whut he's up to, and she jest politely got up and fetched them pickled beans to t'other side of the table. Now, this made Jonathan madder than a wounded bar, and he biled over. He got up, went to t'other end of the table, grabbed them pickled beans, toted 'em back and set 'em by Sadie's plate. Sallie Sue seed thet she'd been outsmarted, and she wuz fightin' mad, too, but she couldn't use none of her powers, kase a witch cain't do nuthin' when they're mad.

"Now, Sallie Sue's old man, Timothy Weyland, seed all of this and he smelt a mouse. When he got Sallie Sue back to their cabin, he told her he'd beat the hell outten her effen she didn't tell him whut wuz a goin' on. So she told him thet she wuz a witch and thet she'd been a messin' 'round with Sadie. Timothy promised he wouldn't beat her effen she'd quit her witchin'.

*Mountain people gathered at different homes to help each other accomplish big tasks that had to be done in a short time, such as harvesting, stringing beans, peeling apples, killing hogs, quilting, log rolling and house raising. Usually, these activities—called "workings"—were made into social affairs often climaxed with a big feast, drinking and sometimes dancing.

**Pickled beans are prepared from green or snap beans which are parboiled and then placed in a strong brine solution in large crocks or barrels. After a few weeks, they become pickled.

"But, onct a witch trades her soul to the Devil, he won't trade back and he'll beat a witch effen she balks 'bout doin' his work, ard he made Sallie Sue keep on a witchin'. She witched some cows, then made some sheep die, and folks told Timothy thet Sallie Sue wuz still witchin' and he orter do sumpthin' 'bout hit.

"Timothy studied over hit fer some days. Then, one day he tuk his rifle-gun and made out like he's a goin' squirrel huntin'. He slipped back to the cabin, pushed thet gun through a crack in the cabin, and shot Old Sallie Sue daid."

COFFIN NAILS

As the cold, black shroud of a February night dissolved into a soggy gray dawn, Billy Jack Mays rolled out of bed feeling as gloomy as a black rain cloud and totally unprepared to face another day. Patrick Addington said Billy Jack told him, "I'd rolled and tossed all night and got nary a bit of sleep. When I glanced under my bed in the mornin', I seen the broom under there. You know, a witch'll come where there's a broom, but won't cross hit. But, onct a broom is in their path, they'll pester and hag ennybody on t'other side of the broom. So, I jest knowed my miseries and shakes wuz kase a witch 'ud ride me all night long."

Patrick went on to tell the rest of Billy Jack's story:

"Now, Billy Jack wuz a high strung onery old codger, and he 'lowed his old woman, Cynthia Fay 'ud put thet broom there to bewitch him. Lately, he'd been under the weather and Cynthia Fay 'ud acted like she couldn't put up with him. He jest knowed she wanted to make a ghost outten him. The very idee made him madder'n a hemmed-in wildcat, but he didn't know 'zactly whut to do. Finally, he hobbled over to Devil's Foot Branch to talk to Eli Culbertson, who wuz a warlock.

"Eli told Billy Jack to hang a checkered cloth over the keyhole every night and to put the broom in frunt of the door. He 'splained thet witches 'ud have to stop at the door to count the checks in the cloth and the straws in the broom and afore they'd get through, hit 'ud be daylight and witches run away as soon as the roosters crow. Also, he wuz to sprinkle a little salt and pepper in his shoes when he went to bed.

"These tricks to skeer the witches away worked jest like Eli sed they would, so fer quite a spell Billy Jack slept like a baby and got moughty peart and spry. Now, he 'lowed this bothered his old woman, kase he felt she wanted to git shet of him ennyhow.

"One mornin', when Billy Jack jumped outten bed and dumped the salt and pepper outten his shoes, out rolled a big ten-penny nail. Now, this really made a sinkin' feelin' way down in

Collected by James Taylor Adams, Big Laurel, Virginia, August 17, 1941. Told to him by Patrick Addington, of Big Laurel, who first heard it from his grandfather, who was a neighbor of Billy Jack Mays.

the pit of his stomach, kase he'd heard sumpthin' 'bout witches a killin' people with nails. The fust thing thet come to his mind wuz to whup the livin' hell outten Cynthia Fay, kase he knowed she wuz in cahoots with them witches. Hit looked like the naked-skinned truth thet she'd been up to her tricks agin. But, he studied over hit a while and then he went back to see Eli Culbertson.

"Eli told Billy Jack thet one way a witch'll kill a person wuz by drivin' nails into his coffin till there's enuf to hold the lid on tight. Then, the person jest withered away and died. The way they drive 'em in the coffin, he sed, wuz to drop a nail in a person's shoes. He told Billy Jack to go home and pick up all the nails 'round the place and, at midnight, at the dark of the moon, to take 'em to the woods and bury 'em alongside a hickory tree, and never to bring no more nails home.

"Billy Jack done jest as Eli 'ud told him. 'Twarn't long afore he got up one mornin', when he dumped the salt and pepper outten his shoes, and out come a whole passel of nails. Now, he really 'lowed sumpthin' wuz in the wind, kase witches couldn't git into the cabin with thet broom and cloth at the door. Hit shore looked like Cynthia Fay wuz the witch thet wuz a usin' him strange, so he jest cut loose and faulted her to her face.

"Course, she jest fumed and fussed and swore she didn't know nuthin' 'bout them nails. She 'lowed the young'uns 'ud been a playin' with 'em on the hearth the night afore atter he'd went to bed. She reckoned mebbe they'd drapped 'em in his shoes. Now, he knowed he'd been foxed, kase there wuzzen't no nails in the house, less she'd brung 'em in.

"I still recollect the hang-dog look on Old Billy Jack's face the last time I seed him. He sed, 'Oh, well! Betwixt my old woman and the witches, I know I hain't long fer this world. The Devil's a goin' to git me. Them nails in my shoes last night makes eleven in my lifetime so fur. You know, hit takes jest thirteen nails to nail down the lid of a coffin, and then you jest up and die sudden like.'"

MATILDA REFUSES THE KNIFE

Most uneducated people believed firmly in witchcraft. When any illness or body disorder such as boils or tumors occurred, these people accused supposed witches of casting spells on them. That is what Matilda Sweet, a former slave from Suffolk, Virginia, thought when she developed boils under her arms. Here is how she told it:

"I've been conjured onct, and that's a plenty. That there conjure spell brung three big risins [lumps] under both of my arms. There wuz three bumps under my right arm and four under the left. They'se so big that the petticoat that I uster tie 'round me up under my arms wouldn't reach and I had to hold it up with straps over my shoulders.

"I couldn't figger out who wuz conjurin' me. They's only one woman who ever come to my house, and she ain't got no cause to conjure me. My old man, Ned, sent me to the root and yarb doctor, Old Doc Andrews, to see what could be done. Well, sir, he musta been a mind reader, a fortune teller and a doctor all rolled up into one, 'cause he told me 'zactly what happened. He sed, 'T'other night, you dreamt of an open drawer at home. The next night you dreamt of an open grave. A coffin was put in the grave and stayed there nine days.'

"Doc Andrews went on: 'You woke up and roused all the chillun and axt them who's been here, but them chillun all sed, "Mammy, 'tain't nobody been here." Then you sed, "Take that bucket to the well and wash it good and clean and bring me back a drink of water."'

"But, Doc Andrews told me that I didn't drink none of the water 'cause, if I hadda, I'd a died right then and there. He told me I had been conjured to die on the ninth day, but he sed, 'Tilda, if you'll give back to that conjure woman what she's give to you, I can cure you. But, if you don't do 'zactly as I say, you're goin' to be a dead duck in nine days.'

"Doc Andrews handed me a long knife and says, 'Do you want to take it and use it on the witch that conjured you?'

"I sed, 'No, Doc, I don't want nuthin' to do with it; and I handed it back to him.

Collected by Cornelia Berry, of Lynchburg, Virginia, May 15, 1939. Told to her by Matilda (Ma Sweet) Perry, an ex-slave of Suffolk, Virginia.

"He sed, 'Tilda, don't you see how to git rid of the spell that's been put to you? You jest put it back on her with this knife.'

"But, I sed, 'No, Doc, Heaven's been promised to me and I ain't got no mind to do nuthin' to break that promise. I b'lieve in God, and I'm lookin' to go to Heaven, 'cause He's prepared a place for me. I ain't goin' to mess up my chance by givin' no spell to nobody.'

"'Bout that time, a cart drove up and Doc Andrews sez: 'Scuse me, Tilda, I want to see how far these folks've come.' He tuk a horseshoe and tied it up over the door. He swung it in, then out, and, when it slowed down, he sed: 'Tilda, you've come twenty miles and they've come thirty, so they've come to fetch you.'

"I sez, 'All right, Doc, I guess I'd better go with 'em.'

"Then, Doc Andrews sez, 'Wait! If you won't take the knife, I'd better give you some medicine.'

"So he give me a bottle of stinkin', ugly, green medicine and he sez, 'When you get home, take a dose, then another jest before you go to bed every night as long as it lasts. On the ninth day, the conjure woman who hagged you will come and confess. Look for her between noon and midnight.'

"So, I went home and took Doc Andrews' medicine jest like he told me to do. Well, bless my soul! On the ninth day betwixt three and four o'clock, Caroline Crip commenced hollerin' and runnin' up and down the neighborhood. She wuz a singin':

Oh yes! Oh yes!
I've been conjurin'.
Oh yes! Oh yes!
I've been killin'.
Fer no cause t'all,
Fer no cause t'all
In dis wide world.

"My old man, Ned got madder'n all hell. We could hear Caroline Crip a way crost them woods singin' all day, 'cause she couldn't help confessin'. Her voice kept gittin' nigher and nigher, and Ned kept gittin' madder'n madder. He sez, 'I swear to God, Tilda, if ennybody ever conjures you agin, I'm goin' to kill them deader than a doornail. And I'm gonta kill that woman.'

"Ned went and got his ax, and wuz shakin' he wuz so mad. I wuz skeered most to death and I begged him not to do nuthin' to Caroline. But, he didn't give in till I set on his lap and sed, 'Ain't I allus been a good woman to you, and done what you've told me? Now, if you kill that woman, they'll take you away to the pen and I won't have no man, and our chillun won't have no pappy, and the house won't have no haid.'

"Ned seed the light, and when old Caroline come into the clearin', he handed me the ax and went out raging to the spring.

"That medicine old Doc Andrews give me shore wuz workin' powerful strong on old Caroline Crip. She stumbled into our yard singin' at the top of her voice,

> Oh yes, Oh yes!
> I conjured you,
> I conjured you.
> No cause in the wide world,
> No cause in the wide world;
> Give me your hand,
> Give me your hand.

"I give her my hand, and I've been all right ever since, 'ceptin' them places where the risins wuz. They gits sore and itches a little every onct in a while."

WHO SHOT MIZE THORPE?

Mrs. Lula Drewry, of Ferrum, Virginia:

"I was a single girl teaching in a one-room school about 1888 out on Shooting Crick. This was an isolated community in Franklin County. While teaching there, I lived in the home of Kevin and Eileen Linklater. After one year of teaching, I married one of the mountain boys, Craig Drewry, and we settled down near the Linklaters.

"After I had been living in the Linklater home for a few weeks, I became intrigued by a very fine rifle which hung on a set of elk horns on the wall. Kevin Linklater was a great hunter and a good marksman, but he never took that particular gun with him on his frequent hunting trips. I was puzzled by this, so one day I asked Eileen if the gun was in good shape and why Kevin never used it.

"'Honey child,' she answered, 'thet's Kevin's bizziness. I 'low effen he'd a wanted you to know 'bout thet gun, he'd a told you. I figger he jest don't like to talk 'bout hit. Jest you axt him and see whut he sez.'

"Now, this just made me more curious about this special gun, but I thought perhaps Kevin didn't know me well enough to trust me, so I didn't ask him. I was careful to do everything I could to make him respect me and trust me.

"As the school year drew near its end and it became known that I was going to marry one of the local boys, I asked Kevin about the gun. I was flattered and surprised when he took me into his confidence and told me the story:

'Many years ago, my nephew, Mize Thorpe, kilt his brother, Nick. They brung him to trial, and sence hit wuz sech a common, clear murder thet everybody 'lowed he'd go to the pen fer life or mebbe even get his neck stretched. But, Mize got him a slick lawyer from the city, and thet lawyer 'splained hit in court so thet the jury warn't 'zactly shore thet Mize had done hit, and effen he did, thet hit wuz an accident. So, the judge and jury turned him scott free. Everybody wuz flabbergasted. For a while, hit looked like the folks

Collected by Raymond H. Sloan, Rocky Mount, Virginia, March 27, 1939. Told to him by P.T. Sloan, a rural mail carrier, about his aunt Lula Sloan Drewry, who lived in Franklin County, in a community near the Patrick County line known as Shooting Creek, about 1888.

183

wuz a goin' to take the bit in their own mouth and hang him, but they didn't.

'Then, as time passed, they wuz signs thet Mize 'ud got to be a witch and wuz a conjurin' folks and things. So, I went over to Greasy Crick, nigh Witch Mountain, in Carrol County, and talked to Josh Seay who's a good conjure man, and he told me whut to do to take away Mize's magic so he wouldn't be a witch no more. He sed I could make a wax doll thet looked like him and stick pins in hit, er I could make me a silver bullet, and draw his picture on a tree and shoot hit with thet bullet.

'Now, I knowed deep down in my heart thet Mize 'ud kilt his brother kase he wuz jealous of him. I vowed I'd git even with Mize and I've jest been a bidin' my time. I melted down a quarter and made me a silver bullet fer thet rifle-gun, loaded hit, and hung hit up there ready to use when the time is right. No indeedy, tain't no use to git shet of this witchin' when I wanted to see thet devil daid.'

"Kevin had grown more and more agitated as he talked, and, before I could question him further, he got up abruptly and left the room. That rifle-gun remained untouched for as long as I stayed there. About a year later, Mize Thorpe was found dead back in the woods with a bullet wound through his heart. They never found out who killed Mize. Course, I don't think they tried very hard, since everybody seemed to be relieved that he was dead.

"It wasn't too many years before Kevin died, and my husband and I went to his wake. As soon as I got in the house, I noticed that the rifle-gun was missing from the elk's horns where it had rested all the time I stayed there. I didn't ask anybody about it, nor did I ever tell anybody, not even my husband, what Kevin had told me. But I think I know how Mize Thorpe met his end."

THE WITCH OF CENECU

Eutiquio Holquin, the healthy young son of a Mexican immigrant, lived in San Elizario, Texas. No one could excel this handsome young man in dancing the fandango. He was usually among the winners on Sunday afternoons when the young men gathered to play games.

Eutiquio was admired by all the young men and adored by the young ladies, but he loved only one girl, Juanita, daughter of a prominent landowner, Pedro Sabinas. Juanita returned Eutiquio's love, but Pedro did not want his beautiful daughter to marry this peasant boy, whom he did not consider her equal. Therefore, he did all in his power to prevent them from seeing each other.

It was rumored in the community that Pedro was having an illicit love affair with Hilda Torres, a well-known bruja [witch] of Cenecu. It was more likely, however, that Hilda held Pedro under a magic spell.

During a dance one night, someone stole one of Eutiquio's gloves. This upset Juanita very much, because she remembered that a wise woman had once told her that if a bruja took a person's glove, stroked it on the belly of her cat nine times, dipped it in the blood of a toad, and then buried it, as it rotted, the owner would be bewitched. But, Eutiquio refused to be worried, and teased Juanita about her superstitious belief.

However, thirteen days after Eutiquio's glove had been stolen, he was stricken quite suddenly with a strange illness. His arms and legs became paralyzed, and he lay helpless in bed. Soon, he had wasted away to a mere skeleton and was at the brink of death.

Eutiquio's mother, with the help and advice of a neighboring granny doctor, treated him with every remedy they knew. They gave him tonics of hot catnip, dog-fennel and snakeroot. They plastered his helpless limbs with crushed puffballs mixed with soot and grease from a young calf, and drenched him with stone-root tea. All of this did absolutely no good.

In the meantime, Pedro had placed severe restrictions on Juanita to prevent her seeing Eutiquio. To get around this, she

A Mexican Witch tale, published in the *Texas Folklore Society Journal*, Volume 10, number 3, 1935.

disguised herself as a nun and came to see him. When she arrived, Juanita suggested that he had been bewitched. She was sure that his glove had been taken by a bruja, possibly Hilda Torres. She confided that on the same night that his glove had been stolen, someone had stolen an amulet from her neck while she slept. This amulet had been handed down from oldest daughter to oldest daughter in her family for generations. It had been placed around her neck at her christening as a charm against evil spirits, since it contained a magic stone. Without this protective charm, Juanita was afraid that something terrible would happen to her, too, and she told Eutiquio that she was going to consult a wise woman to find out how to break the spell over him and find her amulet.

That night, Eutiquio's family was startled from its sleep by his cries, "Look! Look! I have her. Come quick! She is dragging me away!"

Indeed, his mother and sister could see that he was being dragged toward the door, but they could see no one. Suddenly, he fell near the door, and his mother and sister managed to get him back in bed with great difficulty.

"Did you see her?" he whimpered, when he had recovered a little from the shock. "It was the bruja from Cenecu. I felt some evil thing put its invisible hands on my shoulder and pull me out of bed. I cried out and caught hold of her hands, so she dragged me with her as she tried to escape. I wouldn't let go until she bent my fingers backward and my strength left me. Then, I could see her and I recognized her. It was Hilda Torres. I am as sure of this as the morning sunrise."

The next morning, Juanita, this time disguised as a peddler, came to report on her visit with the wise woman. She heard of Eutiquio's experience of the night before with pity and terror. She explained to the family that the wise woman had told her that a bruja's soul could leave her body, roam around doing evil deeds, and then return. She was sure that that was what happened to Hilda Torres, since Eutiquio's mother and sister had seen no one.

Juanita relayed the advice of the wise woman. First, they must all kneel down in prayer and recite the seven Psalms of Pentinence. This they solemnly did.

Second, the wise woman had sent instructions to Eutiquio's mother to kill a black rooster and cut out its heart. Thirteen pins were to be stuck in the heart, and it was to be put on the fire to roast at exactly midnight. She did all this, and when the heart was well roasted, both Eutiquio and his mother saw something shapeless appear near the window.

After this, the spell seemed to be broken, and Eutiquio began to improve. Juanita, variously disguised as a nun, a peddler, and a beggar, came every day to bring him nourishing meats, fruits and milk. As his strength returned, Eutiquio vowed that as soon as he was able to ride his horse, he would go to Cenecu and kill the witch who had almost destroyed him.

Eutiquio arrived at Cenecu early one evening. He had no difficulty in finding the bruja's cottage, since the smoke from all the houses was blowing with the wind, but the smoke from her house was blowing against the wind. A girl answered his knock and told him that her mother was not at home. When he inquired where she was, the girl said she had gone to decorate the church in preparation for a fiesta. Eutiquio didn't believe a word of this. He pushed past the girl and searched the house, but the bruja wasn't there. He demanded that the girl tell him where her mother kept her talismans. The girl refused until he threatened to take his quirt [whip] to her, at which time she showed him an immense gourd under the bed.

Eutiquio dragged the gourd in front of the fire and removed its contents. There were rag dolls of every size and description. Some had thorns stuck in their heads, others in their eyes, stomachs, arms or legs. Each one represented some victim of the bruja's evil powers.

The gourd also contained a witch's ladder,*a dried toad's foot, a wisp of baby hair, three mad-stones, and a beautiful diamond-studded amulet which fit the description Juanita had given him of her stolen one. He clasped the amulet tightly in his hand and asked himself if this charm had been the price the bruja had exacted from Pedro for destroying his daughter's undesirable suitor? He burned with rage at the thought.

Eutiquio stirred up the fire and dumped the gourd's contents on it. As they started to burn, the bruja ran into the house, screaming at the top of her voice. She cornered Eutiquio, and he cringed against the wall, chilled by surprise and fear. He raised his quirt and started lashing her with it. Twice it landed on her forehead and cut a small cross on it. As the cuts started to bleed, the bruja fell to the floor, sobbing. With the burning of her talismans and the drawing of blood, her magic powers had been destroyed.

Eutiquio rushed out of the house, mounted his horse, and rode at top speed to Juanita's house. He returned the amulet to her, and

*See note on page 77.

they confronted Pedro with it. Pedro confessed to his wicked scheme with the bruja to get rid of Eutiquio, but he promised that if they would forgive him, he would not only give them permission to marry, but would give them a sumptuous wedding. They agreed to this, had the most elegant wedding San Elizario had ever seen, and lived happily ever after.

A CONJURE BOTTLE IN THE CHIMNEY

Keith Brian McMinnis, who owned a large farm near Mantee, Virginia, had a whole houseful of children. One of his girls, Millie, had always been strong and healthy until she was about twenty-five years old. Then, all of a sudden, she began to have crazy spells, and some kind of seizures. The family lived in an old log cabin with a wide chimney of logs on the outside; and the inside was made of rocks held together with mud. They had to watch Millie all the time to prevent her from jumping into the fireplace when she would have these spasms.

A city doctor came to see her, but he didn't know what ailed her, and his medicine did her no good. She got worse and worse. The spells came more often, and got more severe. Some of the neighbors said that she acted like somebody who'd been witched. They advised Keith to go over to Winjiner and get Mize Hoge. Mize was a conjure man.

Now, Keith McMinnis didn't believe in witches and conjure men, but he figured he didn't have anything to lose, so he sent for Mize Hoge. Mize came and examined Millie, then waited for her to have one of her spells. He watched her trying to get into the fire, and right off he said, "Keith, it sure looks like she has been conjured. I don't think it's the fire that's bothering her. You get to work and find out what's up that chimney."

At first, they were afraid to investigate, but after a while Mize said, "If you're not going to do something right off, I'm going back home tomorrow."

So, Millie's oldest brothers, Ben and Milt, began to examine the chimney carefully, and they found a bottle hanging down the chimney. They had begun to believe in witches, and were afraid to touch it, so they yelled for Mize. He climbed up the ladder and got the bottle.

When he opened it, he found a little cross, a small ball of hair, and a small bone which looked like a rat's spine. There was also some powdered stuff that looked as if it might have been herbs. Mize knew just what to do with all this. He took the bone and put it

Collected by Roscoe Lewis, Hampton, Virginia, May 6, 1940. Told to him by Milton McMinnis, Millie's grandson.

under the doorstep. Then, he poured the rest of the stuff in the fire and stirred it until it had all burned. Then, he corked the empty bottle and put it in his pocket.

He told Keith that the bottle had been Millie's trouble. She had been witched, and he could tell by what was in it that it was Old Mal Pilynor who had put the hag on her.

By this time, Keith had started to believe in witches and spells, so he told Mize, "I'll give you most anything I've got if you'll just make Millie like she once was, and then drive away the witch that bothered her."

So, Mize said he'd do this for five dollars, if they would take him back home. Early next morning, Ben and Milt went with Mize to Winjiner. They had to cross a river on a ferry to get there. When they got out in the middle of the river, Mize said, "Here goes Old Mal Pilynor," and dropped the empty witch bottle in the water.

Sure enough, in a few days, old Mal Pilynor and her old man pulled up stakes and moved away. They never came back again. Millie got well and never had any more spells.

THE APPLE PEELING

It was a well established custom in the Cumberland Mountains of southeastern Kentucky for the women of a community to assemble at one another's homes to help with such chores as peeling apples, making apple butter, stringing beans, and quilting. So, when Old Nan Seeley let it be known throughout Red Bird Valley that she wanted to have an apple peeling on Friday, about fifteen women showed up at her house early in the morning. To tell the truth, none of them dared stay away, because Old Nan was thought to be a witch and all of them were afraid that, if they did, it would invite trouble.

Although Old Nan was fully aware of her besmirched reputation, she tried to put up a good front. She displayed her hospitality as soon as they had all arrived by serving them milk and cookies. Before long, the milk supply ran low, and Old Nan picked up the pitcher and slipped out the back door to get a fresh supply.

Hattie Mullins, who was a meddlesome busybody, was very curious to know where Nan was getting the milk from, since she didn't have a cow. So, Hattie sneaked into the kitchen, hid behind the door, and peeped through the crack. She saw Nan pull on a knotted string which pulled down a peg on the wall just outside the kitchen door. A stream of fresh milk poured out from the peg into the pitcher. Hattie was afraid of being caught snooping, so she left her observation post before she saw what Nan had done to cut off the milk flow. Nan returned to the front room and served the women all the fresh milk they could drink.

Later in the morning, Nan went to her back yard to stir the apples cooking in the big iron kettle to make apple butter. Hattie Mullins wanted another drink of milk, but she found the pitcher was empty. It occurred to her that she might try the same milk source Nan had used, so she slipped quietly out the door, pulled the knotted string and filled the pitcher from the peg. Then, just as she thought Nan had done, she removed the string and put the peg back in its original position. But, to her dismay, the milk continued to flow. Turn the peg as she might, out came milk and more milk.

Based on a story by James Bickley, age seventy-eight, of Pinsfork, Kentucky, June 10, 1940, who had heard his grandfather tell the story when he was a little boy.

Hattie panicked, and yelled to the women to bring her some pans to catch the milk. They brought her all the pails and pans they could find in the kitchen, but soon they were all full. They went back and emptied the apples on the floor and brought her the apple containers, but soon they, too, were filled.

At the height of the confusion, Old Nan appeared. She was white with rage and scowling like thunder. In a voice that shook the roof, she shrieked, "You damned idiots, why can't you mind your own business? Don't you know that you have drawn all the milk from every cow in the Valley? Now not one of you will get a drop of milk from your cows tonight."

Nan put the string back on the milk peg and turned off the stream of milk. She removed the string, and made Hattie and the others pour all the milk out on the ground. Then, she took the string inside and threw it on the fire. It spewed and cracked and, as it burned, each knot exploded like a shot and splashed hot embers about the room. Each explosion released the most foul and putrid odor they had ever smelled. They began to cough and sneeze and ran from the house. Nan called out after them, "You'll all pay dearly for this as long as you live!"

THE CHAINED DRAGON

A girl by the name of Bessie Sue Boggs fell in love with a handsome young mountain boy, and he sed he wanted to marry her. But jest as they started a makin' plans, all of a sudden he lost interest. 'Course, Bessie Sue got awful upset, and then jealous and madder'n all git out when somebody told her thet her feller wuz a goin' to see Rosa Jean Whittle. She studied 'bout hit fer a long time and decided she'd get even with Rosa Jean fer takin' her feller. She talked to other folks 'bout hit, and made out thet the onliest way she could do hit wuz to be made a witch fer a spell.

One day, a big, black cat showed up at her cabin. She fed and petted hit, but hit wuz wild and soon left. Then, seven days atter this, the cat come back agin. She fed and petted hit and tried to win hit over, but hit went away agin. Three days later, hit come back, and, as she petted hit, Bessie Sue sed she wisht she could turn into a black cat so she could scratch Rosa Jean's eyes out. Well, will wonders never cease! Jest as she sed this, thet cat turned into an old woman. She wuz stooped and wuz wropt in a long black dress. She had a furrowed face, beady black eyes and long, crooked teeth. She sed, "I make out frum whut you sed thet you'd like to be a witch."

Now, Bessie Sue wuzzen't 'spectin' nuthin' like this, so she wuz too skeered and s'prised to answer. Then, she kinda got her feet on the ground agin. She wuz so jealous and mad at losin' her feller thet she forgot her fear of the old woman and sed, "Yep, I'd give nigh ennythin', even my soul, effen I could be a witch fer jest a little whet."

The old woman sed, "Effen you git to be a witch, you'll have to serve the Devil fer the rest of yore life. Now, effen you're willin' to do thet, hit won't be too hard to make a witch outten you, and I'll holp you to do hit."

Bessie Sue studied on hit a little, then she told the old crone, "Yep, I'll serve the Devil the rest of my life effen I can jest git my feller back."

The old woman stopped a minute and sed, "Well, the fust thing you orter do is to git a new cake of soap thet hain't been used. Go

Collected by James Taylor Adams, Big Laurel, Virginia, July 2, 1940. Told to him by Melia Hayes, of St. Paul, Virginia, then seventy-eight years old, who said her grandfather had told her the story forty years prior.

outten the hills and find a branch of clear water thet runs due east outten a spring. Wait till the thirteenth of the month and then, jest one minute atter midnight, go to this branch and wash yore hands and belly with thet soap. Then, stand on yore left foot and jump acrost the branch. Jump back the same way, and do this seven times. Betwixt each jump say, 'I wish my soul as free of the grace of God as my hands and belly air free of dirt.' Do all this fer the next six nights. Then, on the seventh night, I'll come back and tell you whut to do next."

The old woman then changed back into a black cat and scampered away. Bessie Sue had her doubts 'bout all of this. She wondered effen atter she got her feller back she might some way quit bein' a witch. She argued with herself a long whet, then at last she sed to herself, "Shucks! Hit's worth a try." Atter all, the Devil hisself wuz the one who'd have to change her into a witch, and folks wuz allus outsmartin' the Devil.

So, Bessie Sue headed up Lick Branch and walked up the holler nigh onto a mile till she found a spring at the head of the branch. She come back home and waited till the thirteenth of the month, which wuz on a Friday. Then, she slipped away with her cake of new-made soap, up the little branch, to the spring, and done jest as the old woman had told her to do. She done this fer six nights in a row.

On the morning of the seventh day, Bessie Sue set down on her doorstep a wonderin' whut would happen next, when lo and behold: the biggest toad she'd ever seed jumped right outten the weeds and started a hoppin' torge her. This skeered the livin' daylights outten her and she jumped up and hollered and started to run into the cabin. But, afore she could move, thet toad turned into the old crone who had come afore as a black cat. The old woman cackled 'cause Bessie Sue 'ud been so skeered of a toad and sed, "Chile, you hain't got nuthin' to be afeard of. On Friday night, you'll have to do one more thing afore you can be a real witch. Meet me at the crossroads down near the graveyard then."

Atter she'd told Bessie Sue whut to do, the old hag changed back into a toad and, with one big hop, disappeared into the tall weeds. At midnight on Friday, Bessie Sue slipped through the woods and crept along the narrer path to the graveyard. She wuz scared stiff, and thought she seed sumpthin' behind every tombstone ready to jump out at her. Then, she realy did see sumpthin' move on top of one of the stones. She jest froze in her tracks too skeered to run. Right before her very eyes, a big beetle jumped down offen the tombstone, and, as hit teched the ground, hit turned into the old witch. She tuk Bessie Sue's tremblin' hand and sed, "Now, don't be skeered, chile, jest come 'long with me."

She led Bessie Sue up a narrer holler through thick bushes and tall briar vines to an old run-down cabin. When they went into the cabin, Bessie Sue spied a shuttle hole to the loft with a ladder to hit a standin' agin the wall. The old crone whispered low, "Now, chile, you jest climb thet ladder and crawl through thet shuttle hole into the loft. No matter whut you see, don't you git skeered. Nuthin's a goin' to harm a hair on yore haid."

Bessie Sue was skeered outten her wits, and she 'lowed she'd been trapped. But, the old woman could kill her effen she didn't do as she wuz told, so she climbed fearfully up the ladder and laid down on her belly to wait fer whut would happen next.

Hit wuzzen't long afore she seed sumpthin' a crawlin' torge her. Hit had big eyes thet looked like two boiled eggs, and they'se a shinin' like balls of fire. Hit wuz a draggin' a chain thet rattled everytime hit moved, and the sparks 'ud fly jest like the chain wuz red hot.

Bessie Sue laid there, not movin a muscle. She figgered she wuz a goin' to be tied up with thet chain and burned to death. As thet monster got closer and closer to her, she couldn't keep still enny longer and hollered at the top of her voice, "Lord! Have mercy on me!"

Jest as she hollered, them floor boards tilted and she fell through the loft to the floor of the cabin. She landed feet first and sprained her ankle and skinned up her legs. But she wuz so skeered thet she didn't feel no pain. She jumped up and lit out a shuck* down the holler torge home through the bushes and briars jest like the Devil wuz a nippin' at her heels every step of the way.

The next day, her face wuz all scratched and swole, her legs wuz blue and scratched, and she wuz a sight to see. When she 'splained to her family whut had happened, they didn't b'lieve her at fust. But, she swore to 'em thet hit wuz the truth effen ever she told hit, and they all got madder'n hornets.

Right away, her oldest brother, Mart, got a quarter and moulded him a silver bullet. Then, he loaded hit into his rifle-gun and tuk off in a turkey trot torge the old witch's place. He called her to the door and shot her daid as a hammer. Then, he set the cabin on fire to git shet of her body.

Well, sir, the smoke frum thet burnin' cabin 'ud hardly blowed

*See note on page 71.

away afore Bessie Sue's feller bobbed up. He sed he'd never been to see Rosa Jean Whittle, kase he didn't like her. He 'splained thet the same old witch thet 'ud tricked her had spelled him. She'd come to him as a purty young gal with pearly white teeth and golden hair. He went to her place a sparkin' her a good many times, but he 'lowed sumthin' wuz wrong with her. One night, he slipped back to the cabin and saw her turn back into an old crone. Atter thet, he tried to stay away frum her, but her spell wuz too tight on him, and she made him go to see her most every night. Now thet she wuz dead, the spell wuz broke. He had come to axt effen Bessie Sue 'ud marry up with him.

VERMIN AND HAGGED FOOTPRINTS

Mrs. Virginia Shepard, of Norfolk, Virginia, tells this story about her stepfather:

"My stepfather, Phillip Hunter, of Chesapeake, was a former slave. He developed boils all over his buttocks, so he went to a doctor who gave him a jar of foul-smelling salve to rub on them. When he had done this a few times, them risins all burst and live maggott-like things come out of them and crawled all over the floor. This scared the living daylights out of him, and he knew he'd been witched. So, he high-tailed it over to see Zac Wampler, who was a witch doctor. Zac told him what to do, but warned him that the witch would make a ghost out of him before nine days had passed if he didn't do exactly like he was told.

"First, Phillip got a bottle and filled it with stump water that he got from way back in the Dismal Swamp. Then, he cut a little bit of hair from under his right armpit and put it in the bottle. He added a smidgen of salt and a small chunk of his toenail. Then, he cut a sliver from his shirttail and put that in the bottle. At the dark of the moon at midnight, he sneaked around to his front doorstep and buried the bottle under it so he'd step over it every time he came into the house.

"I'll declare, this mess sure did work a magic spell. It kept them witches away from this house for a long time, and his boils all went away and the sore places got well.

"But, by and by, he got poorly again. This time, he couldn't stomach food, he couldn't sleep, he'd fidget, he got all addle-brained, and he was jest pining away. So, he figgered he was witched again, and went to see Zac Wampler about it.

"Now, this was a humdinger and at first old Zac was stumped. He tried all his conjure tricks, but none of 'em worked. Then, he thought mebbe his cards would help, so he put his deck of cards on the table and got out a little bottle with a live bug in it which he put on the table, too. He tied a string to the neck of the bottle, and started asking Phillip exactly what ailed him and for how long.

"Then, he shuffled the cards and asked Phillip to cut them. He

Collected by Roscoe Lewis, Hampton, Virginia, May 15, 1939. Told to him by Mrs. Hayes Shepard, of Norfolk, Virginia.

read the cards, and then looked at the bug in the bottle. He called it his 'Walkin Boy' and pulled the string to make him move. Whichever the direction the bug moved in was the way to go to find the witch.

"Old Zac, grinning like a coon, said, 'Phillip, you're under the spell of that witch again. The witch what put them crawling vermin in you lives on the edge of the Dismal Swamp, jest back of Hickory. He's Old Hurd Poins. Now, when you put them things in your witch bottle and hid it under your doorstep, you got Hurd all hot and bothered 'cause he couldn't get inside the cabin to you. Now, he's trying to get you in his power again.'

"'My Walkin' Boy and my cards tell me that he got a dab of dirt out of the graveyard near where you live and he's scattered it where you've walked in it. If we don't break this spell before wolf moon* you'll be a goner. Right now, he's trying to get some dirt out of the tracks of your left foot. He'll take this over to the graveyard and put it on the newest grave. If he does that, you won't be able to walk t'all.'

"'Now, we're going to have to work fast, and you've got to do exactly as I tell you, because, shore's you don't, your jig is up. You go home and sweep all the dirt out of your cabin. Pick it up and put it in a poke. Tonight, at exactly midnight, take it to the graveyard and scatter it over the newest grave there. Then tomorrow, at the first light of day, find your tracks in the yard. Spit in your left foot track, turn around three times, and say, "In the name of the Father, and the Son and the Holy Spirit, do away with this spell." Then, you spit three times in your right foot track. Then, back off seven steps before you start walking home.'

"Of course, Phillip was scared stiff and was as white as a duck egg, but he did just as Zac told him. And, sure enough, the witches haven't pestered Phillip any more."

---

*By an old Indian lunar calendar, the first full moon in February.

THE THUNDERSTORM BRINGS A WITCH

One of the areas where mountain people most frequently consulted witches involved matters of the heart. When a girl or boy wanted to win the love of a person who was indifferent to him, or when the affections of someone seemed to cool, young people often consulted a witch and followed her prescriptions.

Vergil Ray was down-hearted when his bussy, Naomi Sue Sadler, ditched him and bucked up to Dewey Horne. Vergil had his mind set on marryin' her and effen he didn't, he wuzzen't 'bout to let Dewey er ennybody else have her. He didn't rightly know whut to do, so he thought on hit fer a spell, then went over to Bear Cove and got his head together with Polly Searce, who wuz a powerful witch. They soon hatched up a scheme.

'Twarn't too long atter this when, late in the day, clouds black as midnight come acrost the sky and lightnin' flashed and thunder rumbled over the ridge. Hit come closer till streaks of lightnin' and loud thunder seemed to bounce from the top of one hill to annuder. There come a bright flash of lightnin' and a loud crack of thunder thet rattled the winders in Naomi Sue's cabin, and hit started to pour down rain. When hit wuz quiet fer a few seconds, there wuz a knock on the door. Hit scared Naomi stiff, but she walked slowly torge hit and opened hit.

In stepped a stooped old woman who shook the water from her long dirty skirt, peered at Naomi with her dark, piercing eyes, and sed, "I'm Polly Searce, and I wonder effen a good gal like you 'ud take me in till the storm passes."

Now, Naomi wuz sorry fur her, so she axt her to set in a rockin' cheer afore the fire and dry herself. Naomi wuz nervous, so she tried to talk to the old woman and axt her whut she wuz a doin' out in the storm. But, Polly dodged most of her questions and instead axt Naomi some pryin' ones. At last, the storm died away to jest a patter of raindrops, and Polly started to keep time with 'em by thumpin' her gnarled fingers against the arm of her cheer and by a pattin' her foot on the floor. These sounds over and over seemed to cast a spell over Naomi.

Collected by Gertrude Blair, Roanoke, Virginia, June 9, 1939. Told to her by Helen Prilliman, a long-time resident of the community. Everybody in the community had heard this story, and the older people believed it.

Then, the old woman rose and sed that, sence the storm wuz 'bout over, she'd be on her way. As she passed Naomi, she waved her hand quick-like in front of her face, but didn't tech her. Then, she slipped into the dark night. Naomi wuz worn to a frazzle and drowsy, so she went right to bed.

The next mornin', when Naomi awoke, she could move her fingers and toes, but she couldn't git up. As the day passed, she sank lower and lower into a kinda sleep. Then, she got so she could only open and close her eyes, and, atter a whet, she wasted away 'most to a skeleton.

T'warn't long afore Dewey Horne lost all interest in Naomi and quit a comin' to see her. Soon, he found him annuder bussy, and in no time t'all, they wuz married.

So, Vergil went to see Polly Searce to git her to lift the spell from Naomi. He had paid her a pretty penny to put the spell on, and now she axt fur a lot more to take hit off. But, Vergil paid her with no back talk.

Right off, Naomi started to git stronger, and soon she wuz as frisky as a colt, and as purty as a red heifer in a strawberry patch. She soon forgot all 'bout Dewey Horne when Vergil started to spark her agin. Afore long, they wuz married and lived a long life. She raised him a whole passel of young'uns.

THE FINDER AND THE CHARM DOCTOR

Grandpappy Floyd Ashworth, of Coeburn, Virginia, told this story:

"Everybody figgered Old Beverly Freeman wuz not only a charm doctor, but thet he could work magic, too. Bev lived over in Flatwoods, and folks fer miles 'round b'lieved thet he could allus find ennythin' thet'd been lost. When they'd send fer him, he'd come and go straight to where the lost thing wuz. 'Course, some folks sed he done this by sneakin' 'round at night, takin' a man's ax, er plow pint, er t'other tools off and hidin' 'em. Then, when they'd send fur him to find 'em, he'd go straight to where he'd hid 'em and show the feller where they wuz.

"One of the magic tricks old man Freeman wuz s'posed to know wuz how to stop bleedin' effen he wuz nowhere nigh the person who wuz a bleedin'. All he needed to know wuz thet they wuz a bleedin' and wanted him to stop hit.

"Onct, my mammy-in-law, John Eaton's widder Betty, had a bleedin' in her lungs. Hit got so bad thet she wuz 'bout to bleed to death. She wuz shore thet Bev Freeman could stop hit, so she sent me to git him to doctor her. So, I rid over on my hoss to fetch him, but he wouldn't come. 'Sted of thet, he turned his back on me and reached his arms torge the Heavens like he wuz an angel. Then, he mumbled some words thet I couldn't make out, and made some quare moves with his arms and hands jest like he wuz a swimmin. Then, he drapped his arms to his sides and stood as still as a mouse fer a little spell. Atter he cut all these monkeyshines, he turned torge me and sed, 'You go right back and tell Betty Eaton thet she's a goin' to be all right!'

"Well, I'll swanny, twarn't no time t'all till Widder Eaton got better. Purty soon she wuz up and goin' 'bout frisky as a spring colt. She lived fer many, many years atter thet, and raised a big family. She wuz an old woman when she died of smallpox.

"Now, I'm not too certain effen Old Bev Freeman had ennythin' to do with stoppin' her bleedin', but hit shore could make a believer outten some folks."

Collected by James Taylor Adams, Big Laurel, Virginia, November 7, 1941. Told to him by Floyd A. Ashworth, a cobbler from Coeburn, Virginia, who was then ninety-five years old.

FIRM BELIEVERS IN WITCHCRAFT

The Reverend J. H. Coleman of Norton, Virginia, tells this story from his younger days:

"I wuz born a slave in a one room log cabin. I've heard my pappy tell 'bout how folks got to be conjurers and how they practiced magic. 'Course, I didn't b'lieve there wuz ennythin' to hit. I figgered hit must be tricks thet wuz played on folks fer money.

"Onct, there wuz two men who made up their minds to be conjurers, so they got in touch with the Devil and he told 'em whut to do. Fust, they had to kotch somebody's black tomcat and tote hit out to Drake's Crossroads nigh Scott's Crick clost to Longview graveyard.

"They done this, and when they got there, they drawed a big ring on the ground 'bout fifteen er twenty feet acrost right in the middle of the crossroads. Then, they sed some magic words the Devil 'ud told 'em, and built a fire in the middle of the ring. They filled a pot with water and put hit on to bile. When hit got to bilin, they throwed thet live black tomcat right into hit. Atter all the meat biled offen his bones, they throwed hit into Scott's Crick. Bless my soul, the conjure bone from thet cat floated upstream whilst all the rest went downstream. They hustled up the stream and fetched thet conjure bone outten and brung hit back to the fire.

"Then, the Devil come outten the graveyard, and the three of 'em got their haids together and laid out some schemes. They 'lowed their fust job 'ud be a bedfast old couple thet lived 'bout a mile away on Stoney Ridge.

"So, the very next night, one of 'em sneaked up nigh this couple's place and buried a bottle thet had two spiders, a toad's toes, some sulfur, and the conjure bone in hit. The next day, t'other man went to the cabin and axt these old folks a whole passel of foolish questions and told 'em a big pack of lies. Atter a while, they got thet old man and woman so flabbergasted thet they didn't know one end from annuder. Thet wuz 'zactly how they wanted hit to be.

"Then, he told 'em that they'd been witched by somebody, and thet wuz why they'se sick in bed. He 'splained thet he knowed

Collected by James Taylor Adams, Big Laurel, Virginia, October 1, 1940. Told to him by the Reverend J.H. Coleman, of Norton Virginia, who said he had been born a slave. This story was told to him by his father.

whut wuz a keepin' the spell on 'em, and he'd break hit fur five dollars. Then, they'd be well agin and could git outten the bed.

"At fust, the old couple didn't b'lieve him, but he sed he'd prove hit. He told 'em the witch 'ud hid a bottle with some magic stuff in hit and he'd show hit to 'em. He bargained with 'em thet he'd find the stuff and use hit to break the spell so they'd get well.

"Sence there wuzzen't much else they could do, they agreed to pay him the five dollars. The conjurer then made a bee-line to where his friend 'ud told him he'd buried thet bottle. He didn't have to look very long afore he found hit and fetched hit back to the cabin. He showed hit to the old folks, and they paid him the last five dollars they had.

"Then, he sneaked the conjure bone outten the bottle and told 'em to watch when he throwed the bottle with the spider and the frog's toes and sulfur into the fire. When the bottle broke and thet stuff hit the fire, the sulfur burnt with a blue flame, and t'other stuff made an awful stink.

"Did them sick people b'lieve him? Did they get well?" Rev. Coleman asked and answered himself. "Of course they did. They jest b'lieved so strong in witches and their magic thet nacherally they got better when they thought the spell wuz broke. In no time t'all they'se up and potterin' 'round.

"Folks air like thet, you know. Effen they b'lieve strong enuf, hit'll jest be like thet."

THE WITCH AND THE OVERSEER

Miles and miles of rich plantation land stretched from the Salt River, near the Texas border, eastward to the Red River, in southern Oklahoma. The labor of more than one hundred slaves produced a bounteous yield from this land which enabled its owner, Jed Horner, to support lavishly his stunning young wife of less than five years, Irene, and his two step-daughters. Jed, a plain man in his late fifties, had a heart as big as Texas and a generosity that flowed like the Rio Grande. He bought the most expensive jewelry and finery for his beautiful wife and her two young daughters. He was generous and kind to his slaves, who he liked to consider as his partners in creating a good life for them all.

However, their happiness had been marred by tragedy in each of the past four years. In each of these years, they had lost their overseer by death. Jed had always insisted on a first-rate man who would manage to get high yields from the land, but who would be kind and considerate toward the field hands, as well as compatible with his family. He had never quibbled about salary when he thought he had the right man.

One day, soon after Christmas, a man came riding down the lane to the plantation house and asked for Mr. Jed Horner. He said that he had heard that they needed an overseer and that he would like to apply for the job.

Jed replied, "I am Jed Horner and I do need an overseer, but I am afraid when I tell you why I need one, you may not be interested in the job."

"I am Rod Stevens from near Norman, Oklahoma," the man replied. "I was born on a plantation and have worked land all my life. The terrible tornado we had six months ago killed my family, destroyed my home and outbuildings and most of my cattle. I just couldn't bear to stay there and live, so I sold my land and cattle to my brother, and have been looking for work for the past few weeks. I hope you'll give me a chance to start life over here."

"Well, come over to my office in the yard and we'll talk more about it. If you and I can agree, then I feel sure we can work out a deal. If I hire you, I will pay you well."

Based on "Following the Drinking Gourd," which appeared in the *Texas Folklore Society Journal*, volume 10, number 7, 1938.

Rod was encouraged by these words. His loneliness, sorrow, and wandering about looking for a job had been making him feel very downcast.

Jed began, "I have hired an overseer the first of each year now for four years. No overseer has held the job quite a full year. They always work satisfactorily until Christmas. Each has gone to bed on Christmas Eve hale and hearty, and, on Christmas morning, each has been found dead in bed. No one has been able to find out what has killed them. There is never any evidence of violence, nor of illness."

"I will take my chance on this," Rod assured Jed. "That is, if I meet your expectations otherwise."

Jed answered, "In that case, you are hired."

Rod was very pleased at this, and, at the overseer's private quarters, at the rear of the house, Jed explained that he would have his meals with the family, and that he hoped he would become another member of the family. He was then taken to meet Mrs. Horner and her two daughters, Anita and Rinez.

Rod's association with the Horners helped soften his sorrow at the loss of his own family. He loved brown betty,* and often Irene would have some made especially for him and delivered to his cottage by one of her little girls whom Rod always enjoyed having as a visitor. In a short time, he had developed into a splendid overseer and everything was going along smoothly.

Early the following December, Jed Horner was in Frederick for two weeks of jury duty. The crops had all been harvested, and Rod was able to relax after a successful year as overseer. One cold and dreary night, he had just settled himself before the blazing fire in his cabin to read his Bible before retiring, when there came a faint knock on his door. He wondered who would be visiting so late, or whether some emergency had arisen in which he was needed.

When he opened the door, he was so taken aback that he couldn't utter a word. He stood face to face with the beautiful Mrs. Irene Horner. She was clad in a full length robe, open in front, and revealing a sheer black nightgown. She held a small square pan of brown betty, capped with a golden brown crust.

"I hope you're not too surprised," she said in a soft voice. "With Jed away and the servants and children in bed, I was lonesome and hungry, so I thought you'd perhaps enjoy sharing some brown betty with me."

*A baked pudding made of fresh apples or other fruit, with bread or pie dough, sugar, butter and spices. Sometimes, it is sweetened with honey.

Rod had been friendly to Mrs. Horner, but only in a fatherly way. He had carefully avoided anything in his conduct which might in any way encourage undue familiarity, and he had no intention of becoming illicitly involved with Jed Horner's young wife. He searched for words which would be polite and at the same time avert an ugly situation. Finally, he replied calmly, "Mrs. Horner, it was sweet and thoughtful of you to be so concerned about me. But, I am neither lonely nor hungry tonight, and I am sure it would be best if you did not come in."

He was unable to maintain his calm, though, and he suddenly lost his self-control and blurted out: "You ought to be ashamed of yourself. You know what your trusting husband would do to both of us if he knew you'd come to my cottage. I wouldn't dare tell him that you have been here tonight."

Burning with rage, Irene dashed the pan of brown betty on the floor and whispered, "You'll live to regret this." Then, she wheeled from the door and ran off.

From the next morning, Rod made it a point to be late for meals and sometimes he didn't come at all. Mrs. Horner avoided him as well. The next two weeks dragged along slowly, and Rod thought he ought to leave the plantation. But, in view of what had happened to the other overseers at Christmas, he reasoned that Jed would think him a coward for leaving before then, so he resolved to leave as soon after Christmas as he could.

Early on the day before Christmas, Jed went into Frederick to purchase gifts for the families on the plantation and candies and toys for the children. It took him until past midnight on Christmas Eve to distribute these gifts with personal season's greetings to each family. This custom had been started by his grandfather, continued by his father, and Jed thoroughly enjoyed keeping it alive.

That night, Rod sat before the fire in his cottage. The past two weeks had been difficult for him: he hadn't been able to relax nor to forget the terrifying experience with Mrs. Horner. The silence seemed to contain an ominous presence, and he thought about what had happened to the other overseers in this house. He got out his hunting knife and laid it on the arm of his chair. Then, he chuckled at his stupid fears. There was nothing in the room: he was just letting his imagination run away with him.

He shrugged his shoulders, reached for his Bible and began to read. He had just started when he heard a soft "meow" at the door. He opened the door and the most beautiful white cat he had ever seen dashed in. Rod had never seen the cat about the plantation before, and he wondered where it had come from. It ambled around the room and then sat down before the fire.

Thinking that the cat might be hungry, Rod gave her a piece of buttered bread. She ate it with relish, licked her paws and face and started wandering about the room again. Then, she sat down before the fire, and Rod resumed his seat and began to read his Bible.

Soon, he heard another "meow" at the door, and the white cat called out, "Come in!"

Rod jumped up from his chair and stared at the cat. He knew he had really heard the cat speak! He pulled himself together and sat down again and pretended to read his Bible.

"Who said so?" asked a soft voice outside.

"Rod Stevens said so," the white cat answered.

A second cat—smaller than the first—came in, and, after exploring the room, sat beside the first cat. Rod was filled with apprehension, and he nervously watched the cats from the corner of his eye.

Soon, he heard another cat at the door, and the larger cat answered again, "Come in."

"Who said so?" was the query.

"Rod Stevens said so," was again the response.

The third cat came in, explored the room and then sat down on the hearth beside the other two cats. After a while, the first cat got up, yawned and walked slowly about the room as if she were searching for a mouse. She reared up with her forefeet on the arm of Rod's chair, and it seemed that she was about to jump into his lap. At this, Rod lost his self-control, grabbed his hunting knife and slashed at her with it. She dodged, but the knife came down on her forefeet and sliced them off. When this happened, all three cats disappeared like a streak of light.

Rod tossed the severed paws on the table. As soon as they hit it, they changed into human hands. They were as white and graceful as they could be, and the fingers were adorned with gorgeous rings which gleamed in the firelight. They were obviously the hands of a beautiful woman.

Rod was so frightened that he wanted to take off like a scared rabbit. But, he felt weighted down, and he could barely move. He felt as if something or somebody was in the room and watching him, but again he told himself there was nothing in the room—that it was his imagination. To keep from going completely out of his mind, he picked up his Bible again and began to read. He didn't know whether he actually read or if he were in a trance. Finally, daylight appeared.

Rod sat there, trance-like, until he was startled by a soft knock. He jumped from his chair and called out faintly, "Come in." The early morning visitor was Jed Horner, who had come in trepidation to check on his overseer on Christmas morning. When he saw that Rod was alive and well, he was much relieved.

When Jed entered the cottage, Rod gestured toward the severed hands on the table and asked him in a trembling voice if he recognized them.

"I'm not so sure about the hands, Jed replied, "But I could swear to those rings. That one especially," and he pointed to a ring which he had so recently given Irene. "How did you come by these hands? Have you killed my wife? Where is her body?"

Jed's voice had risen with rage, and Rod was afraid that he was going to attack him. He told Jed to calm down and he would tell him what had happened. This he proceeded to do, while Jed listened in agony and bewilderment. "Had Rod lost his mind under the strain of expecting the same fate which had overtaken the other overseers?" Jed wondered.

As he listened, Jed began to put together other things which had happened. He vowed to Rod that he'd find out for himself whose hands they were, and he rushed out of Rod's cottage.

He went upstairs to his wife's bedroom and found her and her two daughters in the same bed, which was unusual. He called out, "Irene, are you alright?"

When he got no answer, he came closer and saw that Irene's chalky white face was a mask of anguish. The film of death covered her eyes. He rushed out of the room to get the servants to help him examine the bodies. Anita and Rinez had been beheaded. Irene's hands had been severed and were missing. There was a pool of blood in the bed which indicated that she had bled to death.

Jed hurried back to the overseer's cottage to retrieve the hands and to question Rod further about this horrible tragedy. He found Rod gone, and no one ever saw him or heard from him again.

CURED FROM A DISTANCE

"Hit's the truth, so holp me, there's a lot of folks here in these hills thet'll tell you tales 'bout Old Ben Cordle 'zactly like mine," Ebb Bond vowed.

"Hit's more'n twenty-five year ago when I wuz a livin' at the Pound thet I got moughty porely. I wuz sore as a bile all over. I couldn't raise my arms ner set one foot afore t'other. There wuz no rest fer my body ner my soul, so I went to a doctor. I tuk his bitter physic and foul drenches fer weeks, but kept a goin' down hill.

"Then, I went to see Granny Lipps, who wuz the best yarb doctor hereabouts. She brewed teas and simples, kivvered me with poultices and plasters, dosed me with catnip and sheep dip teas, and give me physic. Still, I jest kept a inchin' nigher and nigher to death. Then, Granny Lipps sed she'd done all she knowed to do fer me, and I 'lowd the jig wuz up fer me sure. But, she told me thet mebbe effen I'd see preacher Ben Cordle out on Cumberland, he mought holp me. He wuz one of them faith doctors.

"By this time, I wuz too much under the weather to go ennywhere. But, Dale Bolling wuz a carryin' the mail from the Pound, over on Cumberland, and on his route he passed right alongside where Ben Cordle lived. I axt Dale effen he'd see Ben and axt him to doctor me. Effen he would, I'd git somebody to fetch me over there in a wagon. Dale done whut I axt him, and come back and told me this story.

"'Ebb,' Dale sed, 'Reverend Ben Cordle axt me all sorts of things 'bout you, like, When did you git so porely? How many young'uns did you have? Had you ever seed a doctor? Had a yarb doctor treated you? Had you seed a conjure doctor? Then, he ended up by axtin' effen I thought you b'lieved he could holp you.'

"'So, I told him all the ins and outs he wanted to know as best I could. I told him thet you're worser than all git out, and felt lower than a snake's belly. I sed they's no two ways 'bout hit, you shore did b'lieve he could holp you.'

"'Then, the Reverend Cordle turned his face straight torge where you live, closed his eyes, raised his hands torge Heaven, and

Collected by James Taylor Adams, Big Laurel, Virginia, June 6, 1940. Told to him by Elbert J. Bond, of Pound, Virginia. This story is said to have happened to Mr. Bond's father.

mumbled a lot of strange jabber thet I couldn't make out. Atter he'd done this, he whirled 'round torge me and sed, "You can tell Ebb he'll be all right now. He won't have to come over here to see me. Jest tell him as soon as he's able to roam the woods and to walk over here, he can go out and dig 'bout a pound of 'snag roots and fetch 'em to me.'"

"Well, hit's the truth effen ever I told hit, I started to mend right there and then. Thet wuz on Toosday, and by Saturday, I'd straightened up and wuz a feelin' as peart as a bumblebee in June. In less time then hit takes fer a funeral prayer, I dug them 'snag roots and traipsed over the ridges on my mare's shank to Cumberland and paid thet preacher. I told him I wuz much obleeged to him kase he'd saved my life.

"Now, I hain't never felt a tech of thet ailment sence, and thet's been nigh onto twenty-five year ago."

THE BURNING MILL

"If you get any meal here, you'll have to pay for it like anybody else," snorted Ramp Dilby to Old Nan Feeney. "While it's true that your drunken old husband, Mize, worked for me until the day before he drowned in my mill pond, that don't oblige me to give you corn and meal the rest of your life."

Ramp stepped in front of Old Nan, hemming her into a corner, and continued, "Now you listen to me, you crotchety old hag, the last few days Mize worked for me, he was drinking so much that his tongue got loose at both ends. He bragged to me that you had a big gourd full of rough diamonds. He said that everytime it rained and washed the soil away from them, you'd take your old yellow cat and hustle over to the Crater of Diamonds* and come back with some. He said that that cat could spot a rough diamond a mile away on a moonlight night. Now, I allow if you'd sell some of the diamonds, you'd be able to pay for all the things you need like everybody else."

Old Nan cringed and was silent until she had squirmed around to the door. Then, as she stepped outside, she rounded on Ramp and hissed angrily, "Ramp Dilby, you white-livered skinflint, everything you said is a black lie. You'll regret till your last breath cheating and abusing a poor helpless widow."

Then, Nan whirled around and took off up the narrow path through the woods toward her cabin. As she disappeared, Ramp muttered, "Good riddance to bad rubbish." He was glad the day was over; it was Christmas Eve and he had had a busy day, so he began to close up. He lived alone in a cabin about a hundred yards from the mill.

Ramp went to bed early, but was aroused from a sound sleep by a loud crashing noise. He rushed to the window and peered out. The noise he had heard was the roof of his mill falling in. All he could see of it was thick black smoke and orange flames. The mill was totally destroyed, and it was obvious to Ramp that the fire had

Told by Jasper Minnick, Eudora, Arkansas, June 3, 1950, who heard this story from a retired schoolteacher when he was a boy.
*A diamond field, near Murfreesboro, Arkansas, where diamonds can sometimes be found after a hard rain. Now a part of the Arkansas State Park System.

been set.

The mill had been built by Ramp's grandfather, at Diamond Cove, on the Little Missouri River, in western Arkansas. It was important to the community, as well as being Ramp's only means of making a living. So, Ramp rebuilt the mill with borrowed money, and was soon back in business. He kept a watch at night for several weeks after it was completed, but as nothing happened, he gradually left off the watch.

But, next Christmas Eve, just before midnight, Jonas Spense roused Ramp and said he thought something was wrong at the mill. They rushed to it, Ramp unlocked the door, and they went in. They found a pile of empty sacks smouldering under a stack of dry corn cobs. After Ramp had doused the fire, Jonas explained that he had been on his way home from the village when, just as he was passing the mill, his horse had been frightened by a varmint with shiny eyes which had run across their path. When he dismounted to calm his horse, he smelled smoke and saw a flicker of light in the mill.

After this attempt to set his mill on fire, Ramp checked it nightly for several weeks. Again, when he saw nothing unusual, he relaxed his vigilance.

But, when Christmas Eve rolled around again, he thought he had better return to check the mill that night. On his way along the dark path, he thought he felt something furry and warm brush against his leg, but he saw nothing. He found the door locked and the windows barred just as he had left them, but there was another pile of smouldering sacks in the same spot as they had been the year before on Christmas Eve. Ramp poured a bucket of water on them, and then inspected the building to see how anyone might have entered it. The only possible opening was where the sluice passed into the mill, but this was much too small to admit anything but a cat or dog, and they would have had to wade through water. But, his own cat was in the house and he knew of no stray dogs in the neighborhood. Suddenly, he thought of the furry thing which had brushed against his leg on the path, and of the varmint that had frightened Jonas' horse the year before. Whatever it was, it had gone now, so Ramp went home to bed.

When the next Christmas Eve rolled around, Ramp was determined to catch the person or thing that was trying to burn down his mill. He brought down the makings of a beef stew early in the evening, built a fire, and put on the pot of stew. He stirred it with a long ladle and, when it was done, filled a bowl and sat down in his chair to enjoy it. He was prepared to spend the night in the mill. He didn't have a gun, but he had brought along his Civil War sword which he placed beside him on a wooden box.

While he was eating, a whole troup of cats entered the mill through the sluice opening and padded across the floor toward him. The thought that these cats might possibly be witches had just flashed across his mind when his suspicion was confirmed. One of the cats spoke in a low, human voice. He said: "Mouskin, go sit by Rampskin."

At this suggestion, a beautiful white cat ambled over to Ramp and sat down by his side. She licked her tongue as if begging for some of the stew whose inviting aroma filled the mill. Ramp dipped the big ladle into the pot, filled it with hot liquid, and dashed it in the cat's face. It caught her completely off guard, and she let out an anguished howl. She wiped the hot liquid from her eyes, hissed, and drew back her right front paw with its sharp claws as if to claw his eyes out. Ramp snatched up his sword and brought it down on the paw hard enough to cut it completely off.

When this happened, all of the cats disappeared like a shadow when a light is turned on. Ramp picked up the severed paw and tossed it on the box beside him. Instantly, the paw turned into the leathery, wrinkled hand of an old woman. One finger wore a ring set with a huge, uncut diamond. Ramp recognized it as the hand of Old Nan Feeney. The arson incidents of the past four years were now explained. Obviously, Old Nan had been carrying out her threat to curse him.

As soon as dawn broke the next morning, Ramp, mad as a hornet, wrapped the cold wrinkled hand in a cloth and hurried to Nan Feeney's cabin. There was no answer to his knock, but he pushed on the door in his rage and found it unfastened. He walked in and found the cabin empty. In the middle of the floor, there was a puddle of blood and beside it was a large bloody gourd. It was empty except for three rough diamonds which had stuck to the sides with dried blood. There was a trail of blood leading from the cabin through a field and into the woods. Ramp followed the trail until he lost it in the woods.

Ramp gave up the search for Old Nan, and nobody saw or heard anything of her for two years. Then, one day some hunters found what appeared to be a woman's skeleton in a remote section of the woods. It was complete except for the bones of the right hand. Only two small rough diamonds were found under the bones. If Old Nan indeed had a whole gourd full of diamonds, no one has yet found them.

MONT AND DUCK

Once, a queer, shabbily dressed old couple—Mont and his wife, Duck—appeared from nowhere in the hill country which lies along the slopes of the Blue Ridge Mountains, in Franklin County, Virginia. They moved into an abandoned cabin on a run-down farm. They didn't have any farm animals or farm tools, and they never mentioned their past lives. Folks in the community were suspicious of all strangers, but especially of those who had no worldly goods at all.

Soon after they moved in, there was an epidemic of sickness and death among the farm animals of the region. Nobody knew what caused it, and one of their neighbors accused Mont and Duck of having cast a spell on their sick cow. Old Mont awed his accuser by readily admitting that his wife, Duck, had the power of evil, and that he could break the spells. Shortly after this, he began to offer to cure ailing animals by removing the spells on them in return for a bushel of potatoes or some other vegetables, or even a piece of meat.

For several years, this queer couple lived by selling their knowledge of good and bad witchcraft. Their black magic was so feared by the mountain people that they gave them anything they asked when they had to consult them, and avoided them whenever possible.

One day, a young man in the neighborhood began to act very strangely, and his family thought that he'd fallen under one of Duck's evil spells. So, they bargained with Mont to treat him, which he did with success. They paid him well for this, but after the boy was almost well, they stopped paying Mont. Soon after this, the young man disappeared, and it was several weeks before his body was found in the back woods. Although this young man was probably the victim of an emotional disorder, the mountain folks all attributed his death to the two witches, Mont and Duck.

When Duck died, Mont followed three days later. Most of the mountain folk had given their cabin a wide berth during their lifetimes, but as news of their death spread, many people who

Collected by Raymond T. Sloan, Rocky Mount, Virginia, April 7, 1939. Told to him by Phil Wolfe, of Patrick County, whose father had told him this story when he was a little boy.

would never have dared cross their doorsill now came through curiosity. They found very little that was useful in the dirty little cabin, but they did discover a large cave back of the house which was filled with the food and other objects which had been given them for their practice of magic.

Even today, curious folks visit the gloomy hollow where the graves of Mont and Duck are marked with two stones from the mountain.

WITCHES WITH STINGERS

Grandpappy Lamp Griffin lit out at the crack of dawn one day in the harvest season to pick some apples outten his orchard atop of Foggy Ridge above the Clinch River. This orchard had been handed down to him from his grandpappy, who'd cleared the land and planted the trees during pioneerin' days. They had allus given bumper crops, but this mornin' Lamp found that some of the trees nigh the edge of the orchard had been stripped of their fruit.

Now, this flustered and stumped Grandpappy Lamp, kase afore this, nobody had ever pilfered his apples, since he'd allus give his neighbors some, whether er no they wuz a good crop. So, he studied 'bout hit fer a spell, and then figgered mebbe hit wuz some witches a pesterin' him.

Lamp lit a shuck over to old Zeb Patton's place so'se they could git their haids together and hatch some scheme to kotch the rogues. Zeb wuz a warlock and had a knack of grabblin' with sperets and witches. Lamp wuz a bilin' over, and he told Zeb he'd do most ennythin' to git shet of them witches.

While Lamp had been blowin' his top, Zeb smiled a sly grin, kase he knowed somethin' Lamp didn't know. But, he was long-headed and sharp as a briar when hit come to strikin' a bargain, and he got Lamp to promise thet, effen he'd git shet of them thieves, Lamp 'ud give him a ham, a young calf and 'ud keep him in fruit fer three years. Lamp agreed, and Zeb knowed his word wuz as good as his bond, so he started workin' on the case.

Fust, Zeb went out and found him some lightnin' dust which is worm dust from a tree kilt by lightnin'. Hit'll scare thieves and cross 'em up so they'se afeard to use ennythin' they steal. Then, he got some burnt wood, beat hit into black powder, mixed some flour with hit, added a little water, rolled hit up into little balls, and put hit into a black rag. He made thirteen of these balls. He cut some short hairs from his horse's tail, tied a string to every one of the bags, dipped 'em in molasses, and then rolled 'em in the horse hairs. Then, he made a bee-line fer Lamp's orchard and tied them witch balls on the lower limbs of some trees nigh those thet 'ud

Collected by James Taylor Adams, Big Laurel, Virginia, April 7, 1939. Told to him by Mose Lane who heard the story from his grandfather.

been stripped. Soon as them balls dried, the bumblebees, yaller jackets, hornets and honeybees jest went hog-wild a swarmin' over 'em.

Thet night, Zeb hid in the orchard, and purty soon a thief come to one of them trees and started a pickin' apples and puttin' 'em in a poke. Afore he'd pulled more'n a dozen, he rubbed agin one of them witchballs and upset a yaller jacket er a hornet er some other bee. Ennyhow, hit stuck hit's stinger smack dab 'bout three inches into thet rogue's hand. He cut loose with a yell like a dog thet 'ud been slapped by a bar, and cleared outten thet orchard like a house afire.

Zeb laughed fit to kill, kase he knowed all the time thet a batch of Melungions and gypsies 'ud settled over the ridge and wuz a pilferin' the country and a livin' off the land. He knowed thet they'se more afeard of witches than ennythin' in the world, and they knowed thet all night-witches had stingers. Hit waren't long afore word got 'round among them thet they'se witches in them fruit trees. The Melungions never bothered Lamp's orchard enny more, and Zeb never told him how he found out who wuz a gittin' the fruit ner how he'd got shet of 'em.

CAN'T STEAL

Pidgeon Creek twisted down the narrow valley from where it originated in a large spring under a cliff, made one last sharp turn, and then dropped over a rock ledge fifteen feet high. Many years ago, an enterprising pioneer had built a mill race at the head of the falls to operate his grist mill below. The mill, built from hewn logs, had stood the years well and was now encased in a growth of wild honeysuckle. The fungus-covered shakes glistening in the moonlight gave the mill the same hoary appearance as its present eccentric owner, Nathan Lee Purky.

Now Old Nath was a warlock, and he spelled his mill so'se nobody could steal from hit. He was so sure thet his spell'ud work thet, he didn't even have locks on the doors.

Everybody sed thet effen ennybody tried to steal from Nathan's mill they allus got caught. Old Jim Tom McCoy, from out on Buck's Knob was the seventh son of a seventh son. This gave him some magic powers, but they were effective only when he had his magic buckeye in his possession. The buckeye had a seven carved on the eye, and had been hung around his neck by his grandfather at his birth.

Old Jim Tom was as mean as a pile of rattlesnakes when he was drinking. And he liked to brag. He said he'd show Old Nath Purkey thet he wuzzen't skeered of his witched mill. So, he got his magic buckeye and lit out one night for the mill. 'Course, he found hit open, so he went in and found some sacks of corn settin' on the floor.

He heisted a sack of shelled corn to his shoulder, and reached down in his pocket for his magic buckeye. But, bein' tipsy, he struck his hand agin the meal trough and drapped thet buckeye on the floor. When he reached down to pick hit up, he lost his balance and fell on thet buckeye and the sack of corn he'd been totin' fell on top of him. 'Course, Jim Tom wuz a big, strong man, and he could've rolled thet sack away with one hand, but when he tried, he found thet he couldn't move neither his arms ner his legs.

Collected by Gertrude Blair, Roanoke County, Virginia, June 30, 1939. Told to her by Joe Adkins, a local story teller, coon hunter and dog lover, who lived about ten miles south of Roanoke.

Well, there's no doubt 'bout hit, Jim Tom wuz fit to be tied. Though he couldn't move his arms er legs, his tongue wuzzen't tied, and he cut loose with cuss words till the air wuz blue 'round him. But, as the likker wore off, Jim Tom, who wuz clearheaded when he's sober, knowed he'd been foxed. So, he laid there with thet sack of corn a pushin' down on him and thet conjure bone a cuttin' his buttocks like a rock in a shoe. He wuz so outdone thet he wanted to cuss hisself fer gittin' in sech a mess.

Soon atter cock crow, Nath showed up at the mill. With a jeerin' laugh and a frown, he sed, "Howdy, Jim Tom. I kinda 'spected to find you here. Hope you hain't too tired totin' thet sack of corn to holp me unload this wagon of corn."

'Course the spell wuz broke as soon as Nath spoke, but Jim Tom wuz so cowed thet he jest rolled over thet sack of corn. Then, he picked up his conjure bone and lit out a runnin' like the devil wuz atter him, and he didn't let up till he got to his cabin nigh onto two miles away. Atter Jim Tom's bungersome caper in the mill, nobody who ever knowed 'bout hit ever tried to steal any of Nath's corn.

THE WITCH OF LAS NORIAS

Midnight darkness and stillness lay over Las Norias, Texas, where Don Gonzales slept fitfully in the little hut he shared with his aged mother. He was roused from slumber by the type of screeching an owl would make at a stray wolf, and he knew that Old Nita Pescadito, the bruja* was flying overhead on wings borrowed from the Devil. She was going south to Raymondsville, some twenty miles away, where she would get a new supply of poisons and other tools of her trade to use against her enemies and their livestock.

It had been less than a month since Old Nita had threatened Don for refusing to sell her Brindle, the cow from which he and his mother got most of their subsistence. A childhood illness had left Don with a withered leg, and he had found it difficult to supply their meager needs since his father had died. His landlord, Ricardo Valdez, a prosperous and kind man, had found enough light work for Don to keep him on as a tenant.

Don limped over to the small window and peered up into the black and cloudy sky. He could see Old Nita's lantern and the waves of her black dress rippling in the wind as she glided by overhead. Tonight she was traveling alone, but sometimes she would be joined by two other witches from a nearby village, who belonged to her coven. Together they would extract poisons and make potions from monkshood, henbane, hellbore and manioc roots.

Whether alone or with her evil companions, these nocturnal excursions brought forebodings of some new calamity to the poor residents of the little town. Don grasped the window sill and shuddered as he remembered how she had harassed others who had dared to displease her. Had not Atwood Bruni's sheep been struck by some mysterious disease and died after he had disputed with her about a load of firewood? He recalled with pity how Juan Mirando's little four-year-old angel had suddenly become covered with lice which caused her face to become contorted, her eyes to roll and her body to twist until she was permanently deformed. And all this because Juan had refused to give Old Nita some of his fruit. On other occasions, when she had become angry with the whole town,

Based on "Witches," published in the *Texas Folklore Journal*, volume 10, number 6, 1931.

*The Spanish word for witch or sorceress.

she had brought on droughts which had caused the river to run dry, pastures to burn up and livestock to die. Completely unnerved by these terrifying recollections and with apprehension as to what she could do to him, Don shuffled back to bed and uttered a prayer to his guardian saint not to forsake him.

For several days, Don found excuses for not going to the ranch house where Nita worked, but finally he had to go for seed and other supplies. As he left the house, Nita insisted that he take some rum and a package of her homemade cake to his mother. Don graciously accepted them, but threw them into a stream on his way back to his hut. He feared that they were poisoned.

When weeks passed and Nita hadn't bothered them, Don began to think that she wasn't going to punish them at all. During this time, it got drier and drier. Pastures were parched, and small streams dried up. One morning both Don and his mother became milk-sick. No doubt their cow had eaten some snakeroot in the absence of grass.

Don felt better in a day or two, but his mother was unable to eat or drink for several days. Don drank the milk his mother was unable to use. In about three days, he felt a prickling and tingling in his throat. Then, a kind of numbness and contraction seized the roof of his mouth and his tongue. He realized the bruja had somehow put some monkshood juice in his milk pail.

He hurriedly prepared a glass of honey, vinegar and salt water and took several big swallows. This made him violently ill and he disgorged the contents of his stomach. But, the prickling spread over his body, his throat became constricted, and his fist and jaws began to clench convulsively. This seizure lasted for several hours before the effects of the poison wore off. At that point, Don realized how nearly he had been fatally poisoned by this evil witch. Needless to say, he did all he could to see that his tracks and Old Nita's saw as little of each other as possible for the rest of his days.

THE DISAPPEARING WITCH

Tobias Seawell ran a country store and post office at the crossroads of Capahosic, on the York River, in Gloucester County, Virginia. The community seemed to be full of witches who'd been hagging a lot of folks in the neighborhood. They'd get into people's houses in some mysterious way and would manifest themselves as some kind of animal, often a black cat or a feist dog.

One night, Tobias, his wife and nine children went to bed early. He had locked up the house and all his valuables and had his keys under his pillow. He also slept with a hunting knife under the pillow. It was a cold December night, so he had built up the fire in the fireplace before going to bed. Everybody was asleep but Tobias, who lay awake watching the fire.

Suddenly, two black cats, a large one and a small one, appeared on the hearth. The small one stretched out before the fire as if it were ready for a night's sleep, but the large one started prowling about the room like a fox smelling a chicken house. Tobias pretended to be asleep, but he was peeking nervously at the cats from under his eyelids. After a few minutes, the large cat started edging toward the bed, and Tobias decided that they were witches looking to rob him.

As that cat inched close to Tobias' bed, he kept still, but moved his hand slowly under the cover and got hold of his hunting knife. When that cat got close enough for him to touch it, it turned into an old crone. She was dressed in a dirty black dress. Her stringy white hair hid most of her face, but her long, crooked teeth showed through her grinning little mouth. She reached out her bony withered hand towards the pillow for the keys, but Tobias grabbed the old woman by the dress. As she pulled away from him, he slashed at her with his hunting knife. But all he cut was a little piece out of her dress.

She lunged toward the fireplace and Tobias leaped from the bed after her. But, before he could get to her, she changed back into a black cat, and both cats disappeared as strangely as they'd come.

Collected by Lucille B. Jaynes, Capahosic, Gloucester County, Virginia, September 3, 1939. Told to her by Aunt Holly Bowser, who at that time was eighty-four years old. Aunt Holly had heard the story as a child from her grandmother.

Since there was no door or window through which they could have escaped, Tobias thought they must have gone up the chimney or through the keyhole.

The next day, Tobias went to his farm up river to supervise some work his men were doing, and, on the way, he saw an old woman with a cut in her skirt. He pulled out the piece of cloth he'd cut from the witch's dress, and saw that the shape matched perfectly. Of course, he knew he'd found the witch, but he said nothing to her because he wanted to catch the other one, too.

Now, this all happened a few weeks before Christmas, and some men in the community had ordered extra Christmas liquor which they had not yet picked up from the store. This was known generally throughout the community, and so some of the warlocks got together and decided to raid the store to get some liquor and some other things for Christmas. They gathered in front of the store one night, each with a bottle of special lotion. They rubbed this on themselves to make them shrink small enough to get through the keyhole.

The first warlock to reach the door said, "Through the keyhole I go." He shrank and slipped right through the keyhole.

The next one said, "After you I go," and he disappeared.

The third one, who was the husband of the old crone who'd entered Tobias' house, was stupid and had forgotten the magic words, so he said, "Inside the keyhole I go." He lunged toward the keyhole, but only banged hard against the door. He tried again, this time saying, "Right through the keyhole I go." He bumped the door again, but this time succeeded in getting through.

Of course, Tobias had been expecting a robbery attempt, since it had happened in past years, so he was sleeping in the store. The noise of the bumbling witch had awakened him, but he lay still and pretended to be asleep. The warlocks collected the liquor, some money and other goods on the counter, and then decided to sample some of the liquor on the spot. They opened a bottle and started drinking and Tobias leaped up to catch them. Two of them shrank quick as a wink and escaped through the keyhole. But, the stupid old man who'd had trouble getting in, got confused again, so Tobias caught him and locked him in a closet.

The next morning, the old crone walked into the store and asked Tobias if he'd seen her old man. Tobias told her he had, and if she'd just wait a minute, he'd get him. Instead, he sent for two of his neighbors who'd been hagged by witches, and the three of them took the old man and the old woman back into the woods to hang them. They tied their hands behind them, put a hood over their heads, a rope around their necks and put each on a horse. They tied one end of the rope to a tree and were ready to drive the horses from under the witches.

But bless my soul! A flock of large black crows swooped right down over those witches and said, "Caw! Caw! Caw! Up! Up! Up! in the air we go."

The old crone replied, "And I after you," and she flew right out of the rope and up in the air and disappeared like a puff of smoke.

Well, the old man was so surprised at this that he was too confused to figure out how to follow her. When she flew up, she scared the horses so bad that they both ran away, leaving the old man dangling from the rope.

After this hanging, the witches got scared and the community was never bothered by them again.

IZZY SNIPES' SOUL IS DELIVERED
TO THE DEVIL

Pale moonbeams filtered through the lone glass pane in the window of the log cabin and pierced the thick gloom. A foul stench filled the one room where Izzy Snipes, a withered old crone, squirmed her stinking, pain-racked body about on a bed covered with dirty quilts. Her once bewitching black eyes, now strange and beady, mirrored the agony of her body and soul. Bed sores and rheumatic joints made sharp twinges of pain go through her body so that she groaned aloud.

Her pitiful moans brought Zollie Snipes, her wasted and wizzened husband, to her side. He bent over her and gently pleaded in his wispy little voice, "Izzy, why don't you pray. Shorely God'll pay more mind to yore prayers than to yore moans and groans."

"Like Hell, I orter pray", Izzy exploded. "You know damned well, you old hypocrite, why I can't pray. God knows it, too. I can't cry! I can't scream! I can't even die! Effen I could git shet of this sufferin' here on earth and go on to hell where I know I'm a goin' ennyhow, I'd be better off! Hit's annuder one of the Devil's ways of punishin' me."

A tear ran down her sunken, wrinkled cheek. "Zol, you're pokin' fun at me 'bout prayin. I'd be the laughin' stock of God and all of his angels effen I tried to pray. No, Zol, hit's too late now even effen I could pray.

"I told you onct how I sold my soul to the Devil when I wuz a purty young gal. He promised to keep me purty, to give me money, and to give me power over folks. Yep, he kept me purty fer a few years, but he never give me no money, and the little bit of power I had over folks ain't a doin' me a bit of good now. And the Devil'll cheat every time, and even He's turned agin me now. Right now, his angels air a thrashin' my body with a bundle of thorns."

Izzy gasped and lay still for a few seconds to catch her breath, then continued, "Now, kase I told you I wuz a witch and some of the secrets 'bout witchin' and makin' witch balls, the Devil's a

Collected by James Taylor Adams, Big Laurel, Virginia, June 11, 1941. Told to him by Mrs. Virginia Croft, of Wise, Virginia, who had heard the story from her grandmother.

punishin' me by leavin' me here sick, drawed up, kivvered with bed sores and a stinkin' and a hurtin'. No, Zol, God won't have my soul, and the Devil hain't ready fer hit yet."

Zollie, exhausted from weeks of harried nights filled by Izzy's moans and cries, sprawled his weary body across the bed hoping to steal a few moments of rest. But, the brief stillness was broken by Izzy's weak voice wailing, "Now! Now! I feel the Devil's clammy hand with his sharp claws a tearin' away at my soul. Oh! Effen he'd jest rip hit outten and throw hit into the eternal hellfire!"

Gasping, she writhed her skinny body. Her claw-like hands twitched, then death's stillness took over. At the very moment when Izzy's tormented soul finally left her body, some force which Zollie could feel but not see yanked his right arm from the bed and jerked him upright. As he sat on the bed, he saw Izzy's familiar, a big black cat, appear.

A dark, shapeless shadow seemed to rise from Izzy's body and hung momentarily just above Zollie's head. Then, as he sat there horrified, he saw it float slowly down toward the black cat. It hung over it for a moment, then seemed to be engulfed by the cat. The cat, with a blood-curdling cry, lunged through one of the rag-filled window spaces, bearing the soul of the Devil's servant back to its master.

The whole community breathed a sigh of relief when the last clod of dirt thudded down on Izzy's grave. Many tales of her evil doings were now related, which folks had never dared speak of during her life.

PIERRE AND THE DEVIL

A young man by the name of Pierre Petit left his home to seek his fortune because his parents were no longer able to keep him. He walked through the forest all day and, toward evening, he came upon a huge stone castle with a moat around it. When he reached the front of the building, he heard a horn blow, the drawbridge came down, and a beautiful girl met him at the great iron door.

"My name is Pierre," he said, "and I am looking for a place to spend the night."

"You must go away from here," she replied. "My father is the Devil and he will kill you."

"I'm not afraid of the Devil," boasted Pierre. "Let me come in and take me to him."

So, the girl led Pierre through the iron gate, up the castle steps and into a huge room. "This is where my father stays," she said, leaving quickly.

The Devil was sitting alone at a large table, absorbed in a game. He had before him an enormous bottle and a large glass.

When he looked up and saw Pierre, he asked, "Well, Well, who are you? How dare a puny little human like you walk into my presence? But, now that you are here, come a little closer."

"Sir, I am looking for a place to stay tonight," explained Pierre, shivering from the Devil's bellow.

"Sit down," commanded the Devil, pouring himself a huge glass of liquor from his enormous bottle. "You are just in time to play a game of cards with me. Here, take a drink."

"I don't drink," answered Pierre, as he sat down at the table.

"You don't what?" asked the Devil as he filled another tumbler. "You'll either drink this down or I'll crush you into a small ball," he threatened. Then, he bolted down his drink at one gulp, snorted and wiped his mouth on his sleeve. Pierre drank also, trembling as the fiery liquor made his hair stand on end and his throat burn.

"Now, we'll play cards," the Devil announced. "Put up your money."

Based on a folktale of French Louisiana by Calvin Claudel, and published in the *Southern Folklore Quarterly*, volume 9, number 4, 1945.

Not daring to refuse, Pierre took all his money out of his pockets and laid it on the table. They began to play and Pierre soon lost all his money. He really didn't know how to play, and besides, the Devil seemed to have a dozen ways to get the best cards.

"I've won all your money," said the Devil with an evil smile. "Now, I'll play you another game. If you win, you'll get all my money, but if I win, you'll work for me for the rest of your life."

They played another game, and Pierre lost. "Tomorrow you'll begin work for me," the Devil announced. Then, he ordered, "Come with me and I'll show you your room."

Pierre followed the Devil, carrying a flickering candle as he stumbled up the steps. After climbing a long way on the twisting stairway, they reached a little cell with a bed of corn shucks on the bare floor.

"Sleep here, and be sure not to talk to any of my three daughters. If you do, I'll kill you instantly," threatened the Devil, as he shut the door.

In spite of his rough bed, Pierre fell asleep instantly. The next morning, he was awakened by a gruff voice saying, "Wake up and come with me."

As he rubbed his eyes, Pierre thought he had had a terrible dream. But, he realized it was not a dream when he saw the Devil towering over him. He noticed that the Devil had horns growing from his head, and his feet were cloven hoofs.

He followed the Devil outside, where he was given an ax, a spade, and a hoe. He was taken to a huge forest about fifty acres square. "By noon, you must have all this land cleared and corn planted," the Devil announced, and left him.

Pierre began to cut one small tree from all the thousands and thousands of trees in the forest. The ax soon broke into bits because, like all the other tools, it was made of wood. Poor Pierre was in despair.

Suddenly, the Devil's beautiful daughter came toward him and asked him how he was getting along. "Badly," Pierre responded. "I must cut all of the forest and plant corn by noon today. If I fail, your father will kill me."

"Don't worry," the girl advised. "Here, I've brought you a drink of water."

Pierre took the water and drank it. When he looked toward the forest again, all the trees were gone, and corn was sprouting up. "I'll be back again to help you," the girl promised and went away again.

Soon, the Devil came up and said, "Well, Pierre, it seems that you are a good worker. Now, by sundown all of this corn must be full grown, harvested, ground into meal, put into sacks, and taken to the castle ready to be used."

Pierre almost fainted at this, for the corn was just above the ground. Just then, the girl reappeared, carrying something wrapped in a napkin. "Here is some food for you," she said.

"But, I don't have time to eat," he complained. "Your father wants the corn grown, harvested, ground into meal, and ready at the castle by sundown."

"Eat," she commanded. "I'll take care of the corn."

So, Pierre sat down in the shade and ate his meal. He noticed a large barge filled with sacks of meal floating down the river. "There is the meal," the girl said.

"Oh, you have been so wonderful!" Pierre cried. "How can I ever repay you, pretty mademoiselle? Will I see you again?"

"Perhaps," she answered, "but we must watch out for my father. He'll kill you if he finds his youngest daughter with you." She said good-bye and left.

Pierre began to steer the barge toward the castle just as the sun began to set in the west. But, soon, black clouds appeared and a great storm came up. Peals of thunder were heard, and a torrential rain began to pour down. But, before the meal could get wet, the Devil's daughter reappeared and used her magic powers to help Pierre land the barge safely and store the meal without lifting a sack.

"You are indeed the kindest person I know, and I don't know how to thank you. I love you and want to marry you," Pierre vowed.

"We shall have trouble getting away to be married," the girl warned. My father is very crafty. But, tomorrow at daybreak we'll try to escape."

Just then, the Devil strode up, fuming with rage. "So, Pierre, this is how you do your work," he exclaimed angrily. I might have guessed you were helping him, daughter. Go inside quickly while I do away with this young buck."

"Don't do that father," pleaded the youngest daughter, "Pierre loves me and wants to marry me."

"Ho! Ho! Does he? Does he? We shall see about that. All right, young fellow, I'll give you one more chance. If you can pick her out from my other daughters, you may have her. But, if you fail, I'll kill you."

After they were inside the castle, the girl whispered to Pierre,

"When you come to see us, remember, I'll have an iron ring on my finger."

Finally, the Devil called Pierre into a large room which had a crack in one wall. Through this crack were sticking four fingers. "Now," explained the Devil, "through that crack are sticking out four fingers. One belongs to my wife, two to my daughters, and one to my youngest daughter. If you pick her finger, you may have my youngest daughter, but if you pick the wrong one, I'll cut off your head."

Pierre examined the fingers, and saw that one wore a gold ring, one a silver, one a copper and the fourth an iron ring. He picked the finger wearing the iron ring. "You have won my youngest daughter, and tomorrow you'll be married," promised the Devil.

That night, the girl came to Pierre's room and said, "Pierre, we must be off, because my father plans to kill you tonight. Make a dummy and put it in your bed so he'll mistake it for you."

Pierre made a wax dummy, placed it on his bed, and covered it. Then, they went out to the stables, where they saddled the Devil's two horses, Thunder and Lightning. When Thunder pawed the ground, thunder rumbled in the sky, and when Lightning snorted and pawed, lightning flashed. Pierre put the girl on Lightning and he rode Thunder. Off they went with a thunder clap and a flash of Lightning.

The Devil came to Pierre's room that night with an ax. He severed the head of the dummy with one stroke and went back to bed laughing. The next morning, he found his two horses gone and came back to Pierre's room. When he found the dummy with the severed head, he realized how he had been tricked.

He immediately went to the stables and saddled his giant bull, Bally-Lo, who could leap five miles at a jump. The animal stomped and snorted and leaped over forest and mountain at great speed. Before long, the Devil saw the lovers in the distance. But, they heard him coming, and when they looked back and saw Bally-Lo just behind them, the girl called to Pierre to throw some of Thunder's sweat behind him. He scooped up some of the lather from the horse's flank and flung it behind him.

Immediately, a great wall of water separated the lovers from the Devil. He had to detour around the water, but eventually he caught up with them. They could feel Bally-Lo's warm breath on their backs. Then, the girl took off her iron ring and tossed it behind them. Immediately, a great forest grew up which entangled Bally-

Lo. The Devil had to go back to get an ax to cut his way through the forest.

Meantime, the lovers had time to reach the church. They were inside being married when they heard the crashing of hooves and the snorting of the bull.

When the Devil reached the entrance of the church, he started to rush in, but he suddenly became as weak and helpless as a child. His magic powers deserted him as he touched the threshold. He finally remounted the bull and sped away. But, on the trip home, the bull threw him and trampled him.

Pierre and the Devil's youngest daughter were married and lived happily afterwards.